WARNINGS TO THE KINGS AND
ADVICE ON RESTORING SPAIN

THE
OTHER VOICE
IN
EARLY MODERN
EUROPE

A Series Edited by Margaret L. King and Albert Rabil Jr.

### RECENT BOOKS IN THE SERIES

María de Guevara

# WARNINGS TO THE KINGS AND ADVICE ON RESTORING SPAIN

*A Bilingual Edition*

჻

*Edited and Translated by*
*Nieves Romero-Díaz*

THE UNIVERSITY OF CHICAGO PRESS
*Chicago & London*

*María de Guevara, d.* 1683

*Nieves Romero-Díaz* is associate professor of Spanish at
Mount Holyoke College.

The University of Chicago Press, Chicago 60637
The University of Chicago Press, Ltd., London
© 2007 by The University of Chicago
All rights reserved. Published 2007
Printed in the United States of America

16  15  14  13  12  11  10  09  08  07      1  2  3  4  5

ISBN-13: 978-0-226-14080-3 (cloth)
ISBN-13: 978-0-226-14081-0 (paper)
ISBN-10: 0-226-14080-6 (cloth)
ISBN-10: 0-226-14081-4 (paper)

The University of Chicago Press gratefully acknowledges the generous support
of James E. Rabil, in memory of Scottie W. Rabil, toward the publication of this book.
Publication of this book has been aided by the Dean of Faculty's Office at
Mount Holyoke College.

Library of Congress Cataloging-in-Publication Data
Guevara, María de, d. 1683.
  Warnings to the kings and advice on restoring spain / María de Guevara ; edited
and translated by Nieves Romero-Díaz.
     p.   cm.
  English and Spanish.
  Includes bibliographical references and index.
  ISBN-13: 978-0-226-14080-3 (cloth : alk. paper)
  ISBN-10: 0-226-14080-6 (cloth : alk. paper)
  ISBN-13: 978-0-226-14081-0 (pbk. : alk. paper)
  ISBN-10: 0-226-14081-4 (pbk. : alk. paper)
  1. Spain—History—Philip IV, 1621–1665. 2. Women—Spain—History—17th
century. I. Romero-Díaz, Nieves, 1970–   II. Title.
DP185.G84  2007
946′.052—dc22

2007013778

# CONTENTS

# ACKNOWLEDGMENTS

I would not have been able to complete this project had it not been for some very important people and institutions; I wish to express my sincerest gratitude to them all.

First, to Mount Holyoke College and the Office of the Dean of Faculty, for generously funding my summer research in Spain over the past few years. MHC was also kind enough to grant me a sabbatical leave, which allowed me to complete a first draft of the manuscript. Second, I need to thank Spain's Program for Cultural Cooperation between Spain's Ministry of Culture, Education and Sports and Colleges and Universities in the U.S. This program financially supported me during two months of archival research in Spain; for that I am very grateful.

Also, I wish to thank those who attended the numerous conferences and symposiums where I presented different parts of the introduction; in particular, those who attended the conferences held by the Asociación de Escritoras de España y las Américas (1300–1800). The scholars and members of the public at those talks encouraged me with their praise and guided me with their questions and suggestions.

Encouragement and guidance also came from numerous manuscript readers—those colleagues and friends who gave me excellent advice and very valuable comments. In particular, Lerice Martin, Amanda Powell, Barbara Simerka, Sally Sutherland, Lisa Vollendorf, and Julian Weiss. Special thanks to translator Samuel Martin, who was always available to respond to my questions, doubts, and complaints about the ever-challenging English language. I am also indebted to Margaret Greer, who recommended me for this translation, and to the anonymous reader as well as to Albert Rabil and Margaret King, the editors of the Other Voice in Early Modern Europe

series, for their invaluable suggestions on ways of improving my English and my ideas.

Last, but certainly not least, I wish to thank my family in Spain for their unconditional love and support. And above all, thanks to Alex Martin-Romero, *mi enanillo,* who came into my life in the middle of this project and whose wonderful smiles and incomprehensible babble have brought new light and meaning to everything I do.

I dedicate this book to my mother, Josefa Díaz Catalán, for being a voice of strength and love in my life.

*Nieves Romero-Díaz*

# THE OTHER VOICE IN EARLY MODERN EUROPE: INTRODUCTION TO THE SERIES

*Margaret L. King and Albert Rabil Jr.*

## THE OLD VOICE AND THE OTHER VOICE

In western Europe and the United States, women are nearing equality in the professions, in business, and in politics. Most enjoy access to education, reproductive rights, and autonomy in financial affairs. Issues vital to women are on the public agenda: equal pay, child care, domestic abuse, breast cancer research, and curricular revision with an eye to the inclusion of women.

These recent achievements have their origins in things women (and some male supporters) said for the first time about six hundred years ago. Theirs is the "other voice," in contradistinction to the "first voice," the voice of the educated men who created Western culture. Coincident with a general reshaping of European culture in the period 1300–1700 (called the Renaissance or early modern period), questions of female equality and opportunity were raised that still resound and are still unresolved.

The other voice emerged against the backdrop of a three-thousand-year history of the derogation of women rooted in the civilizations related to Western culture: Hebrew, Greek, Roman, and Christian. Negative attitudes toward women inherited from these traditions pervaded the intellectual, medical, legal, religious, and social systems that developed during the European Middle Ages.

The following pages describe the traditional, overwhelmingly male views of women's nature inherited by early modern Europeans and the new tradition that the "other voice" called into being to begin to challenge reigning assumptions. This review should serve as a framework for understanding the texts published in the series The Other Voice in Early Modern Europe. Introductions specific to each text and author follow this essay in all the volumes of the series.

## TRADITIONAL VIEWS OF WOMEN, 500 B.C.E.–1500 C.E

Embedded in the philosophical and medical theories of the ancient Greeks were perceptions of the female as inferior to the male in both mind and body. Similarly, the structure of civil legislation inherited from the ancient Romans was biased against women, and the views on women developed by Christian thinkers out of the Hebrew Bible and the Christian New Testament were negative and disabling. Literary works composed in the vernacular of ordinary people, and widely recited or read, conveyed these negative assumptions. The social networks within which most women lived—those of the family and the institutions of the Roman Catholic Church—were shaped by this negative tradition and sharply limited the areas in which women might act in and upon the world.

GREEK PHILOSOPHY AND FEMALE NATURE. Greek biology assumed that women were inferior to men and defined them as merely childbearers and housekeepers. This view was authoritatively expressed in the works of the philosopher Aristotle.

Aristotle thought in dualities. He considered action superior to inaction, form (the inner design or structure of any object) superior to matter, completion to incompletion, possession to deprivation. In each of these dualities, he associated the male principle with the superior quality and the female with the inferior. "The male principle in nature," he argued, "is associated with active, formative and perfected characteristics, while the female is passive, material and deprived, desiring the male in order to become complete."[1] Men are always identified with virile qualities, such as judgment, courage, and stamina, and women with their opposites—irrationality, cowardice, and weakness.

The masculine principle was considered superior even in the womb. The man's semen, Aristotle believed, created the form of a new human creature, while the female body contributed only matter. (The existence of the ovum, and with it the other facts of human embryology, was not established until the seventeenth century.) Although the later Greek physician Galen believed there was a female component in generation, contributed by "female semen," the followers of both Aristotle and Galen saw the male role in human generation as more active and more important.

In the Aristotelian view, the male principle sought always to reproduce

---

1. Aristotle, *Physics* 1.9.192a20–24, in *The Complete Works of Aristotle,* ed. Jonathan Barnes, rev. Oxford trans., 2 vols. (Princeton, 1984), 1:328.

itself. The creation of a female was always a mistake, therefore, resulting from an imperfect act of generation. Every female born was considered a "defective" or "mutilated" male (as Aristotle's terminology has variously been translated), a "monstrosity" of nature.[2]

For Greek theorists, the biology of males and females was the key to their psychology. The female was softer and more docile, more apt to be despondent, querulous, and deceitful. Being incomplete, moreover, she craved sexual fulfillment in intercourse with a male. The male was intellectual, active, and in control of his passions.

These psychological polarities derived from the theory that the universe consisted of four elements (earth, fire, air, and water), expressed in human bodies as four "humors" (black bile, yellow bile, blood, and phlegm) considered, respectively, dry, hot, damp, and cold and corresponding to mental states ("melancholic," "choleric," "sanguine," "phlegmatic"). In this scheme the male, sharing the principles of earth and fire, was dry and hot; the female, sharing the principles of air and water, was cold and damp.

Female psychology was further affected by her dominant organ, the uterus (womb), *hystera* in Greek. The passions generated by the womb made women lustful, deceitful, talkative, irrational, indeed—when these affects were in excess—"hysterical."

Aristotle's biology also had social and political consequences. If the male principle was superior and the female inferior, then in the household, as in the state, men should rule and women must be subordinate. That hierarchy did not rule out the companionship of husband and wife, whose cooperation was necessary for the welfare of children and the preservation of property. Such mutuality supported male preeminence.

Aristotle's teacher Plato suggested a different possibility: that men and women might possess the same virtues. The setting for this proposal is the imaginary and ideal Republic that Plato sketches in a dialogue of that name. Here, for a privileged elite capable of leading wisely, all distinctions of class and wealth dissolve, as, consequently, do those of gender. Without households or property, as Plato constructs his ideal society, there is no need for the subordination of women. Women may therefore be educated to the same level as men to assume leadership. Plato's Republic remained imaginary, however. In real societies, the subordination of women remained the norm and the prescription.

The views of women inherited from the Greek philosophical tradition became the basis for medieval thought. In the thirteenth century, the su-

2. Aristotle, *Generation of Animals* 2.3.737a27–28, in *The Complete Works*, 1: 1144.

preme Scholastic philosopher Thomas Aquinas, among others, still echoed Aristotle's views of human reproduction, of male and female personalities, and of the preeminent male role in the social hierarchy.

ROMAN LAW AND THE FEMALE CONDITION. Roman law, like Greek philosophy, underlay medieval thought and shaped medieval society. The ancient belief that adult property-owning men should administer households and make decisions affecting the community at large is the very fulcrum of Roman law.

About 450 B.C.E., during Rome's republican era, the community's customary law was recorded (legendarily) on twelve tablets erected in the city's central forum. It was later elaborated by professional jurists whose activity increased in the imperial era, when much new legislation was passed, especially on issues affecting family and inheritance. This growing, changing body of laws was eventually codified in the *Corpus of Civil Law* under the direction of the emperor Justinian, generations after the empire ceased to be ruled from Rome. That *Corpus*, read and commented on by medieval scholars from the eleventh century on, inspired the legal systems of most of the cities and kingdoms of Europe.

Laws regarding dowries, divorce, and inheritance pertain primarily to women. Since those laws aimed to maintain and preserve property, the women concerned were those from the property-owning minority. Their subordination to male family members points to the even greater subordination of lower-class and slave women, about whom the laws speak little.

In the early republic, the *paterfamilias*, or "father of the family," possessed *patria potestas*, "paternal power." The term *pater*, "father," in both these cases does not necessarily mean biological father but denotes the head of a household. The father was the person who owned the household's property and, indeed, its human members. The *paterfamilias* had absolute power—including the power, rarely exercised, of life or death—over his wife, his children, and his slaves, as much as his cattle.

Male children could be "emancipated," an act that granted legal autonomy and the right to own property. Those over fourteen could be emancipated by a special grant from the father or automatically by their father's death. But females could never be emancipated; instead, they passed from the authority of their father to that of a husband or, if widowed or orphaned while still unmarried, to a guardian or tutor.

Marriage in its traditional form placed the woman under her husband's authority, or *manus*. He could divorce her on grounds of adultery, drinking wine, or stealing from the household, but she could not divorce him. She could neither possess property in her own right nor bequeath any to her

children upon her death. When her husband died, the household property passed not to her but to his male heirs. And when her father died, she had no claim to any family inheritance, which was directed to her brothers or more remote male relatives. The effect of these laws was to exclude women from civil society, itself based on property ownership.

In the later republican and imperial periods, these rules were significantly modified. Women rarely married according to the traditional form. The practice of "free" marriage allowed a woman to remain under her father's authority, to possess property given her by her father (most frequently the "dowry," recoverable from the husband's household on his death), and to inherit from her father. She could also bequeath property to her own children and divorce her husband, just as he could divorce her.

Despite this greater freedom, women still suffered enormous disability under Roman law. Heirs could belong only to the father's side, never the mother's. Moreover, although she could bequeath her property to her children, she could not establish a line of succession in doing so. A woman was "the beginning and end of her own family," said the jurist Ulpian. Moreover, women could play no public role. They could not hold public office, represent anyone in a legal case, or even witness a will. Women had only a private existence and no public personality.

The dowry system, the guardian, women's limited ability to transmit wealth, and total political disability are all features of Roman law adopted by the medieval communities of western Europe, although modified according to local customary laws.

CHRISTIAN DOCTRINE AND WOMEN'S PLACE. The Hebrew Bible and the Christian New Testament authorized later writers to limit women to the realm of the family and to burden them with the guilt of original sin. The passages most fruitful for this purpose were the creation narratives in Genesis and sentences from the Epistles defining women's role within the Christian family and community.

Each of the first two chapters of Genesis contains a creation narrative. In the first "God created man in his own image, in the image of God he created him; male and female he created them" (Gn 1:27). In the second, God created Eve from Adam's rib (2:21–23). Christian theologians relied principally on Genesis 2 for their understanding of the relation between man and woman, interpreting the creation of Eve from Adam as proof of her subordination to him.

The creation story in Genesis 2 leads to that of the temptations in Genesis 3: of Eve by the wily serpent and of Adam by Eve. As read by Christian theologians from Tertullian to Thomas Aquinas, the narrative made Eve

responsible for the Fall and its consequences. She instigated the act; she deceived her husband; she suffered the greater punishment. Her disobedience made it necessary for Jesus to be incarnated and to die on the cross. From the pulpit, moralists and preachers for centuries conveyed to women the guilt that they bore for original sin.

The Epistles offered advice to early Christians on building communities of the faithful. Among the matters to be regulated was the place of women. Paul offered views favorable to women in Galatians 3:28: "There is neither Jew nor Greek, there is neither slave nor free, there is neither male nor female; for you are all one in Christ Jesus." Paul also referred to women as his coworkers and placed them on a par with himself and his male co-workers (Phlm 4:2–3; Rom 16:1–3; 1 Cor 16:19). Elsewhere, Paul limited women's possibilities: "But I want you to understand that the head of every man is Christ, the head of a woman is her husband, and the head of Christ is God" (1 Cor 11:3).

Biblical passages by later writers (although attributed to Paul) enjoined women to forgo jewels, expensive clothes, and elaborate coiffures; and they forbade women to "teach or have authority over men," telling them to "learn in silence with all submissiveness" as is proper for one responsible for sin, consoling them, however, with the thought that they will be saved through childbearing (1 Tm 2:9–15). Other texts among the later Epistles defined women as the weaker sex and emphasized their subordination to their husbands (1 Pt 3:7; Col 3:18; Eph 5:22–23).

These passages from the New Testament became the arsenal employed by theologians of the early church to transmit negative attitudes toward women to medieval Christian culture—above all, Tertullian (*On the Apparel of Women*), Jerome (*Against Jovinian*), and Augustine (*The Literal Meaning of Genesis*).

THE IMAGE OF WOMEN IN MEDIEVAL LITERATURE. The philosophical, legal, and religious traditions born in antiquity formed the basis of the medieval intellectual synthesis wrought by trained thinkers, mostly clerics, writing in Latin and based largely in universities. The vernacular literary tradition that developed alongside the learned tradition also spoke about female nature and women's roles. Medieval stories, poems, and epics also portrayed women negatively—as lustful and deceitful—while praising good housekeepers and loyal wives as replicas of the Virgin Mary or the female saints and martyrs.

There is an exception in the movement of "courtly love" that evolved in southern France from the twelfth century. Courtly love was the erotic love between a nobleman and noblewoman, the latter usually superior in

social rank. It was always adulterous. From the conventions of courtly love derive modern Western notions of romantic love. The tradition has had an impact disproportionate to its size, for it affected only a tiny elite, and very few women. The exaltation of the female lover probably does not reflect a higher evaluation of women or a step toward their sexual liberation. More likely it gives expression to the social and sexual tensions besetting the knightly class at a specific historical juncture.

The literary fashion of courtly love was on the wane by the thirteenth century, when the widely read *Romance of the Rose* was composed in French by two authors of significantly different dispositions. Guillaume de Lorris composed the initial four thousand verses about 1235, and Jean de Meun added about seventeen thousand verses—more than four times the original—about 1265.

The fragment composed by Guillaume de Lorris stands squarely in the tradition of courtly love. Here the poet, in a dream, is admitted into a walled garden where he finds a magic fountain in which a rosebush is reflected. He longs to pick one rose, but the thorns prevent his doing so, even as he is wounded by arrows from the god of love, whose commands he agrees to obey. The rest of this part of the poem recounts the poet's unsuccessful efforts to pluck the rose.

The longer part of the *Romance* by Jean de Meun also describes a dream. But here allegorical characters give long didactic speeches, providing a social satire on a variety of themes, some pertaining to women. Love is an anxious and tormented state, the poem explains: women are greedy and manipulative, marriage is miserable, beautiful women are lustful, ugly ones cease to please, and a chaste woman is as rare as a black swan.

Shortly after Jean de Meun completed *The Romance of the Rose*, Mathéolus penned his *Lamentations*, a long Latin diatribe against marriage translated into French about a century later. The *Lamentations* sum up medieval attitudes toward women and provoked the important response by Christine de Pizan in her *Book of the City of Ladies*.

In 1355, Giovanni Boccaccio wrote *Il Corbaccio*, another antifeminist manifesto, although ironically by an author whose other works pioneered new directions in Renaissance thought. The former husband of his lover appears to Boccaccio, condemning his unmoderated lust and detailing the defects of women. Boccaccio concedes at the end "how much men naturally surpass women in nobility" and is cured of his desires.[3]

---

3. Giovanni Boccaccio, *The Corbaccio, or The Labyrinth of Love*, trans. and ed. Anthony K. Cassell, rev. ed. (Binghamton, N.Y., 1993), 71.

WOMEN'S ROLES: THE FAMILY. The negative perceptions of women expressed in the intellectual tradition are also implicit in the actual roles that women played in European society. Assigned to subordinate positions in the household and the church, they were barred from significant participation in public life.

Medieval European households, like those in antiquity and in non-Western civilizations, were headed by males. It was the male serf (or peasant), feudal lord, town merchant, or citizen who was polled or taxed or succeeded to an inheritance or had any acknowledged public role, although his wife or widow could stand as a temporary surrogate. From about 1100, the position of property-holding males was further enhanced: inheritance was confined to the male, or agnate, line—with depressing consequences for women.

A wife never fully belonged to her husband's family, nor was she a daughter to her father's family. She left her father's house young to marry whomever her parents chose. Her dowry was managed by her husband, and at her death it normally passed to her children by him.

A married woman's life was occupied nearly constantly with cycles of pregnancy, childbearing, and lactation. Women bore children through all the years of their fertility, and many died in childbirth. They were also responsible for raising young children up to six or seven. In the propertied classes that responsibility was shared, since it was common for a wet nurse to take over breast-feeding and for servants to perform other chores.

Women trained their daughters in the household duties appropriate to their status, nearly always tasks associated with textiles: spinning, weaving, sewing, embroidering. Their sons were sent out of the house as apprentices or students, or their training was assumed by fathers in later childhood and adolescence. On the death of her husband, a woman's children became the responsibility of his family. She generally did not take "his" children with her to a new marriage or back to her father's house, except sometimes in the artisan classes.

Women also worked. Rural peasants performed farm chores, merchant wives often practiced their husbands' trades, the unmarried daughters of the urban poor worked as servants or prostitutes. All wives produced or embellished textiles and did the housekeeping, while wealthy ones managed servants. These labors were unpaid or poorly paid but often contributed substantially to family wealth.

WOMEN'S ROLES: THE CHURCH. Membership in a household, whether a father's or a husband's, meant for women a lifelong subordination to oth-

ers. In western Europe, the Roman Catholic Church offered an alternative to the career of wife and mother. A woman could enter a convent, parallel in function to the monasteries for men that evolved in the early Christian centuries.

In the convent, a woman pledged herself to a celibate life, lived according to strict community rules, and worshiped daily. Often the convent offered training in Latin, allowing some women to become considerable scholars and authors as well as scribes, artists, and musicians. For women who chose the conventual life, the benefits could be enormous, but for numerous others placed in convents by paternal choice, the life could be restrictive and burdensome.

The conventual life declined as an alternative for women as the modern age approached. Reformed monastic institutions resisted responsibility for related female orders. The church increasingly restricted female institutional life by insisting on closer male supervision.

Women often sought other options. Some joined the communities of laywomen that sprang up spontaneously in the thirteenth century in the urban zones of western Europe, especially in Flanders and Italy. Some joined the heretical movements that flourished in late medieval Christendom, whose anticlerical and often antifamily positions particularly appealed to women. In these communities, some women were acclaimed as "holy women" or "saints," whereas others often were condemned as frauds or heretics.

In all, although the options offered to women by the church were sometimes less than satisfactory, they were sometimes richly rewarding. After 1520, the convent remained an option only in Roman Catholic territories. Protestantism engendered an ideal of marriage as a heroic endeavor and appeared to place husband and wife on a more equal footing. Sermons and treatises, however, still called for female subordination and obedience.

## THE OTHER VOICE, 1300–1700

When the modern era opened, European culture was so firmly structured by a framework of negative attitudes toward women that to dismantle it was a monumental labor. The process began as part of a larger cultural movement that entailed the critical reexamination of ideas inherited from the ancient and medieval past. The humanists launched that critical reexamination.

THE HUMANIST FOUNDATION. Originating in Italy in the fourteenth century, humanism quickly became the dominant intellectual movement in Europe. Spreading in the sixteenth century from Italy to the rest of Europe,

it fueled the literary, scientific, and philosophical movements of the era and laid the basis for the eighteenth-century Enlightenment.

Humanists regarded the Scholastic philosophy of medieval universities as out of touch with the realities of urban life. They found in the rhetorical discourse of classical Rome a language adapted to civic life and public speech. They learned to read, speak, and write classical Latin and, eventually, classical Greek. They founded schools to teach others to do so, establishing the pattern for elementary and secondary education for the next three hundred years.

In the service of complex government bureaucracies, humanists employed their skills to write eloquent letters, deliver public orations, and formulate public policy. They developed new scripts for copying manuscripts and used the new printing press to disseminate texts, for which they created methods of critical editing.

Humanism was a movement led by males who accepted the evaluation of women in ancient texts and generally shared the misogynist perceptions of their culture. (Female humanists, as we will see, did not.) Yet humanism also opened the door to a reevaluation of the nature and capacity of women. By calling authors, texts, and ideas into question, it made possible the fundamental rereading of the whole intellectual tradition that was required in order to free women from cultural prejudice and social subordination.

A DIFFERENT CITY. The other voice first appeared when, after so many centuries, the accumulation of misogynist concepts evoked a response from a capable female defender: Christine de Pizan (1365–1431). Introducing her *Book of the City of Ladies* (1405), she described how she was affected by reading Mathéolus's *Lamentations*: "Just the sight of this book . . . made me wonder how it happened that so many different men . . . are so inclined to express both in speaking and in their treatises and writings so many wicked insults about women and their behavior."[4] These statements impelled her to detest herself "and the entire feminine sex, as though we were monstrosities in nature."[5]

The rest of *The Book of the City of Ladies* presents a justification of the female sex and a vision of an ideal community of women. A pioneer, she has received the message of female inferiority and rejected it. From the fourteenth to the seventeenth century, a huge body of literature accumulated that responded to the dominant tradition.

4. Christine de Pizan, *The Book of the City of Ladies*, trans. Earl Jeffrey Richards, foreword by Marina Warner (New York, 1982), 1.1.1, pp. 3–4.

5. Ibid., 1.1.1–2, p. 5.

The result was a literary explosion consisting of works by both men and women, in Latin and in the vernaculars: works enumerating the achievements of notable women; works rebutting the main accusations made against women; works arguing for the equal education of men and women; works defining and redefining women's proper role in the family, at court, in public; works describing women's lives and experiences. Recent monographs and articles have begun to hint at the great range of this movement, involving probably several thousand titles. The protofeminism of these "other voices" constitutes a significant fraction of the literary product of the early modern era.

THE CATALOGS. About 1365, the same Boccaccio whose *Corbaccio* rehearses the usual charges against female nature wrote another work, *Concerning Famous Women*. A humanist treatise drawing on classical texts, it praised 106 notable women: ninety-eight of them from pagan Greek and Roman antiquity, one (Eve) from the Bible, and seven from the medieval religious and cultural tradition; his book helped make all readers aware of a sex normally condemned or forgotten. Boccaccio's outlook nevertheless was unfriendly to women, for it singled out for praise those women who possessed the traditional virtues of chastity, silence, and obedience. Women who were active in the public realm—for example, rulers and warriors—were depicted as usually being lascivious and as suffering terrible punishments for entering the masculine sphere. Women were his subject, but Boccaccio's standard remained male.

Christine de Pizan's *Book of the City of Ladies* contains a second catalog, one responding specifically to Boccaccio's. Whereas Boccaccio portrays female virtue as exceptional, she depicts it as universal. Many women in history were leaders, or remained chaste despite the lascivious approaches of men, or were visionaries and brave martyrs.

The work of Boccaccio inspired a series of catalogs of illustrious women of the biblical, classical, Christian, and local pasts, among them Filippo da Bergamo's *Of Illustrious Women*, Pierre de Brantôme's *Lives of Illustrious Women*, Pierre Le Moyne's *Gallerie of Heroic Women*, and Pietro Paolo de Ribera's *Immortal Triumphs and Heroic Enterprises of 845 Women*. Whatever their embedded prejudices, these works drove home to the public the possibility of female excellence.

THE DEBATE. At the same time, many questions remained: Could a woman be virtuous? Could she perform noteworthy deeds? Was she even, strictly speaking, of the same human species as men? These questions were

debated over four centuries, in French, German, Italian, Spanish, and English, by authors male and female, among Catholics, Protestants, and Jews, in ponderous volumes and breezy pamphlets. The whole literary genre has been called the *querelle des femmes*, the "woman question."

The opening volley of this battle occurred in the first years of the fifteenth century, in a literary debate sparked by Christine de Pizan. She exchanged letters critical of Jean de Meun's contribution to *The Romance of the Rose* with two French royal secretaries, Jean de Montreuil and Gontier Col. When the matter became public, Jean Gerson, one of Europe's leading theologians, supported de Pizan's arguments against de Meun, for the moment silencing the opposition.

The debate resurfaced repeatedly over the next two hundred years. *The Triumph of Women* (1438) by Juan Rodríguez de la Camara (or Juan Rodríguez del Padron) struck a new note by presenting arguments for the superiority of women to men. *The Champion of Women* (1440–42) by Martin Le Franc addresses once again the negative views of women presented in *The Romance of the Rose* and offers counterevidence of female virtue and achievement.

A cameo of the debate on women is included in *The Courtier,* one of the most widely read books of the era, published by the Italian Baldassare Castiglione in 1528 and immediately translated into other European vernaculars. *The Courtier* depicts a series of evenings at the court of the duke of Urbino in which many men and some women of the highest social stratum amuse themselves by discussing a range of literary and social issues. The "woman question" is a pervasive theme throughout, and the third of its four books is devoted entirely to that issue.

In a verbal duel, Gasparo Pallavicino and Giuliano de' Medici present the main claims of the two traditions. Gasparo argues the innate inferiority of women and their inclination to vice. Only in bearing children do they profit the world. Giuliano counters that women share the same spiritual and mental capacities as men and may excel in wisdom and action. Men and women are of the same essence: just as no stone can be more perfectly a stone than another, so no human being can be more perfectly human than others, whether male or female. It was an astonishing assertion, boldly made to an audience as large as all Europe.

THE TREATISES. Humanism provided the materials for a positive counterconcept to the misogyny embedded in Scholastic philosophy and law and inherited from the Greek, Roman, and Christian pasts. A series of humanist treatises on marriage and family, on education and deportment, and on the nature of women helped construct these new perspectives.

The works by Francesco Barbaro and Leon Battista Alberti—*On Marriage* (1415) and *On the Family* (1434–37)—far from defending female equality, reasserted women's responsibility for rearing children and managing the housekeeping while being obedient, chaste, and silent. Nevertheless, they served the cause of reexamining the issue of women's nature by placing domestic issues at the center of scholarly concern and reopening the pertinent classical texts. In addition, Barbaro emphasized the companionate nature of marriage and the importance of a wife's spiritual and mental qualities for the well-being of the family.

These themes reappear in later humanist works on marriage and the education of women by Juan Luis Vives and Erasmus. Both were moderately sympathetic to the condition of women without reaching beyond the usual masculine prescriptions for female behavior.

An outlook more favorable to women characterizes the nearly unknown work *In Praise of Women* (ca. 1487) by the Italian humanist Bartolommeo Goggio. In addition to providing a catalog of illustrious women, Goggio argued that male and female are the same in essence, but that women (reworking the Adam and Eve narrative from quite a new angle) are actually superior. In the same vein, the Italian humanist Mario Equicola asserted the spiritual equality of men and women in *On Women* (1501). In 1525, Galeazzo Flavio Capra (or Capella) published his work *On the Excellence and Dignity of Women*. This humanist tradition of treatises defending the worthiness of women culminates in the work of Henricus Cornelius Agrippa *On the Nobility and Preeminence of the Female Sex*. No work by a male humanist more succinctly or explicitly presents the case for female dignity.

THE WITCH BOOKS. While humanists grappled with the issues pertaining to women and family, other learned men turned their attention to what they perceived as a very great problem: witches. Witch-hunting manuals, explorations of the witch phenomenon, and even defenses of witches are not at first glance pertinent to the tradition of the other voice. But they do relate in this way: most accused witches were women. The hostility aroused by supposed witch activity is comparable to the hostility aroused by women. The evil deeds the victims of the hunt were charged with were exaggerations of the vices to which, many believed, all women were prone.

The connection between the witch accusation and the hatred of women is explicit in the notorious witch-hunting manual *The Hammer of Witches* (1486) by two Dominican inquisitors, Heinrich Krämer and Jacob Sprenger. Here the inconstancy, deceitfulness, and lustfulness traditionally associated with women are depicted in exaggerated form as the core features of witch

behavior. These traits inclined women to make a bargain with the devil—sealed by sexual intercourse—by which they acquired unholy powers. Such bizarre claims, far from being rejected by rational men, were broadcast by intellectuals. The German Ulrich Molitur, the Frenchman Nicolas Rémy, and the Italian Stefano Guazzo all coolly informed the public of sinister orgies and midnight pacts with the devil. The celebrated French jurist, historian, and political philosopher Jean Bodin argued that because women were especially prone to diabolism, regular legal procedures could properly be suspended in order to try those accused of this "exceptional crime."

A few experts such as the physician Johann Weyer, a student of Agrippa's, raised their voices in protest. In 1563, he explained the witch phenomenon thus, without discarding belief in diabolism: the devil deluded foolish old women afflicted by melancholia, causing them to believe they had magical powers. Weyer's rational skepticism, which had good credibility in the community of the learned, worked to revise the conventional views of women and witchcraft.

WOMEN'S WORKS. To the many categories of works produced on the question of women's worth must be added nearly all works written by women. A woman writing was in herself a statement of women's claim to dignity.

Only a few women wrote anything before the dawn of the modern era, for three reasons. First, they rarely received the education that would enable them to write. Second, they were not admitted to the public roles—as administrator, bureaucrat, lawyer or notary, or university professor—in which they might gain knowledge of the kinds of things the literate public thought worth writing about. Third, the culture imposed silence on women, considering speaking out a form of unchastity. Given these conditions, it is remarkable that any women wrote. Those who did before the fourteenth century were almost always nuns or religious women whose isolation made their pronouncements more acceptable.

From the fourteenth century on, the volume of women's writings rose. Women continued to write devotional literature, although not always as cloistered nuns. They also wrote diaries, often intended as keepsakes for their children; books of advice to their sons and daughters; letters to family members and friends; and family memoirs, in a few cases elaborate enough to be considered histories.

A few women wrote works directly concerning the "woman question," and some of these, such as the humanists Isotta Nogarola, Cassandra Fedele, Laura Cereta, and Olympia Morata, were highly trained. A few were profes-

sional writers, living by the income of their pens; the very first among them was Christine de Pizan, noteworthy in this context as in so many others. In addition to *The Book of the City of Ladies* and her critiques of *The Romance of the Rose*, she wrote *The Treasure of the City of Ladies* (a guide to social decorum for women), an advice book for her son, much courtly verse, and a full-scale history of the reign of King Charles V of France.

WOMEN PATRONS. Women who did not themselves write but encouraged others to do so boosted the development of an alternative tradition. Highly placed women patrons supported authors, artists, musicians, poets, and learned men. Such patrons, drawn mostly from the Italian elites and the courts of northern Europe, figure disproportionately as the dedicatees of the important works of early feminism.

For a start, it might be noted that the catalogs of Boccaccio and Alvaro de Luna were dedicated to the Florentine noblewoman Andrea Acciaiuoli and to Doña María, first wife of King Juan II of Castile, while the French translation of Boccaccio's work was commissioned by Anne of Brittany, wife of King Charles VIII of France. The humanist treatises of Goggio, Equicola, Vives, and Agrippa were dedicated, respectively, to Eleanora of Aragon, wife of Ercole I d'Este, duke of Ferrara; to Margherita Cantelma of Mantua; to Catherine of Aragon, wife of King Henry VIII of England; and to Margaret, Duchess of Austria and regent of the Netherlands. As late as 1696, Mary Astell's *Serious Proposal to the Ladies, for the Advancement of Their True and Greatest Interest* was dedicated to Princess Anne of Denmark.

These authors presumed that their efforts would be welcome to female patrons, or they may have written at the bidding of those patrons. Silent themselves, perhaps even unresponsive, these loftily placed women helped shape the tradition of the other voice.

THE ISSUES. The literary forms and patterns in which the tradition of the other voice presented itself have now been sketched. It remains to highlight the major issues around which this tradition crystallizes. In brief, there are four problems to which our authors return again and again, in plays and catalogs, in verse and letters, in treatises and dialogues, in every language: the problem of chastity, the problem of power, the problem of speech, and the problem of knowledge. Of these the greatest, preconditioning the others, is the problem of chastity.

THE PROBLEM OF CHASTITY. In traditional European culture, as in those of antiquity and others around the globe, chastity was perceived as woman's quintessential virtue—in contrast to courage, or generosity, or

leadership, or rationality, seen as virtues characteristic of men. Opponents of women charged them with insatiable lust. Women themselves and their defenders—without disputing the validity of the standard—responded that women were capable of chastity.

The requirement of chastity kept women at home, silenced them, isolated them, left them in ignorance. It was the source of all other impediments. Why was it so important to the society of men, of whom chastity was not required, and who more often than not considered it their right to violate the chastity of any woman they encountered?

Female chastity ensured the continuity of the male-headed household. If a man's wife was not chaste, he could not be sure of the legitimacy of his offspring. If they were not his and they acquired his property, it was not his household, but some other man's, that had endured. If his daughter was not chaste, she could not be transferred to another man's household as his wife, and he was dishonored.

The whole system of the integrity of the household and the transmission of property was bound up in female chastity. Such a requirement pertained only to property-owning classes, of course. Poor women could not expect to maintain their chastity, least of all if they were in contact with high-status men to whom all women but those of their own household were prey.

In Catholic Europe, the requirement of chastity was further buttressed by moral and religious imperatives. Original sin was inextricably linked with the sexual act. Virginity was seen as heroic virtue, far more impressive than, say, the avoidance of idleness or greed. Monasticism, the cultural institution that dominated medieval Europe for centuries, was grounded in the renunciation of the flesh. The Catholic reform of the eleventh century imposed a similar standard on all the clergy and a heightened awareness of sexual requirements on all the laity. Although men were asked to be chaste, female unchastity was much worse: it led to the devil, as Eve had led mankind to sin.

To such requirements, women and their defenders protested their innocence. Furthermore, following the example of holy women who had escaped the requirements of family and sought the religious life, some women began to conceive of female communities as alternatives both to family and to the cloister. Christine de Pizan's city of ladies was such a community. Moderata Fonte and Mary Astell envisioned others. The luxurious salons of the French *précieuses* of the seventeenth century, or the comfortable English drawing rooms of the next, may have been born of the same impulse. Here women not only might escape, if briefly, the subordinate position that life in the family entailed but might also make claims to power, exercise their capacity for speech, and display their knowledge.

THE PROBLEM OF POWER. Women were excluded from power: the whole cultural tradition insisted on it. Only men were citizens, only men bore arms, only men could be chiefs or lords or kings. There were exceptions that did not disprove the rule, when wives or widows or mothers took the place of men, awaiting their return or the maturation of a male heir. A woman who attempted to rule in her own right was perceived as an anomaly, a monster, at once a deformed woman and an insufficient male, sexually confused and consequently unsafe.

The association of such images with women who held or sought power explains some otherwise odd features of early modern culture. Queen Elizabeth I of England, one of the few women to hold full regal authority in European history, played with such male/female images—positive ones, of course—in representing herself to her subjects. She was a prince, and manly, even though she was female. She was also (she claimed) virginal, a condition absolutely essential if she was to avoid the attacks of her opponents. Catherine de' Medici, who ruled France as widow and regent for her sons, also adopted such imagery in defining her position. She chose as one symbol the figure of Artemisia, an androgynous ancient warrior-heroine who combined a female persona with masculine powers.

Power in a woman, without such sexual imagery, seems to have been indigestible by the culture. A rare note was struck by the Englishman Sir Thomas Elyot in his *Defence of Good Women* (1540), justifying both women's participation in civic life and their prowess in arms. The old tune was sung by the Scots reformer John Knox in his *First Blast of the Trumpet against the Monstrous Regiment of Women* (1558); for him rule by women, defects in nature, was a hideous contradiction in terms.

The confused sexuality of the imagery of female potency was not reserved for rulers. Any woman who excelled was likely to be called an Amazon, recalling the self-mutilated warrior women of antiquity who repudiated all men, gave up their sons, and raised only their daughters. She was often said to have "exceeded her sex" or to have possessed "masculine virtue"—as the very fact of conspicuous excellence conferred masculinity even on the female subject. The catalogs of notable women often showed those female heroes dressed in armor, armed to the teeth, like men. Amazonian heroines romp through the epics of the age—Ariosto's *Orlando Furioso* (1532) and Spenser's *Faerie Queene* (1590–1609). Excellence in a woman was perceived as a claim for power, and power was reserved for the masculine realm. A woman who possessed either one was masculinized and lost title to her own female identity.

THE PROBLEM OF SPEECH. Just as power had a sexual dimension when it was claimed by women, so did speech. A good woman spoke little. Ex-

cessive speech was an indication of unchastity. By speech, women seduced men. Eve had lured Adam into sin by her speech. Accused witches were commonly accused of having spoken abusively, or irrationally, or simply too much. As enlightened a figure as Francesco Barbaro insisted on silence in a woman, which he linked to her perfect unanimity with her husband's will and her unblemished virtue (her chastity). Another Italian humanist, Leonardo Bruni, in advising a noblewoman on her studies, barred her not from speech but from public speaking. That was reserved for men.

Related to the problem of speech was that of costume—another, if silent, form of self-expression. Assigned the task of pleasing men as their primary occupation, elite women often tended toward elaborate costume, hairdressing, and the use of cosmetics. Clergy and secular moralists alike condemned these practices. The appropriate function of costume and adornment was to announce the status of a woman's husband or father. Any further indulgence in adornment was akin to unchastity.

THE PROBLEM OF KNOWLEDGE. When the Italian noblewoman Isotta Nogarola had begun to attain a reputation as a humanist, she was accused of incest—a telling instance of the association of learning in women with unchastity. That chilling association inclined any woman who was educated to deny that she was or to make exaggerated claims of heroic chastity.

If educated women were pursued with suspicions of sexual misconduct, women seeking an education faced an even more daunting obstacle: the assumption that women were by nature incapable of learning, that reasoning was a particularly masculine ability. Just as they proclaimed their chastity, women and their defenders insisted on their capacity for learning. The major work by a male writer on female education—that by Juan Luis Vives, *On the Education of a Christian Woman* (1523)—granted female capacity for intellection but still argued that a woman's whole education was to be shaped around the requirement of chastity and a future within the household. Female writers of the following generations—Marie de Gournay in France, Anna Maria van Schurman in Holland, and Mary Astell in England—began to envision other possibilities.

The pioneers of female education were the Italian women humanists who managed to attain a literacy in Latin and a knowledge of classical and Christian literature equivalent to that of prominent men. Their works implicitly and explicitly raise questions about women's social roles, defining problems that beset women attempting to break out of the cultural limits that had bound them. Like Christine de Pizan, who achieved an advanced education through her father's tutoring and her own devices, their bold questioning makes clear the importance of training. Only when women

were educated to the same standard as male leaders would they be able to raise that other voice and insist on their dignity as human beings morally, intellectually, and legally equal to men.

THE OTHER VOICE. The other voice, a voice of protest, was mostly female, but it was also male. It spoke in the vernaculars and in Latin, in treatises and dialogues, in plays and poetry, in letters and diaries, and in pamphlets. It battered at the wall of prejudice that encircled women and raised a banner announcing its claims. The female was equal (or even superior) to the male in essential nature—moral, spiritual, and intellectual. Women were capable of higher education, of holding positions of power and influence in the public realm, and of speaking and writing persuasively. The last bastion of masculine supremacy, centered on the notions of a woman's primary domestic responsibility and the requirement of female chastity, was not as yet assaulted—although visions of productive female communities as alternatives to the family indicated an awareness of the problem.

During the period 1300–1700, the other voice remained only a voice, and one only dimly heard. It did not result—yet—in an alteration of social patterns. Indeed, to this day they have not entirely been altered. Yet the call for justice issued as long as six centuries ago by those writing in the tradition of the other voice must be recognized as the source and origin of the mature feminist tradition and of the realignment of social institutions accomplished in the modern age.

༄

We thank the volume editors in this series, who responded with many suggestions to an earlier draft of this introduction, making it a collaborative enterprise. Many of their suggestions and criticisms have resulted in revisions of this introduction, although we remain responsible for the final product.

### PROJECTED TITLES IN THE SERIES

Ana de San Bartolomé, *Autobiography and Other Writings*, edited and translated by Darcy Donahue

Catharina Regina von Greiffenberg, *Meditations on the Life of Christ*, edited and translated by Lynne Tatlock

Emilie du Châtelet, *Selected Writings of an Enlightenment Philosophe*, edited by Judith Zinsser, translated by Isabelle Bour

# ABBREVIATIONS

*Aut.*       *Diccionario de Autoridades* (1726)
*Cov.*       *Tesoro de la Lengua Castellana,* by Sebastián de Covarrubias (1611)
*EC*       *Diccionario Enciclopédico Espasa-Calpe*
*OCD*       *Oxford Classical Dictionary*

# VOLUME EDITOR'S
# INTRODUCTION

Representation of the world from a woman's point of view has validity.
Constance Jordan, *Renaissance Feminism* (1990)

The real reason why women are not learned is not a defect in intelligence but a lack of opportunity. When our parents bring us up, if, instead of putting cambric on our sewing cushions and patterns in our embroidery frames, they gave us books and teachers, we would be as fit as men for any job or university professorship.
María de Zayas y Sotomayor, *The Enchantments of Love* (1637)

## CONTENT AND CONTEXT OF
## MARÍA DE GUEVARA'S WRITINGS

In seventeenth-century Spain, the aristocrat María de Guevara, countess of Escalante, appealed for strong leadership, protested corruption, and demanded women's inclusion in political decision making. With irony and eloquence, she made arguments that continue to resonate with discussions of human and civil rights in the present world. As a writer and activist, she exemplifies the important yet poorly understood role of women in the emerging nation-state. Guevara's forthright treatises on culture and politics provide strong evidence for women's participation in the public sphere in early modern Europe. For these reasons, María de Guevara must be included in this series: her voice calls out with urgency not only to her leaders but also to us. Guevara shows us that a woman is capable of engaging authoritatively with issues of state.

Her writings, however, remain obscure, sitting on the shelves of archives and libraries, completely unknown to the contemporary reader. Even specialists of early modern Spanish political writing do not know her work. Despite her noble status, Guevara has been constrained by dominant mas-

culine authorities that have repeatedly overlooked women's presence in the public sphere. Guevara herself is conscious of this dynamic:

> Since men made the laws, all are written in their favor, requiring women to be satisfied with the arms of the distaff and the pincushion. For by my faith, if women made use of letters, they would surpass men, which is just what men fear; they do not want women to be Amazons but rather to have their hands tied, making it unbecoming for a woman to leave her corner. (*Disenchantments* II)

In a corner: that is where her texts have been hidden for more than three hundred years. Thanks to this series, her texts are again brought into the light. Guevara's warnings to the kings in early modern Spain open the door to a better understanding of how discourses of politics and gender are interwoven to give birth to a female voice of authority.

## MARÍA DE GUEVARA: BIOGRAPHICAL BACKGROUND

Despite the emphasis patriarchal society has placed on keeping women out of public space, it must be recognized that historically some women have occupied positions of power. As historian Margarita Ortega López notes, during the Spanish Baroque (1565–1700), many women became figures of authority in the world outside their homes, either because of their status as widows, or because they belonged to an illustrious family, or for their strong personalities.[1] Monastery abbesses and, more particularly, noble women who were widows or who were married but remained alone for extended periods of time while their husbands were at war had to care for their estates. They managed the finances and were active "creating bylaws or regulations, naming municipal offices, supervising accounting ledgers, watching over the morality and the behavior in their jurisdictions, disputing or agreeing with their non-conformist vassals, conferring rewards or charity, etc.," as well as, in the case of those who were also mothers, taking care of their families, both in the house and in society.[2] There are many examples of women, some well known, some not, who took action in a society which attempted to contain and control women's public presence. Their existence demonstrates the need of reviewing early modern Spanish historiography

1. Margarita Ortega López, "El período Barroco (1565–1700)," in *Historia de las mujeres en España*, ed. Elisa Garrido González (Madrid: Síntesis, 1997), 321. All quotations from Spanish sources as well as titles, unless otherwise indicated, are translated by me.

2. Ibid., 322. Regarding the power in the public space of aristocratic women during Guevara's times, see also Helen Nader, ed., introduction to *Power and Gender in Renaissance Spain: Eight Women of the Mendoza Family, 1450–1650* (Urbana: University of Illinois Press, 2004), 1–26.

with a view to recovering and studying these women's impacting agency without underestimating them as "merely oppressed victims of patriarchy, whose lives were marked by exclusion, vulnerability, and powerlessness."[3] In *The Empress, the Queen, and the Nun*, for example, Magdalena Sánchez studies three powerful women at the court of Philip III: the Empress María, his sister; Margaret of the Cross, the empress's daughter; and Queen Margaret of Austria, Philip III's wife. The author emphasizes that these women were portrayed at the time as one-dimensional, simple, and pious; however, their political influence was more important than one might suppose. The objective of Sánchez's book is "to examine the degree to which women manipulated the accepted feminine spheres of family and religion to mask—and even justify—entrance into difficult political debates and to affect the outcome of those debates."[4]

María de Guevara (d. 1683) belongs to this group of women. Although she did not inherit the title of countess of Escalante until 1641,[5] her social empowerment is reflected in the complete list of titles she always includes along with her name, as in the memorial she herself wrote in 1654.[6] However, little is known about her life beyond what she tells us in this memorial:

---

3.  Anne Jacobson Shutte, Thomas Kuehn, and Silvana Seidel Menchi, introduction to *Time, Space, and Women's Lives in Early Modern Europe*, Sixteenth Century Essays and Studies, vol 57 (Kirksville, MO: Truman State University Press, 2001), xvi.

Some of these women include the countess of Lemos, the countess of Aranda, Saint Teresa of Avila, and many women from the Mendoza family such as Ana de Mendoza, the princess of Éboli. In the royal sphere, some are, for example, the queens Juana of Austria (sister of Philip II and regent of the Spanish monarchy between 1554 and 1559), Margaret of Austria (first wife of Philip III), and Mariana of Austria (second wife of Philip IV and regent queen while Charles II was not yet of age).

4.  Magdalena Sánchez, *The Empress, the Queen, and the Nun: Women and Power at the Court of Philip III of Spain* (Baltimore: Johns Hopkins University Press, 1998), 10.

5.  In his *Avisos*, José Pellicer reports that after Ana Catalina de Guevara's death in 1641, "the paternal inheritance, title, houses of Avendaño, Valley of Treceño, Urquizu, Olaso, and Beaumonte are given to Doña María de Guevara, daughter of Don Pedro de Guevara, younger brother of the count, married to Don Lorenzo de Guevara, lord of Paradilla." Quoted in Manuel Serrano y Sanz, *Apuntes de una Biblioteca de Autoras Españolas desde el año 1401 al 1833* (1903) facsimile ed., vol. 1 (Madrid: Atlas, 1975), 474.

6.  These are María de Guevara Manrique, countess of Escalante and Tahalú, viscountess of Treceño, lady of the Valley of Valdaliga and of the marquisate of Rucandio and the village of Villareal at Álava, and lady of the houses of Zeballos and Caviedes and Avendaño, Olaso and Orquizo, Arazuri and Montalbán, and Gamboa, Esparza, and Acotayn. They are found in María de Guevara, *Memorial de la casa de Escalante y servicios de ella al Rey Nuestro Señor* (Valladolid, 1654). For this edition, I have translated only the summary of her memorial from the original, housed at the National Library in Madrid, V-Cᵃ 57-13 (see appendix A). The complete memorial can be found on the microfilm that accompanies María del Carmen Simón Palmer's edition, *Escritoras españolas, 1500–1900: Catálogo. Biblioteca Nacional de Madrid*, 2 vols. (Madrid: Chadwyck-Healy España, 1992–93).

In Xerez de los Caballeros, the above-mentioned Don Pedro de Guevara married Doña Francisca de Mendoza y Azevedo, daughter of Gómez Pérez Miñano, native of the mountains of the house of Azevedo, which is in the *Merindad* [district] of Trasmiera, in the village of Iajano, from where her origin has been proved. She has her entailed estate and house at Xerez. They had as offspring Don Antonio and Don José, who died in childhood and are buried in Xerez, in the same chapel as their father. Also they had Doña Maria de Guevara, who succeeded to the house; and Doña Luisa de Guevara, who is married to Don Martín de Saavedra and Guzmán, who was president of the new realm of Granada, member of the Order of Calatrava, native of Cordoba, and they have three children, Don Martín, Doña Francisca, and Doña María, all three of whom are still alive. The third daughter was Doña Ana de Guevara.[7]

Guevara must state that she belongs to a historically powerful family in order to legitimate herself and create a public persona. Guevara is able to trace her origins to Don Pelayo (from the line of Zeballos) and to the founders of the kingdom of Navarre (from the line of Guevara). Writing a memorial is not an original cultural activity, however. Guevara is participating in a genealogical tradition common to early modern Spain: the farther back a family could trace its origin, the better its nobility could be established and proved.[8] It was not unusual for titled nobles to write those treatises. For most of them, paying attention to historical matters, including their own genealogical history, was a "feature of distinction," a way of boasting of being antiquarian.[9] Knowing history, their own history, writing it, and making it public was a political form of positioning themselves with regard to the society. That is, by writing her own *Memorial*, Guevara distinguishes and authorizes herself in the game of political and social dominance. The extension of her domains in Santander, the Basque country, Navarre, and Extremadura symbolizes the extension of her domains at higher and more important levels of national participation. In fact, this economic and social power allows her to request that the king return certain noble privileges—as well as rewards and economic compensations—to her house, her family, and herself.

7. *Memorial*, 19r.

8. During the sixteenth and seventeenth centuries, the importance of demonstrating historical continuity within noble families gave rise to a proliferation of the genealogical genre. See Antonio Domínguez Ortiz, *La sociedad española del siglo XVII. El estamento nobiliario* (1963) facsimile ed. (Granada: University of Granada, 1992), 164–66.

9. Fernando Bouza, *Corre manuscrito: Una historia cultural del Siglo de Oro* (Madrid: Marcial Pons, 2001), 257.

Guevara most likely lived between the court (Madrid), Valladolid, and her estates, where, as Isabel Barbeito Carneiro points out, "[she] establish[ed] a direct and personal communication with all her vassals."[10] It was while she was at one of her estates in 1660 that the royal family passed by, stopping in Vitoria and the province of Guipúzcoa, on its way to France for the marriage of Princess Doña Teresa and the duke of Anjou, future King Louis XIV. In an anonymous text of 1660,[11] the reader learns of the organizational skills she shows in arranging her estates and the way her servants respond to her.[12] In this document the author refers to one of her husbands, "the head of the Ganboyno house, which is made up of three provinces, Álava, Vizcaya, and Guipúzcoa."[13] By 1654—the year in which the *Memorial* was published—she already was married to Don Andrés, "Lord of Villaquerin and Sinoba, of the Order of Saint James, son of Don Andres Velázquez, head spy of the kingdom, and Doña Josefa de Guzmán, sister of the Marquis of Palacios," at that time "serving your Majesty in the army at Bordeaux."[14]

Luis Ballesteros Robles tells us that Luis Andrés Velázquez de Velasco y Guzmán was born in 1625 and awarded the habit of the Order of Saint James in 1633.[15] As gentleman-in-waiting to Philip IV's bastard son, the great general Don Juan José of Austria, Don Luis Andrés fought in many wars, in particular the one against Portugal, in which he distinguished himself and was rewarded highly by the king. Nothing is known of Don Luis Andrés de Velázquez after 1663, the year of the Entremoz and Évora campaigns during the war with Portugal. In "Fragments of the History of the Spanish Infantry," Don Serafín Estébanez Calderón refers to the loss of fifteen regiments led by the count of Escalante during that campaign.[16] In Don Antonio Alvares da Cunha's account of the campaign from the Portuguese perspective, the

---

10. *Escritoras madrileñas del siglo XVII. Estudio bibliográfico-crítico,* (Ph.D. diss., Universidad Complutense de Madrid, 1986), 2: 297.

11. "Relación de la jornada que al Condesa de Escalante hizo a la ciudad de Vitoria a besar la mano a su Majestad." Translated for this edition; see appendix B.

12. The report appears in the entry dedicated by Manuel Serrano y Sanz to María de Guevara in his *Apuntes,* 474–80.

13. Judging by the dates, this must be Don Andrés Velázquez de Velasco, also mentioned in the *Memorial* along with her previous two husbands, "Don García Bravo Osorio, marquis of Villar, lord of the entailed estate of Ocaña, founded by Pero Alvarez de Osorio, second son of the marquis of Astorga," and "Don Lorenzo Ladrón de Guevara, lord of Paradilla and the Arcor de Campos, page of my house and member of the order of Saint James," with neither of whom did she have an heir. *Memorial,* 19r.

14. *Memorial,* 19v.

15. *Diccionario biográfico matritense* (Madrid: Ayuntamiento, 1912). This information was not provided in what María de Guevara said of him.

16. "Fragmentos de la Historia de la Infantería Española," in his *Obras Completas,* ed. Jorge Campos (Madrid: Atlas, 1955), 2: 180.

name of Don Luis Andrés de Velázquez appears among the lists of prisoners in June of 1663.[17] However, Ballesteros informs us that he was freed and named by the king general sergeant of battle in the Badajoz army. It is likely that he was still alive in 1668, since there is a letter by Guevara in which she reproaches both Don Juan José of Austria and her *pariente*[18] for not responding to her letters.[19] It is worth noting, however, that in the bibliographical entry, Ballesteros highlights that Don Luis Andrés was married to "María de Guevara, countess of Escalante and Tahalú, lady of great wit,[20] who in 1656 wrote and printed a *Memorial of Her House*, and who ruled very successfully in her husband's absence."[21] Thus her wit and her governmental skills, characteristics that imbued her life and her writings, are pointed out in a masculine genre (the military biography) in which women's lives are practically erased. No more is known of her life except that she perhaps died in 1683.

We know of four texts written by María de Guevara.[22] In addition to these, two more texts about her must be kept in mind. The first is the report, already mentioned, of the day journey to Vitoria (1660), probably ordered by her and sent to the king; the second is a proof of pedigree won by the countess (1669).[23] In the report of the journey, Guevara comes across as a woman of strong character, with great leadership skills as owner and administrator of her estates, along with a very good sense of humor, and as one who is well connected socially and who is respected by the highest dignitaries of Spain (see appendix B). Her writings show that the social circle in which she moved so comfortably included the most important and influential figures of her time: from monarchs (Philip IV and Charles II, to

17. *Campanha de Portugal: Pella provincia do Alentejo* (Lisbon: Na officina de Henrique Valente de Oliveira, 1663), 98.

18. At that time, *pariente* could refer to a husband or to any family member of the same lineage (*Cov.*).

19. Letter dated July 9, 1668, MSS 18.655, box 26, number 26, National Library, Madrid.

20. Wit in the seventeenth-century sense, that is, intelligent and cutting (*Cov.*).

21. *Diccionario biográfico matritense*, 663.

22. These four texts are her *Memorial* (1654); a nonautograph manuscript entitled *Tratado y advertencies hechas por una mujer celosa del bien de su Rey y corrida de parte de España* [Treatise and Warnings by a Woman, Concerned for the Good of Her King and Affronted by Part of Spain] (1663); a discourse of seven chapters shrouded in anonymity, with the title *Desengaños de la Corte y mujeres valerosas* [Disenchantments of the Court and Valorous Women] (1664); and an autographed letter to Don Juan José of Austria, which comes accompanied by a gazette (1668).

23. *Ejecutoria ganada a pedimento de la Condesa de Escalante, del pleito que en esta Real Audiencia ha tratado con Antonio Abad de Arizaga y Bartolomé de Gárate y otros consortes, vecinos de la villa de Elgoibar* [Proof of Pedigree Won by the Countess of Escalante, in the Lawsuit She Has Brought in This Royal Court against Antonio Abad de Arizaga and Bartolomé de Gárate and Other Colitigants and Neighbors of the Town of Elgoibar] (Valladolid, 1669), MSS 19.085, National Library, Madrid.

whom the texts translated in this edition are addressed), to the queen, prime ministers (e.g., count of Haro and duke of Medina), exemplary military figures (e.g., Don Juan José of Austria), and other nobles.

Culturally, Guevara demonstrates that she has a good command of Spain's history, past and present, and that she is an avid reader of daily gazettes as well as other literary and nonliterary texts of her time. It is likely that she was strongly influenced by her great-great-uncle, the well-known chronicler, courtier, and bishop Father Antonio de Guevara (1481–1545),[24] as well as by her ancestor Pero López de Ayala (1332–1407).[25] From both men, Guevara inherited the willingness to learn from history and to contribute to it. It comes as no surprise, then, that she insists on a king's reading histories and chronicles, activities that will allow him to act according to his rank. She also dispenses other advice about political, economic, social, religious, and military matters. All of her words aim to fulfill one goal: to educate the prince.

In solitude—either from having husbands away at war or from being a widow—Guevara creates a persona that is allowed to break with the traditional models of women's conduct of her age. To enter into the public space and leave the written evidence of her texts, Guevara has to encode herself through a rhetorical play of boldness and submission. No woman who "is worth two men," as some soldiers say of her in the "Report," can openly attempt to criticize the king. Her family and her social persona, along with the unstable political period in which she lived and the important literary examples that preceded her, all allowed her to have a space in which to air her critical voice.

## HISTORICAL BACKGROUND: THE END OF THE HABSBURGS

> I looked at the walls of my native land, once strong, now dilapidated, worn out by the racing of time, which now causes their bravery to fail. I went out into the fields; I saw that the sun was drinking the brooks freed from ice, and the cattle were complaining of the mountain, whose shadows were stealing the light of day. I entered my house; I saw that, all stained, it was the remnants of an ancient habitation; my cane, more bent and less strong. I felt my sword to be conquered by age, and I found nothing on which to set my eyes that wasn't a reminder of death.
>
> Francisco de Quevedo, Psalm 17

24. Father Antonio de Guevara is named in her *Memorial* as the famous chronicler of the Emperor Charles V (10v). His work is fundamental for her almost-governmental recommendations. In particular, *Relox de Príncipes* (1529) and *Menosprecio de corte y alabanza de aldea* (1539).

25. Pero López de Ayala is well known for his *Rimado de palacio* (ca. 1378–1403), an ironic criticism of the society of his time in 8,200 verses (*EC*).

Philip IV (1605–65) and Charles II (1661–1700) were the last two monarchs of the Habsburg dynasty in Spain. Their reigns, each known for its "crisis," coincide with the end of the Spanish empire. When Philip IV came to power in 1621, he was a young man of sixteen confronting a country already in the midst of an economic recession and a seemingly never-ending war in Flanders. Philip IV showed no interest in state affairs. From the beginning of Philip's reign until 1643, the Count Duke Olivares occupied the position of the king's favorite, his "prime minister," and later was succeeded by his nephew, Luis de Haro, from 1643 to1661. Finally, Medina de las Torres, Olivares's son-in-law, acted as favorite during the last four years of Philip's reign. The beginning of that reign was marked by reformation measures against luxuries and imported goods as well as measures to reduce the expenses of the court—expenses which had been sharply criticized during the reign of Philip III.[26] Olivares aimed to rebuild the economy. However, the main focus of Olivares's ministry was rebuilding the unity of a country in crisis. With this goal in mind, Olivares "presented his famous secret memorandum urging Philip to become truly king of *a unified Spain*" in 1624.[27] This effort to strengthen the political unity of Spain under a centralized government in Madrid resulted in a continuous state of war against Flanders, Italy, France, England, and, in the Peninsula, against Catalonia and Portugal. Exacerbating the situation were pirates' assaults on Spanish fleets coming from America filled with gold and other valuable goods. The expensive maintenance of the troops, the loss of goods in the Atlantic, and the mortal plagues in the Peninsula, among other troubles, drove the country into a state of desperation. In fact, Olivares's policies of centralized control and austere economic reforms were criticized by the nobility, particularly the titled nobility, who revolted and eventually managed to oust Olivares from his powerful position in 1643. In the following years, however, there was little improvement. Both Haro and later Medina de las Torres tried simply to maintain a solvent state by keeping "the monarchy on a survival course."[28]

With the death of Philip IV in 1665, another issue arose: that of succession. Philip IV had married Elizabeth of Bourbon, the daughter of King Henry IV of France, with whom he had only two children that survived infancy—a girl, María Teresa, and a boy, Baltazar Carlos. Baltazar Carlos died

---

26. Henry Kamen, *Spain, 1469–1714: A Society of Conflict* (London: Longman, 1983), 201. Also for an extensive account of Philip IV's reign and Olivares's term as "prime minister," see John H. Elliott, *The Count-Duke of Olivares: The Statesman in an Age of Decline* (New Haven: Yale University Press, 1986).

27. Ibid., 202, emphasis added.

28. Ibid., 204.

in 1646. Philip IV then married Mariana of Austria, who was many years younger and originally a bridal candidate for his deceased son. Daughter of the Austrian emperor Ferdinand III, Mariana gave Philip several children, all of whom died young, and, finally, a male successor, Prince Joseph Charles, the future Charles II, weak and unhealthy, popularly called "the bewitched king," who was only four years old when his father died.[29] But these were only the officially recognized children, since Philip also had multiple affairs. The most well known was with actress María Calderón, who gave him a son, Don Juan José of Austria (1629–79), who became famous for his invincibility as a soldier and who was highly admired by the Spanish people, particularly those of Madrid.

The final forty years of the Habsburg dynasty were no less troubled than the previous ones. Although a peace treaty with France was signed in 1659 (the Peace of the Pyrenees) and the war with Portugal ended with the division of the Peninsula into two independent countries in 1668, the conflictive relation with Flanders and France persisted and the economic recession continued. During the regency of Mariana of Austria up until 1675, and also during Charles II's own reign, tensions grew. The nobility felt threatened by the fact that Mariana, not trusting the traditional grandees, relied on advisors who did not belong to the nobility and, most of all, on her confessor, the Austrian Jesuit Juan Everard Nithard, whom she named as general inquisitor.[30] Grandees were divided between those who supported her and those who felt marginalized by the court. Charles II further fueled the flames of dissatisfaction when, in an attempt to revitalize the noble ranks, he created 328 new titles, "reviv[ing] as well old controversies about the role of aristocracy."[31] In the midst of this social conflict, the bastard son of Philip IV, Don Juan José of Austria, played an important role, since he was supported by the aristocrats who stood against the regent queen and her Austrian minister and in favor of a traditional social status quo. Don Juan José was a leader of the people, probably the first in the history of Spain. His positioning against the queen and her allies attracted most of the Spanish states and a strong majority of grandees. From his pseudo-exile in Aragon, he attempted to take the capital of Madrid on two occasions, 1669

29. "The king, an invalid since birth, was never a significant force: he remained chronically ill throughout his life, and when he was twenty-five the papal Nuncio reported that 'he is as weak in body as in mind. Now and then he gives signs of intelligence, memory and a certain liveliness; usually he shows himself slow and indifferent, torpid and indolent. One can do with him what one wishes because he lacks his own will'" (ibid., 257).

30. Ibid., 257–58.

31. Ibid., 246.

and 1677, the latter resulting in the first official coup d'état in the recorded history of Spain. It was after the second failure that he offered his services to Charles II.[32] But his turn was brief and death found him just two years later. The situation in Spain, however, did not improve. Inflation, money devaluation, famine, poverty, plagues, military losses, and the like were commonplace in the last thirty years of the Habsburgs' rule. During the final decade, Charles's government was marked by the lack of succession.[33] Neither of his two marriages, to Marie Louise of Orleans and to Mariana of Neuburg, produced a successor, thus provoking ever-greater clashes in the country over who would be the future king. By the fall of 1700, the decision had been made: Philip V, duke of Anjou, son of Louis XIV and María Teresa (Charles's stepsister), would be the new monarch. With the new dynasty of the Bourbons, Spain finally had the possibility of a fresh start.

María de Guevara lived during this critical period. In *Treatise and Warnings by a Woman* (1663) and in *Disenchantments at the Court and Valorous Women* (1664), she addresses both monarchs, Philip IV and the king-to-be, Charles II. It is clear that she is completely embedded in the politics of her time. She focuses her discourse on two main historical factors. The first is the importance of the appropriate assignments of royal posts, particularly those in the Council of Finance (presently given to Portuguese) and those in the Council of War (given to cowards and inexperienced people). The second factor is the war with Portugal.

Favoritism was rampant in the post of prime minister. Favorites such as the Count Duke Olivares, Philip IV's first prime minister, and the Austrian minister under the queen's regency came between the king and the aristocrats. Plots among the nobility were effective enough to remove important characters from power (such as Olivares) while imposing others (Don Juan José of Austria). Although from the sixteenth century forward a middle-urban nobility was adapting and assimilating to the new political and socioeconomic circumstances, most of the members of the upper nobility, to which María de Guevara belonged, were determined to recreate an old ideology. While grandees and the titled nobility had considerably increased in number in the previous half century, their privileges were challenged and their unity was threatened. In most cases, survival rested on strengthening the ideological principles of sociocultural distinction that traditionally defined them as ideal models of representation. It is therefore not surprising that María de

---

32. Ibid., 258–59.

33. As Kamen declares: "Charles II's health was [meanwhile] decaying rapidly. In 1699 there was a short-lived attempt to use exorcism to cure the King's condition, in particular his inability to produce an heir (his reputation as a 'bewitched king' derives almost entirely from this incident" (ibid., 261).

Guevara authorized her political discourse by relying on her position as a high noble or that she spoke from a socially conservative position.

Guevara did not doubt that she had the authority to advise the king on who would sit at his side in the government. Guevara was echoing the general opinion of courtly noblemen and reformers when she wrote:

> A king is obliged to know and be familiar with those to whom he gives the important positions and not to govern solely on what he is told; because sometimes a person comes along and tells him that so-and-so is appropriate for such and such a position—saying it because he has been paid to do so, or because of some connection by friendship or kinship. The king grants the man that position, and he begins serving the king and governing. Then the man wishes to recover his costs, and much more, and so he accepts bribes and sells lesser positions to men who, for lack of merits, would never have received them without paying for them. Thus they destroy provinces and kingdoms and conceal the fact from the king who, since he speaks directly with none of them, cannot know all this. If this monarch spoke directly with more of those at his side, and inquired of those to whom he gives the posts, he would know his subjects better. (*Disenchantments* IV)

Guevara insisted on the direct personal participation of the king in issues of state. Philip IV's blind trust in his ministers and advisors was overtly criticized by Guevara as well as by many nobles and *arbitristas* (reformers) who blamed the king's lack of interest in politics for the nation's downturn. But Guevara is not rejecting the presence of ministers around the king. As the historian José Antonio Maravall affirms, most of the political writers of the seventeenth century accepted the necessity of having ministers, but ministers who would not be able to diminish the king's power. That is, the king had to fulfill the duties associated with his position: "he must choose good ministers, keep them in their roles, limit them in case that they, out of excess, attempt to surpass those roles, watch over them to see if their actions are appropriate."[34] In particular, these writers were unwilling for the prime minister, or favorite, to act as head of state.[35] The king had to have his subjects under control, especially those with ruling posts in the Councils of Finance and War.

Historians of seventeenth-century Spanish economic policies have demonstrated that the reign of Philip IV can be characterized by the incorporation of Portuguese bankers and merchants into the *asientos* (contracts).

34. José Antonio Maravall, *Teoría del estado en España en el siglo XVII* (Madrid: Centro de Estudios Constitucionales, 1997), 304.

35. Ibid., 308.

From the beginning of his term, the Count Duke Olivares established continuous contacts and contracts with the Portuguese, hoping they would revitalize the country's economy. Indeed, the year 1622 was the beginning of negotiations between Portuguese merchants and the Spanish government in order for the former to acquire contracts. By 1631 the presence of bankers and merchants at the court was "fully consummated."[36] The invitation offered to Portuguese financiers to come to Spain, an invitation that had been extended since the reign of Philip III, made the aristocracy very uncomfortable. Most of these Portuguese were *cristãos novos* (New Christians), and if they were to accept the new positions, Spain had to concede certain conditions such us "freedom for New Christians to marry Old Christians; freedom of movement within Portugal and in the Peninsula; and above all freedom to settle in Castile and engage (with proper Castilian naturalization) in Seville's trade with the Indies."[37] The New Christian *asentistas* (contractors) did not take long to incorporate themselves into some of the most important posts of the Council of Finance and, consequently, into the ruling circles of Madrid. Obviously, Spaniards resented the economic and political power of the Portuguese in their country, particularly after Portugal initiated its war for independence in 1640.

The surrender of Portugal to Philip II in 1580 marked the beginning of the final period during which the two countries on the Iberian Peninsula were together under the same government. In spite of the many promises and oaths the king made at the Cortes in Tomar (Portugal) in 1581, the relationship between the two countries never became good again. In fact, most of the agreements to preserve Portuguese institutions were not respected by the Spanish monarchy, and the situation deteriorated until the reign of Philip IV. While bankers and important financers were moving to Madrid and gaining positions of influence, discontent in Portugal was on the rise. Various riots, particularly that of Évora in 1637, signaled that the country was on the brink of war.[38] By 1640 the revolts had extended to the entire territory of Portugal, being especially strong in the border towns; these marked the beginning of the end of the "ideal" of peninsular unity and also the end of the Spanish empire.

---

36. James Boyajian, *Portuguese Bankers at the Court of Spain, 1626–1650* (New Brunswick, NJ: Rutgers University Press, 1983), 17.

37. Ibid., 17.

38. The popular revolt of Évora in 1637 was due to the imposition of a new tax on the consumption of wine and meat. On top of this was an additional 25 percent sales tax. All this took place during a very bad economic moment for Portugal. Rafael Valladares, *La rebelión de Portugal. Guerra, conflicto y poderes en la Monarquía Hispánica (1640–1680)* (Valladolid: Junta de Castilla y León, 1998), 25.

Although most of the bankers and contractors supported the Spanish position in the war against Portugal, the Spanish population was not very friendly toward the Portuguese. As James Boyajian says, "[i]n Castile after 1640 it was risky just being Portuguese. The day after the rebellion in Portugal there were outbreaks of violence against the 'Portuguese of birth' in Seville, Bilbao, and other places."[39] The revolt in Portugal set off an inevitably negative reaction in Spain—a reaction that had professional as well as religious causes. Many Spanish Christians accused the Portuguese of Judaizing activities and of many other crimes, "ranging from earning usurious profits from the interest charge in the *asientos* and extracting wealth from the Peninsula to enrich Spain's enemies, to sabotaging Spain's foreign policy and military offensives in Flanders."[40] In her writings, María de Guevara echoes this current of opinion: her main claim is that the Portuguese are spies and that from their posts—mainly in the Councils of Finance and War—they are able to betray Spain. Both in her *Treatise* and in *Disenchantments*, Guevara complains that the money the Portuguese have acquired from their service to the Spanish crown—and thanks to which they have become rich—is being used to help Spain's enemies not only in the war in Portugal but also in the war in Flanders. One of the reasons is that they are not Old Christians, and therefore the only solution would be their expulsion from the country (*Treatise*). It was not surprising to Guevara, then, that many Portuguese families were abandoning Spain with all their wealth, an action that did not help the national economy and which, for her, demonstrated that they were not trustworthy.[41]

It should be noted that Guevara's strong position against the Portuguese is expressed principally in the *Treatise* addressed to Philip IV in 1663. This year marked the end of the Spanish successes in the war against Portugal. Indeed, this was the year of the worst of the defeats, that of Entremoz, and by then the Spanish government realized that the end was near. It would, of course, be an unfavorable resolution for Spain. In fact, from the latter half of the 1650s and into the 1660s, the war against Portugal became the focus of Spanish politics. Until that time, the war with France over Catalonia had been occupying the mind, money, and army of the monarchy. The end of the war against France and the signing of the Treaty of the Pyrenees in 1659 coincide with the difficult years of the war against Portugal. What had

---

39. Boyajian, *Portuguese Bankers*, 130.

40. Ibid., 164. Also see Antonio Domínguez Ortiz, *Política y hacienda de Felipe IV* (Madrid: Ed. de Derecho Financiero, 1960), particularly 127–33.

41. A sentiment also recorded by many other political writers of the time, such as Jerónimo de Barrionuevo in his *Avisos* (1654–58) (quoted in Kamen, *Spain*, 136).

been only a succession of border confrontations and poorly organized skirmishes became in 1658—with the Portuguese sieges of Badajoz and Elvas (Yelbes)—the beginning of a new stage in this war in which Portugal occupied the foreground of Spanish foreign policy. The prime minister himself, Don Luis de Haro, commanded the Spanish army in both sieges. After an overly celebrated victory in Badajoz, though, the Spanish army, led by Don Luis, met a terrible defeat; it was, in the words of the Portuguese count of Castallena, "the greatest shame that the Castilians have suffered in a long time, because they fled the quarters, taking with them everything that was inside and leaving behind the fortresses garrisoned with camp masters and people of high rank who surrendered."[42]

From this moment on, the war against Portugal was a nightmare for Philip IV. Hoping to overcome the poor results of the last campaigns, Philip decided to install his bastard son, Don Juan José of Austria, as the leader of the Spanish army. The previous successes of Don Juan José in Flanders, along with his popular and aristocratic support in Spain, made him the perfect candidate to stop the Portuguese troops. However, as Guevara states, Portugal had help from two great powers, France and, more importantly, England. Guevara complains particularly about English participation: England provided the Portuguese army with more than a thousand horses, two thousand infantrymen, and ten warships for eight months, as well as numerous high officials who knew how to organize and lead a war.[43] Meanwhile, the army that Don Juan José led into Portugal was completely different from the one that accompanied him to Flanders—it was made up of "men coming from forced levies, raw recruits with no military experience."[44]

---

42. Quoted in Carlos M. Sánchez Rubio, et al., *Coreographia y descripción del territorio de la plaza de Badaxos y fronteras del Reyno de Portugal confinantes a ella* (Mérida: Junta de Extremadura, 2003), 11.

43. For more on the English-Portuguese alliance, see Valladares, *Rebelión de Portugal*, 171–80.

44. José Calvo Poyato, *Juan José de Austria* (Barcelona: Mondadori, 2003), 87. In fact, most of the accounts of the Portuguese campaigns in which Don Juan José participated referred to the bad behavior of the soldiers, their lack of discipline and obedience, their cowardice, their desertions in large numbers, their excesses, and so on. But the soldiers were not the only cause of a badly configured army: the high-ranking officials were to blame for being poor role models for their subordinates. As Fernando Cortés Cortés summarizes, their general greed as well as their immoral behavior, their almost nonexistent military preparation, their incompetence to lead, their fear, and so on, characterized a poor army, and one which was easily defeated. *Militares y guerra en una tierra de frontera. Extremadura a mediados del siglo XVII* (Mérida: Junta de Extremadura, 1991), 10–16. On different occasions, Don Juan José himself wrote to the king, Philip IV, complaining about the state of the army he had to command and asking for all kinds of support (mostly for experienced economic and military personnel), but his requests were never granted. For example, see MSS 2.388 (National Library of Madrid), in which Don Juan José writes to the king from Arroches (Portugal) on July 11, 1661, requesting from the Council of War money and experienced officers with knowledge about war.

In 1663 the two battles of Évora and, more disastrously for the Spanish army, that of Entremoz-Ameixial (in the province of Alentejo) marked the end of the war.[45] After these two important defeats, Don Juan José's army was completely destroyed. Most of his commanders and officials were killed or imprisoned (including Don Luis Andrés de Velázquez Velasco, Guevara's last husband). At Entremoz, the Portuguese army led by Don Sancho Manoel, count of Villaflor, along with the English troops led by General Frederick Shomberg, achieved the first crucial victory for the independence of Portugal. With Don Juan José retired from the Portuguese campaign, the Spanish army, then commanded by the duke of Osuna, tried but failed to retake Ameida and Castelo Rodrigo in 1664. Finally, in 1665 and under the leadership of the marquis of Caracena, the Spanish suffered the worst defeat of the war, the battle of Villaviciosa. Philip IV died without seeing the conflict's resolution. It would be the regent Mariana of Austria who in 1668 finally recognized Portugal's independence. The Spanish imperial dream of one peninsula, one country was shattered. The border between the two countries was devastated. Many crops were lost and many families impoverished or broken. The fact that this war both threatened Guevara's pride as a Spanish noblewoman and attacked her economically by destroying some of her properties along the Portuguese border made her find the strength to personally contribute to Spanish foreign policy. Through her writings, Guevara spoke up and took part in the (re)construction of the Spanish nation and in the writing of its history.

## A CONFLUENCE OF GENRES: REASON OF STATE AND CONTEMPT FOR THE COURT

*Treatise and Warnings by a Woman, Concerned for the Good of Her King and Affronted by Part of Spain* (1663) as well as *Disenchantments at the Court and Valorous Women* (1664) cannot be easily categorized into a specific genre. The variety of topics, the personal relationship she establishes with her addressees (principally in the treatise), the mix of styles and tones (from very informal to an almost governmental authoritative one), the choice of rhetorical devices, and other factors make it difficult to shoehorn these texts into one particular genre. However, any reader could find some connections with two of the most popular genres of the time: reason of state and contempt for the court.

It is well known that along with the emergence of Spain as a modern state, there arose a consciousness of making history a new discipline, separated from other genres and with its own goal. Historian Richard Kagan

---

45. See the complete report by Alvares da Cunha, *Campanha de Portugal* (1663).

reminds us of the importance of official histories requested by monarchs ever since the age of Their Catholic Majesties. These official histories were used both to legitimate Spain as a modern state and to increase and legitimate the authority and reputation of the monarchs.[46] Along with the national and royal consolidation of the new state, there was a strong need for political debate on topics such as the reason of state and the formation of a good prince. But writings on state theory and the mirrors of princes are not a novelty of the sixteenth and seventeenth centuries. Political thinkers from classical times to the medieval period (Aristotle to Saint Thomas) have a common objective: to educate society politically for the conservation and the prosperity of the state—a goal that would affect the formation of the prince in the first place.

According to Angeles Galino Carrillo, Spanish medieval texts written for the education of princes do not differ from those of the following centuries.[47] A continuity can be appreciated regarding influences, themes, and treatment of these themes, from religious texts and moral-political prose and *sentenciae* to specific mirrors of princes.[48] It was, however, in the sixteenth century that special attention was paid to works concerning themselves either directly or indirectly with the education of the prince as an ideal role model for his subjects. Some historians, such as J. A. Fernández Santamaría, see an increasing frequency in the composition and publication of these types of works, "an impetuous torrent" of them, by the beginning of the seventeenth century.[49] It is then not surprising that Maravall manages to count more than seventy texts immediately after 1625, all dealing with the prosperity of Spain and its prince.[50]

This increase in the number of treatises since the sixteenth century responded to specific elements, two of which must be highlighted: "the influence of Italian humanism, itself an avid explorer of the prince's role on the stage of politics," and the publication of "two masterpieces of *speculum*

---

46. Richard Kagan, "Clio and the Crown: Writing History in Habsburg Spain," in *Spain, Europe, and the Atlantic World: Essays in Honor of John Elliott*, ed. Richard Kagan and Geoffrey Parker (Cambridge: Cambridge University Press, 1995), 81.

47. *Los tratados sobre educación de príncipes (Siglos XVI y XVII)* (Madrid: CSIC, 1948), 2–35.

48. E.g., Juan Manuel's *Lucanor* or the anonymous *Historia del Caballero Cifar*, on the one hand, and Eiximeniç's *Llibre de regiment de princeps* or Valera's *Doctrinal de principes* on the other. The latter works' two major influences are Saint Thomas's *De regimine Principum* (ca. 1269) and Egidius Romanus's *De regimine principum* (ca. 1287), both very popular during the centuries that followed, with numerous editions and translations.

49. *The State, War, and Peace: Spanish Political Thought in the Renaissance, 1516–1559* (Cambridge: Cambridge University Press, 1977), 248.

50. Maravall, *Teoría*, 15–20.

literature—Machiavelli's *Il Principe* and Erasmus's *Institutio.*[51] Machiavelli's work in particular became the impetus for the composition of this sort of Spanish treatise, which did not so much incorporate his ideas as subject them to critical debate. This debate led to the inclusion of Machiavelli's work on the index of prohibited books in 1559 by reason of its lack of Christian virtue.[52] During the sixteenth century both ethicists and realists rejected Machiavelli's ideas.[53] Christianity became less important in the following century. As a result of the political and social crisis in Spain during the seventeenth century, reason-of-state treatises become more critical and pragmatic. That is, as Fernández Santamaría explains, while "the Renaissance asked: what qualities must the prince possess to rule?" the Baroque age wanted to know "the qualities needed by the prince to rule *in his own age.*"[54] The rise of the modern state opened the door to a new political way of thinking in which idealist dreams were changed by realist facts. The art of ruling approached Machiavelli's ideas insofar as "Christianity is not enough to be a good prince."[55] *Prudencia* (prudence) became the most important characteristic of the prince.[56]

In María de Guevara's writings, as in those by the most influential writers of her time,[57] practical recommendations compose the core of her message. Guevara's most common topics are those which other writers also emphasize: the election of the prime minister and other ministers and councilors; the formulation of a more effective military theory for the defense of the commonwealth; and the need to be knowledgeable about history.

In chapter IV of her *Disenchantments at the Court,* Guevara follows most of the political writers of her age by treating the subject "on how kings should act in assigning government posts." She does not reject having ministers

---

51. Fernández Santamaría, *State, War, and Peace,* 248.

52. For a longer account of the differences between Spanish political authors in their response to Machiavelli's ideas, see Fernández Santamaría, *Reason of State and Stagecraft in Spanish Political Thought, 1595–1640* (Lanham: University Press of America, 1983), 3–41; and Teresa Langle de Paz, "En busca del paraíso ausente: 'mujer varonil' y 'autor femenil' en una utopía feminista inédita del siglo XVII español," *Hispania* 86, no. 3 (2003): 469. Also see Maravall's *Teoría,* 230–72.

53. In Fernández Santamaría's *Reason of State,* 7.

54. *State, War, and Peace,* 250.

55. Ibid., 252.

56. See Galino Carrillo's *Tratados sobre educación,* 161–202. She defines prudence as "a moral norm of the practical intellect that gives man enough tact and discretion to organize his life and govern his subjects, in each case doing what seems most pertinent to the observance of virtue" (161).

57. That is, Fernández de Navarrete, Juan Lancina, Pedro de Ribadeneyra, Diego Saavedra y Fajardo, and Jerónimo de Zeballos.

or councilors. In fact, Guevara and her contemporaries accept that these positions are necessary as long as they do not challenge and diminish the king's power. This is why, in order to be a good prince, the king has such obligations as to choose competent ministers, assure himself of their loyalty, reward them fairly, and control them whenever they try to overrule him. Regarding the prime minister or favorite, there is a subtle yet noticeable lack of confidence. Though they are not against that political figure, these theorists ask the king that the person be completely trustworthy and, even then, that the king be always aware of what this figure does or says.[58] The same could be said about other councilors, mainly in relation to the knowledge and expertise they are expected to have in the area for which they are appointed. It is not surprising that in the middle of the seventeenth century, when defeats on different fronts were bringing the Spanish empire to an end, most of these writers insist on having the "right" person in the Council of War—someone who can be trusted and who has experience on the battlefield. No army can be governed by bureaucrats and courtiers with no knowledge of war.

It is war, its theory and practice, that becomes a repeated subject in each of the treatises addressed to the prince. According to Juan Saavedra and Juan Sánchez Belén, at the end of the sixteenth century military literature begins to become fashionable "due to the reforms that Maurice of Nassau had realized in the army of the United Provinces to halt the advance of the Spanish army—although many were a copy or adaptation of those that were already in force in the Spanish army in Flanders, mainly regarding hierarchical subordination and military training."[59] The number of military treatises is enormous, and the subject of war is treated not only in texts on the topic of war. It also forms part of every text dedicated to the education of the good prince. As one writer explains, "to govern an army well is an art for the empire and a worthy science for a good king."[60]

The warnings of María de Guevara echo most of those presented by the political writers of her time, which are characterized by a "tone of severity

---

58. The attention paid to the figure of prime minister and other ministers and councilors is reflected in the publication of specific books to advise them. Such is the case with, among others, Antonio de Guevara's *Aviso de privados y doctrina de cortesanos* (1539) and Furió Cerol's *Consejo y consejeros del príncipe* (1559) in the sixteenth century, and Lorenzo Ramírez de Prado's *Consejo and consejeros de Príncipes* (1617) and José Laynez, *El privado Christiano* (1641) during the seventeenth century.

59. Introduction to *Teoría y práctica de guerra*, by Bernardino de Mendoza (1595), ed. Juan Saavedra and Juan Sánchez Belén (Madrid: Ministerio de Defensa, 1998), 13.

60. Gerónimo de Zeballos, *Arte real para el buen gobierno de los Reyes, y Príncipes, y de sus vasallos* (Toledo: By the author, 1623), 146.

rarely surpassed."[61] Writers like Gerónimo de Zeballos[62] or Juan Baños de Velasco[63] prescribe who should go to war, at what age, of what social class, and with which experiences and characteristics; who should lead the army during battle and who should govern from the posts of the Council of War; how to deal with bribes and desertions; how to create a spirit of trust between soldiers and their leaders; and how to handle salaries and rewards.

In order to select good ministers who will know how to practice the military art, nothing becomes more important than the knowledge of history. Guevara herself affirms that

> in order for kings to know what each house is worth and how well their owners have served you and how much value to place upon each, it is well that from the moment princes begin to talk, they should be taught to read histories and chronicles, so that they may know what level of esteem to bestow upon each one. (*Treatise*)

Guevara establishes a dialogue with contemporary political writers and recognizes that history is more important than experience, since it "enables the rulers to meet an obligation held sacred by the Baroque: to acquire and to preserve political power."[64] Knowledge of history, in particular the history of Spain, is useful for the proper exercise of public policy. As Maravall says, history was transformed into an entirely new discipline during the seventeenth century. Separated from poetry, history became more pragmatic and with an exemplary goal. Two theorists who saw history as an independent genre and who clearly defined the role of this new discipline are Luis Cabrera de Córdoba and Jerónimo de San José.[65] Cabrera de Córdoba says that "the aim of history is far more than merely narrating great events in order to rescue them from oblivion. Rather, it is to teach us to live by the experience of those who individually contributed to perfect prudence. The end of history is the public good."[66] Prudence and history are closely related, since history supplies the prince with many experiences from the past that will allow him to multiply his personal experience and to be able to rule prudently. With knowledge of the past, the good prince will organize the present and

---

61. Maravall, *Teoría*, 340.

62. See n. 60.

63. Juan Baños de Velasco, *Política militar de príncipes* (1680).

64. Fernández Santamaría, *Reason of State*, 158.

65. Luis Cabrera de Córdoba, *De historia, para entenderla y escribirla* (1611); Jerónimo de San José, *Genio de la historia* (1651).

66. Cabrera de Córdoba, *De historia, para entenderla y escribirla* (Madrid: Luis Sánchez, 1611), fol. 19.

anticipate the future.[67] The prince will rule by following the proper models; he will distinguish between good and bad ministers or councilors according to previous examples; he will know how to reward his vassals fairly, taking into consideration what their predecessors did and how well the ancestors of those vassals served the crown. History will accompany the rise of the modern state for the good of the prince and the conservation and prosperity of Spain and its monarchy.

Among the models that the prince finds in history to imitate are the lives of figures from classical antiquity. Father Antonio de Guevara chooses Roman emperors as protagonists in two of the most influential works of sixteenth- and seventeenth-century Spain.[68] His *Relox* is considered a "best-seller" for its time, surpassed in popularity only by Father Luis de Granada's works.[69] In her *Memorial*, Guevara highlights her relationship with Antonio de Guevara, "bishop of Mondoñedo, and chronicler of the Lord Emperor, who was born in the house of the village of Treceño."[70] Throughout her writings, the countess displays this relationship, noticed clearly in intertextual influences. Indeed, she adapts most of Antonio de Guevara's idealized political advice into something more practical and personal. It is in her *Disenchantments* where this influence can be best appreciated. Without naming the source, she uses Marcus Aurelius's words to authorize her own and to advise the king-to-be, Charles II. Significantly, every reference to Marcus Aurelius corresponds not with his *Meditations*, but to Antonio de Guevara's life of Marcus Aurelius.[71] From common topics regarding the prince's moral characteristics, the selection of good ministers or judges, or the key to cleaning the "empire" of rogues, to specific topics on women, their intelligence, or how husbands should behave with their wives, María de Guevara takes into account Antonio de Guevara's utopian portrait of Marcus Aurelius and uses it to give specific and personal advice to her king-to-be.

There is yet another influence in her writings coming directly from Antonio de Guevara and the very popular humanist topic of contempt of

---

67. Maravall, *Teoría*, 67.

68. *Una década de césares* (1539) and, more importantly, the *Libro aúreo de Marco Aurelio* (1528), later added to and corrected by the author under the title *Vida del famosísimo Emperador Marco Aurelio, con el Relox de príncipes*, better known simply as *Relox de Príncipes* (1529).

69. Keith Whinnom, "The Problem of the Best-Seller in Spanish Golden Age Literature," *Bulletin of Hispanic Studies* 57 (1980): 193–94.

70. *Memorial*, 10v.

71. Antonio de Guevara, *Vida del famosísimo Emperador Marco Aurelio, con el Relox de príncipes* (1529), ed. Emilio Blanco, 2 vols. (n.p.: ABL/ Conferencia de Ministros Provinciales Franciscanos de España, 1994).

the court and praise of the village. Guevara herself makes a direct allusion to Antonio de Guevara's 1539 work on this subject.[72] The reference is clear from the first part of her work's title, *Disenchantments at the Court*, and from some of its chapters.[73] As in her model, a reader can appreciate the philosophical merging of stoicism and epicureanism. According to María de Guevara, the court can be harmful to both the body and the soul since it contains vices (ranging from those related to morals like envy and ambition to those that affect the physical body like alcoholic drinks and sexual illnesses). Every human being, and aristocrats in particular, should remove themselves from those vices. To leave the court would mean to renounce temptations and embrace what each one is and owns—a goal clearly related to that of the religious literature of ascetic character (*contemptus mundi*) that greatly influenced the Castilian humanism of the fifteenth century and later. Along with the dispraise of the court, there is praise of the village, that is, "intermingled with Séneca's idea, and giving it a different sense, there is an exaltation of what is natural."[74] The village becomes a good alternative not only for the body but also, and more importantly, for the soul. Echoing her great-great-uncle's words, María de Guevara explains how in the village the lord is recognized publicly; he is no longer an anonymous being trying to be noticed such as occurs in the court. At the same time, he will be familiar with his subjects and will govern his vassals with justice, offering them what they need in order to live a harmonious life (e.g., good schools and teachers, active churches with regular preachers). The village is the place to enjoy the resources and pleasures of the countryside, from its food (e.g., partridges, rabbits, and fruits) to a variety of activities (e.g., hunting and fishing). It is also the place where the lord will have time to read the chronicles and learn about houses and lineages. In general, this village is more than an ideal *beatus ille* and is closer to a realist vision of life that opposes that of the court.[75]

In summary, María de Guevara's writings perfectly match the literary tastes of her time. She engages in dialogue with the most important con-

---

72. Antonio de Guevara, *Menosprecio de corte y alabanza de aldea. Arte de Marear*, ed. Asunción Relló (Madrid: Cátedra, 1987).

73. "Disenchantments at the Court and Valorous Women" (chap. 1), "On the Disenchantments at the Court and the Quiet Life in the Village" (chap. 5), and "On How Lords Who Live on their Estates Should Behave" (chap. 6).

74. Asunción Relló, in her introduction to Antonio de Guevara, *Menosprecio de corte*, 65.

75. As Relló says in her introduction (67–68), this realist vision has a literary precedent in the *Rimado de palacio* (ca. 1378–1403) by Pero López de Ayala (another of Guevara's ancestors) and in Sánchez de Arévalo's *Espejo de la vida humana* (1491). For more information on María de Guevara's position with regard to the praise of the village, see Langle de Paz, "En busca," esp. 465–66 and 470–71.

temporary political writers and makes use of the most popular topics and genres of seventeenth-century Spain. Guevara demonstrates that she is an avid reader of history, chronicles, and treatises, as well as any sort of book that relates to Spain's conservation and prosperity.

## GUEVARA'S WRITINGS: AN ANALYSIS

In her determination to educate kings, María de Guevara proposes a political and social reorganization of Spain and at the same time rewrites its history. María de Guevara knows how to authorize herself by using some of the most popular genres of her time. However, her advice on the reorganization of Spain and the rewriting of its history is from a gendered perspective, and this is what makes her work original. Guevara herself wonders, "Who is a woman to meddle in this?" (*Treatise*). Guevara recognizes that being a woman can be an obstacle, not so much with regard to writing itself as to writing about overtly masculine topics and in overtly masculine genres. Guevara had to employ certain rhetorical tools and ideological mechanisms in order to create a space of authority for herself in a world of political and military writing and make her conceptual position known with regard to Spain, its history, and its identity.

### A Rhetorical Fencing Game

> For I am repeating what people are saying and what reaches my ears as a good vassal who wishes to serve your Majesty, whom I beseech to forgive me and accept my genuine concern. Would that I were an Amazon at this moment, and that everyone in Spain were an Amazon, to return her honor and the honor of my king. May God watch over you for a thousand centuries and grant you a long succession and protection for these kingdoms.

With this paragraph, María de Guevara, countess of Escalante, concludes her *Treatise and Warnings by a Woman, Concerned for the Good of Her King and Affronted by Part of Spain*. These words summarize the contradiction that characterizes her discourse: on the one hand, there is an active "feminism" in her plea to defend Spain; that is, this defense can succeed only in the hands of women, a notion that subverts the law of the father, the law of the king. On the other hand, Guevara's political challenge is counteracted by a submissive female exposition in which she uses rhetorical techniques that will help her to distance herself from feminism and submit herself to the law of the father, the law of the king.

To represent this contradiction, Guevara utilizes the image of the Amazon. Instead of the sixteenth- and seventeenth-century aberrant monster of nature (although attractive and extraordinary at the same time), Guevara

chooses a favorable image of the Amazon. This positive image reminds us of the work of Christine de Pizan, the first woman to write about this mythological figure as a symbol of female transcendence.

> [W]hile male authors waved the swords of vengeance and retribution and used the Amazon image to glorify themselves, Christine de Pizan created Amazons of strength, sensuality, prowess, and competence and made them speak for women. While men continued to dream, at least for the next few centuries, of conquering Amazons, even of carving up Amazons, Christine de Pizan demonstrated that women could use the Amazon to stake a claim to share in the art and work of civilization.[76]

Guevara's Amazon is powerful, with "superb" strength, and her competence extends from the military space into every type of "art and work of civilization." Indeed, along with women who literally fight in the battlefield and whom she admires and praises in her writings (e.g., the women of Ávila, Queen Isabella of Castile), Guevara recreates the image of an intellectual Amazon, for whom the sword is nothing less than her pen, that is, the learned woman.[77] In this way, the military Amazon is on the same level as the intellectual one, her physical strength on the same level as her mental competence. This connection is confirmed in other texts of hers, such as *Disenchantments at the Court and Valorous Women*, from 1664, in which Guevara writes that "they [men] do not want women to be Amazons but rather to have their hands tied, making it unbecoming for a woman to leave her corner" (*Disenchantments* II).

In her desire to restore honor to Spain, Guevara takes up her pen and challenges her kings, thereby taking part in a rhetorical fencing game in which she wields the weapons of both modest submission and bold warnings. This association between fencing and rhetoric is not arbitrary. In 1611, the sport of fencing was defined as

> the practice and movements of fighting with each other, which, since it was done as entertainment, was given the name "game"; although it is said half in jest, it is customary to dish out many good bumps to the head. The fencing masters teach postures, bravery, the attempt at making a diagonal cut from right to left and from left to right, and

---

76. Abby Wettan Keinbaum, *The War against the Amazons* (New York: New Press/McGraw-Hill, 1983), 68.

77. Regarding the learned woman as a symbol of her time, see Margaret King, *Women of the Renaissance* (Chicago: University of Chicago Press, 1991), 190 ff.

also the attempt at the straight-on touch, the attack, the retreat, the parry and avoidance of the touch, and everything else that concerns defending oneself and attacking.[78]

María de Guevara's wordplay follows a rhetoric of defense and attack. Despite playing only a rhetorical "game" and being neither insulting nor irreverent toward the monarchs, Guevara cannot avoid giving "many good bumps to the head." Therefore, by following the model of the treatises of reason of state, which were so popular in the seventeenth century, Guevara faces the kings as an intellectual Amazon. She educates and advises them on subjects of state, mainly those of governance and the military art. Guevara is challenging the dominant sexual politics of her time, rejecting the submissive role for women regarding matters of state and breaking her silence in order to rewrite the history of Spain.

Philip IV and the king-to-be, Charles II, are her addressees in *Treatise* and *Disenchantments*, respectively. The change of addressee is a response to despair. By 1664, the year *Disenchantments* is written, Philip IV's government was rapidly decaying and most of the critical political and social issues were still unresolved. Guevara addresses her second work to the "Great Prince of Spain," Don Charles Joseph, the future Charles II, and hopes that the Spanish kingdoms may "all be restored and turned once again to proper obedience of such a great monarch" (Dedication). In fact, in this text Philip IV has disappeared completely from the scene. With the lapse of only a year, Guevara decides to change addressees in an attempt to reach the son in a way she could never reach the father. The tone differs as well. In *Treatise* Guevara is very personal and direct. For example, while in *Disenchantments* the addressee is present only in the dedication, in the *Treatise* Philip IV is continuously brought into the conversation by specific strong recommendations and warnings. Indeed, the *Treatise* adheres more closely to a conversational format; in this way, Guevara succeeds in putting herself on the same level as her addressee. This technique is dangerous, not only because she is a woman but because it is a king with whom she maintains this direct conversation. In *Disenchantments*, on the contrary, Guevara prefers to adhere more closely to the norms of the genre and eliminates the direct speech to the future king. That is why in the *Treatise* it is easier to observe Guevara's rhetorical fencing techniques.

The *Treatise* is consciously structured: as the discourse moves forward, Guevara's meddling in state matters grows. Initially presented as the result of "curiosity," the *Treatise* quickly becomes an insistent recommendation at almost the governmental level. The greatest difficulty lies, as I mentioned,

78. Sebastián de Covarrubias, *Tesoro de la lengua castellana* (1611).

in making her voice competent and authoritative. The treatise opens with Guevara addressing her interlocutor, his Majesty Philip IV. First, she points out his ignorance of foreign policy by mentioning his advisors' incompetence: "If someone would tell your Majesty what is taking place, you would certainly try to prevent it, and we would not have such a poor outcome." Second, she singles out one man as incompetent, a man who is to blame for all the military defeats, and whom, maybe out of discretion, it would be better not to mention. Guevara chooses precisely not to name Don Juan José of Austria, the "unfortunate" man leading the Spanish army in Portugal during 1663, when the treatise is written. Since she is a faithful admirer and friend of Don Juan José, her silence is significant when compared with the allusion to the king's ignorance.

After the opening accusation of the treatise, Guevara retreats from her first attack with a contradictory affected modesty: "Your Majesty may say: who is a woman to meddle in this? To which I respond: how sad that we women come to understand what is happening as well as men do, but feel it even more." The countess tries to keep the addressee and the general reader on her side by admitting that she is a woman who dares to accuse the king. Following the Ciceronian topic of the *praemunitio*,[79] Guevara advances her womanhood as defense against the objections that may arise with regard to the points she is going to expand upon. "How sad"—she says modestly—that "we women come to understand what is happening," implying the supposed intellectual inferiority into which women have been plunged historically and which has kept them with their "hands tied" and pushed into the "corner." However, not only have women reached the same intellectual level as men but, paradoxically, thanks to the capacity for feeling that supposedly diminishes them in relation to men, women have become superior to them.[80] Guevara is conscious of the sexual politics of the time in separating "mind" and "feelings"; in order to authorize herself, she takes into account the misogynist discourse and uses it against itself, highlighting instead the superiority of women.[81]

79. Cicero's *praemunitio*: a defense "by anticipating objections to some point we propose to make later." See Lee A. Sonnino, *A Handbook to Sixteenth-Century Rhetoric* (New York: Barnes and Noble, 1968), 144.

80. It is important to notice that *entender* (understand)—the intellectual meaning of the word *sentir* (to feel) in Covarrubias's *Tesoro*—has already disappeared in the 1726 edition of the *Diccionario de Autoridades* (*Aut.*)

81. This technique is similar to the one used by María de Zayas y Sotomayor in the prologue "To the Reader" of her first collection of short stories, *The Enchantments of Love: Amorous and Exemplary Novels* (1637), trans. H. Patsy Boyer (Berkeley: University of California Press, 1990), 1–2. In this prologue, "Zayas, ironically, plays with dominant patriarchal ideology and her biological condition as a woman. She takes advantage of patterns of masculine legitimation

After a paragraph in which she refers to the decadence of traditional nobility in relation to its function, Guevara advances and subtly attacks the royal ignorance, and then again retreats with another excuse: "Forgive me, your Majesty, but since I have read so much, I pride myself on being curious, and I dare speak to you in this manner." Following the classic and, according to Ernst Curtius, "favorite" topos in the *exordia* of the need of imparting and teaching what each knows, Guevara joins the political writers of her time in their duty to educate the king.[82] Guevara insists on the value of history and is explicit about the king's lack of knowledge in this area. To compensate for her boldness, which she herself recognizes, she takes up the topos of false humility and boasts of being "curious," another negative characteristic associated with women in most of the moralist treatises of the age.[83] The bold insult is thereby softened.

However, from this moment on, no expression of modesty or humility is used until the end of the discourse. Her "I dare speak to you in this manner" that closes the introduction opens the door to a list of arguments about military techniques and the art of war. As explained previously, Guevara echoes most of the warnings presented by other writers. And, like some extremists (e.g., Zeballos and Lancina), she even makes specific allusions to the rewards and pensions that the wives and children of dead or disabled soldiers should be given, as well as to the direct participation of women, either in the field or in the rearguard. To authorize herself in this dominantly masculine subject, she utilizes some linguistic strategies. She poses as an "impersonal authority," distancing herself from these military statements so as not to impose her advice upon her addressee. In this part, Guevara's is a non-gender-marked discourse that simply follows what male political writers of her time were already saying. Guevara explicitly disclaims having any

---

and of a socially and literarily accepted *topos*, that of female submission and inferiority, in order to authorize her voice." Nieves Romero-Diaz, *Nueva nobleza, nueva novela: Rescribiendo la cultura urbana del Barroco* (Newark: Juan de la Cuesta, 2002), 111–12. See the entire section on the prologue, entitled "'Clase dominante, grupo dominado': El marco discursivo de María de Zayas" (107–15).

82. Ernst Curtius, *European Literature and the Latin Middle Ages*, trans. Willard Trask (New York: Harper and Row, 1963), 87.

83. See, for example, the chapter entitled "Cómo no es buena la demasiada curiosidad, en especial en las mujeres" (Why too much curiosity is not good, especially in women), in the book of conduct for women by Father Juan de la Cerda, *Vida política de todos los estados de mugeres, en el qual se dan muy provechosos y christianos documentos y avisos, para criarse y conservarse debidamente las mujeres en sus estados* (Alcalá de Henares: Juan Gracián, 1599). Also, for the study of the "false humility" topos, see the book by Alison Weber, entitled *Teresa of Ávila and the Rhetoric of Femininity* (Princeton: Princeton University Press, 1990), in particular chapter 2, "*The Book of Her Life* and the Rhetoric of Humility" (42–76).

knowledge on the subject by referring to other sources: "And so it is written of the army and so say some of those who have returned." More importantly, during this first exposition on military politics she resorts to the royal "we" ("in the histories we see," "as we have seen," "since we have seen that in this case") and to the use of passive structures in which no active subject of the action is named ("if in the villages a soldier is requested," "such men as these should be put in prisons, to be disciplined and trained there"). That is, Guevara makes use of certain mechanisms of depersonalization to neutralize her gender and to avoid involving herself in the accusations or in her direct attacks on the king.

This authorization by depersonalizing that she uses in the first part of her warnings changes radically the moment she introduces the war against Portugal. Her authority then becomes "personal," not only because of her stake in the subject but also because of the literal use of the first person. After a demand that the "right" person be assigned as war councilor, the "I" appears in the discourse in a way that establishes a comparison between the author and the councilor. This "personal authority" is introduced by an "I affirm." In Sebastián de Covarrubias's *Tesoro de la lengua castellana* (1611), it is explained that "in the fencing game and in the gladiatory art, to affirm is the equivalent of moving steadily toward your adversary, maintaining the tip of the sword always in his face, the tip unmoving except in the thrust." That is, if up till now the author has been attacking and retreating, offending and then defending, from this moment on her advice and warnings are affirmed with complete authority, by an intellectual Amazon who directly attacks her adversary with a pen in place of a sword.

First, Guevara bases her attacks on strong ethnic-religious beliefs, speaking from her dominant class position (as a noble conservative woman). The war against Portugal is really a crusade, says Guevara, since "the heretic Englishmen come to bring them victories," and because most of the Portuguese are not noble but plebeians. "And, although everywhere the fewest are the nobles and never the plebeians, in Portugal the plebeians are also Jews that King Ferdinand expelled from Castile and that Portugal welcomed. But since they are rich and that kingdom is so poor, they mixed with the common people. The consequence is obvious: the war is not against Christians." In so characterizing the Portuguese, Guevara is following a current of opinion popular at the time. Miguel Herrero García declares that along with an ideological tendency toward admiration for and racial identity with the Portuguese, Castilians also felt antagonism toward them, mainly because of the so-called "arrogance" of the Portuguese. The Portuguese were thought to be willing to surpass Castilians and to occupy high positions at

the court and posts such as traders, bankers, contractors, and sellers in the city, that is, all positions that were traditionally associated with Jews.[84] In fact, Guevara strongly criticizes the presence of Portuguese in important court posts—since they end up betraying the monarchy. So the countess challenges her king by recommending an "expulsion as was done with the *moriscos.*" This would be the only way to "put a stop" to the social disorder. Guevara manifests a strong anti-Semitic sentiment that was very common during her time. Her belonging to the dominant class puts her in a position of combating Olivares and the government's pro-Portuguese policies. Guevara distrusts and criticizes the presence of Portuguese not only at the court but in the whole Spanish territory. Like many other people, Guevara contributes to the growth of "a particular kind of Castilian nationalism in which . . . popular xenophobia and anti-Semitism . . . intertwined."[85] As James Boyajian explains,

> The prevailing anti-semitic and anti-Portuguese mood of the court in the post-Olivarean period and the heightened Inquisitorial activity contributed to an atmosphere in which the least credible rumors and claims about the Portuguese gained rapid acceptance. A populace that suspected the Portuguese New Christians of *Judaizing* was easily convinced that the Portuguese committed other crimes, ranging from earning usurious profits from the interest charges in the *asientos* and extracting wealth from the peninsula to enrich Spain's enemies, to sabotaging Spain's foreign policy and military offensives in Flanders.[86]

In a sense, Guevara as a noble is constructing an "other" so that her message as a woman will be authoritative enough. Her gendered nationalism becomes one of her stronger ideological arms.

With this authorization given by her class position, Guevara is able to attack the king from the standpoint of a dominated group: women. Guevara advocates the participation of women in reorganizing the country and insists that women should take an active part in this reorganization by fighting directly:

---

84. "Los Portugueses," in *Ideas de los españoles del siglo XVII* (Madrid: Gredos, 1966), 134–78.

85. Richard Kagan and Abigail Dyer, ed. and trans., *Inquisitorial Inquiries: Brief Lives of Secret Jews and Other Heretics* (Baltimore: John Hopkins University Press, 2004), 112. Chapter 4 includes inquisitorial cases against *Judaizing* New Christians, some with Portuguese connections, such as Francisco de San Antonio. As the editors explain, many *converso* persecutions during Olivares's time targeted "Portuguese New Christians residing in Madrid, . . . persecutions [that] culminated in the great *auto de fe* staged in Madrid's Plaza Mayor in 1632 that sentenced seventeen *judaizantes*, all Portuguese, to be burned at the stake" (112).

86. Boyajian, *Portuguese Bankers*, 164.

Send even troops of women, because this war is against a second Spanish *Cava*. Do this so that when we women are not fighting, we shall remain in the fortress serving as foot soldiers. I shall be the first, as well as four more on my behalf, though they be of inferior rank.

Also, and more importantly, women should fight intellectually by writing, as she herself does. As she points out, "Your Majesty knows quite well that I can write books and memorials, which is why I dare to write this one." The "I affirm" that opened this section of the treatise on the war against Portugal reappears on different occasions, and in a similar manner she also uses "I stake my life on it." With the tip of her sword in his face, Guevara tells the king how to organize the war against the Portuguese and how the Councils of War and Finance should deal with it (e.g., who should be leading the army from the court, who should determine the salaries as well as the rewards for soldiers, and so on). In the middle of this explanation, Guevara reaches the height of her attack. She definitely scores a touch against her adversary by figuratively removing the king and placing herself instead at the head of the state. Guevara establishes a correlation between herself and the regent queen of Portugal, Luisa de Gusmão, who promoted the revolt from within Portugal and later its independence: "So, my Lord, since a woman is encouraging them there, let there be another to encourage our men from here." With her as the head of state and with women fighting with swords and pens, Spain would become a country of Amazons who could restore its lost honor.

The thrust has been carried home. However, to end the treatise, Guevara positions herself on guard and again takes up the game of offense and defense that characterized the introduction. She turns to the classic topos of modesty and submission: the discourse is once again depersonalized and the vox populi becomes the owner of her boldness. "I am repeating what people are saying," she writes, "and what reaches my ears as a good vassal who wishes to serve your Majesty." But as she is playing a rhetorical fencing game, this modesty is set against a declaration of her being "an Amazon" and her wish that "everyone in Spain were an Amazon." The restoration of Spain can come only from imitating the valor and carrying out the role of the mythical Amazon women. These women, of whom she is setting the example with her pen, become then the ideal model for Spanish citizens, the king included. Guevara thus achieves a double thrust: a diagonal cut from left to right and a second from right to left.[87]

---

87. This double thrust is called in Spanish "cortar de tajo y de revés" (*Cov.*).

*Rewriting History: A Model of Womanhood for a New "Matriotic" Spain*

One year after writing *Treatise*, Guevara develops an ideal model for Spain in *Disenchantments at the Court and Valorous Women*[88] In this new Spain, "Amazons" are the only ones able to restore honor to the country. Patriotic nationalistic sentiments are thus transformed by Guevara into new "matriotic" ones: Guevara inspires a strong loyalty for a "mother" country and attempts to reconstruct its history by the recovery of heroic women from the past who will mark the road for the future. To better understand the past, she rewrites the history of Spain from a gendered perspective and takes into account female models, religious and secular, national and international; in essence, women are the active protagonists in the history of the country since, in her opinion, "incapable" (male) kings and advisors are unable to do much.

Although women are present in all of her writings, the second chapter of her *Disenchantments* (1664) entitled "Concerning Valorous Women" is worth special consideration. This chapter resembles a catalogue of valorous women that finds its roots in Hesiod's *Catalogue of Women* from around 700 B.C.E. and continues with the work of Giovanni Boccaccio in Italy and Christine de Pizan in France and with that of Álvaro de Luna, Juan Rodriguez del Padrón, Diego de Valera, and Juan Pérez de Moya in Spain. But from a rhetorical point of view, Guevara creates an "original" way of cataloguing, using a perspective that is gendered and generic. Guevara is arguably the first woman in Spain who consciously elaborates a catalogue of women as such, rather than the list of illustrious foremothers that normally appears in prologues and dedications, a list whose goal is to justify women's participation in the world of writing.[89] Nor does she follow the traditional tripartite division established in Spain by Álvaro de Luna,[90] namely, women from the Bible, those from antiquity, and Catholic saints. She does not even

---

88. For this section, I am gratefully indebted to Nina Scott, who provided me with two of her articles which have proved fundamental. They are "'La gran turba de las que merecieron nombres': Sor Juana's Foremothers in *La Respuesta a Sor Filotea*" (in *Coded Encounters: Writing, Gender, and Ethnicity in Colonial Latin America*, ed. Francisco Javier Cevallos et al. [Amherst: University of Massachusetts Press, 1996], 206–23), and "Los espíritus tutelares de la Avellaneda," in *Mujeres latinoamericanas: Historia y Cultura, siglos XVI al XIX*, ed. Luisa Campuzano [Mexico City: Casa de las Américas, 1997], 2: 187–93).

89. This type of list intends to authorize women's own literary adventures. One important example is that of María de Zayas in her prologue "To the Reader" from *The Enchantments of Love* (1–2). For a complete study of Zayas's foremothers, see Margaret Greer, *María de Zayas Tells Baroque Tales of Love and Cruelty of Men* (University Park: Pennsylvania State University Press, 2000), 72–79.

90. Álvaro de Luna, *Libro de las virtuosas y claras mujeres* (1446) (Madrid: Sociedad de Bibliófilos Españoles, 1891).

follow a chronology from the past to the present, or gather them by any sort of affiliation like Diego de San Pedro[91] or by moral virtues like Juan Pérez de Moya.[92] Guevara's women are organized nondiachronically, by neither virtues nor affiliation; rather they are women of different ages and places, chosen solely for their political and military power, thus giving a sense of order to an apparent disorder. Guevara elaborates an original catalogue that has a specific goal: creating a feminine political sisterhood on which she bases the historical past and future of Spain. In this sense, Guevara's words on women cannot be studied in isolation but instead must be considered as part of the larger debate about the proper role of women in society, the *querelle des femmes* which was ongoing in most of Europe from the fifteenth to the seventeenth century. Like female writers such as Christine de Pizan in France and Moderata Fonte in Italy, María de Guevara comes to us with a list of, in her case, "valorous women," women of action who, through arms and wit, use their power to create for themselves a place in a dominantly masculine world, women among whom Guevara includes herself.[93] She wants to make it clear that she is not an exception but belongs to the sisterhood of women that is part of a history still to be told. These women might be a threat, indeed, but a threat that has to be exposed, in Guevara's ideological world, for the good of the Spanish state.

Taking into account the women who appear in *Treatise* and in *Disenchantments* (mostly in the second chapter dedicated exclusively to "valorous women"), the catalogue is made up of women from the Bible,[94] women from classical antiquity and mythology,[95] saints of the church,[96] famous European queens,[97] and women from Spanish history.[98] To these can be added a few women who are not named, in some cases because they or their descendants

---

91. Diego de San Pedro, *Cárcel de amor* (first edition 1492), in which women are grouped into Christians, Gentiles, and Jews.

92. Juan Pérez de Moya's compilation, *Varia historia de sanctas e ilustres mujeres en todo género de virtudes* (1583), in which women are gathered according to their virginity, chastity, obedience, and so on.

93. A good example of the connection between the *querelle des femmes* and a Hispanic woman writer (Sor Juana Inés de la Cruz) is presented by Stephanie Merrim in her introduction to *Early Modern Women's Writing and Sor Juana Inés de la Cruz* (Nashville: Vanderbilt University Press, 1999), xi–xliv.

94. The Virgin Mary, Queen Michal, Abigail, Judith, Bathsheba, Rebecca, Magdalene, the seven wise virgins and the seven foolish virgins.

95. The Amazons, Zenobia, Penelope, Lucretia, Helen of Troy.

96. Saint Isabel of Hungry and Saint Mary of Egypt.

97. The regent queen of Portugal, the queen mother of France, and Queen Giovanna of Naples.

98. Like herself, Queen Catalina, Doña Sancha Queen of León, Doña Ximena, Doña Blanca of Navarre, the women of Ávila, Antona García, Queen Isabella the Catholic, the seven maidens

are still alive and their reputations are at stake. Significantly, more than a third of these women are queens.[99] It is not surprising that Queen Elizabeth of England does not appear in the list, given Guevara's strong feelings against the "heretic" English people who are helping the Portuguese to win the war.

It is a well-known fact that women's role as rulers challenged the sexual politics of Guevara's time. As Merry Wiesner-Hanks writes:

> Beginning in the sixteenth century, the debate about women also became one about female rulers, sparked primarily by dynastic accidents in many countries that led to women serving as advisors to child kings or ruling in their own right . . . . Both as rulers and as regents, women held politically sanctioned authority, not simply operating as the "power behind the throne," but their ability to do so was often challenged.[100]

Two examples of this debate belong to two specific historical moments and three countries: first, around the time of Queen Isabella in Spain (fifteenth century) and Queen Elizabeth in England (sixteenth century), an important polemic was raised regarding the queen's two bodies (sexual and political).[101] Second, and closer to Guevara's time, in France under the regencies of Catherine de Medici, Marie de Medici, and Anne of Austria, a new mode of feminist writing attempted to portray a specific female image, that of the *femme forte*.[102] This *femme forte* is famous for her patriotism, constancy,

---

of Simancas, the Biscayan women of Fuenterrabía, the Cava, Queen Catalina of Navarre, and Doña Mencía.

99. The Queen of Angels the Virgin Mary, Queens Michal, Zenobia, Penelope, Dido, (regent of Portugal) Luisa de Gusmão, the queen mother of France (probably Catherine de Medici), Giovanna of Naples, Saint Queen Isabel of Hungary, Catalina of Navarre, Doña Sancha of León, Queen Regent Catalina, and Isabella the Catholic.

100. Merry Wiesner-Hanks, "Women's Authority in the State and Household in Early Modern Europe," in *Women Who Ruled: Queens, Goddesses, Amazons in Renaissance and Baroque Art*, ed. Annette Dixon (Michigan and London: Merrel/University of Michigan Museum of Art, 2002), 30.

101. For a recent study on Isabella of Castile, see Barbara Weissberger's *Isabel Rules: Constructing Queenship, Wielding Power* (Minneapolis: University of Minnesota Press, 2004). In the case of Elizabeth of England, see, for example, Michael Dobson, *England's Elizabeth: An After Life in Fame and Fantasy* (Oxford: Oxford University Press, 2002), or Susan Doran, *Queen Elizabeth I* (New York: New York University Press, 2003).

102. See Ian MacLean, *Woman Triumphant: Feminism in French Literature, 1610–1652* (Oxford: Clarendon Press, 1977), 64–87. MacLean explains the concept of the *femme forte* in the context of the time and in relation to a new popular feminist literature, in which the *"femme forte* becomes a description linking pagan and Christian virtues, as does *amazone chrestienne* which is also encountered quite frequently in these works" (82). The two most important contemporary texts on this topic are those by Jacques Du Bosc, *La femme heroique, ou les heroines comparées avec les heros*

fidelity, resolution, energy, valor, true devotion, and openly heroic acts—all these at the same time as she "retain[s] the advantages of the female psyche and physique, for she is both compassionate and beautiful."[103] It is uncertain how much of this new feminism influenced Spanish politics and literature of Guevara's age. As demonstrated by Barbara Weissberger (in relation to Isabella of Castile) and Magdalena Sánchez (regarding the Austrian women around Philip III), royal female figures served as public protagonists, able to "manipulate the accepted feminine spheres of family and religion" and also "mask—and even justify—entrance into difficult political debates and to affect the outcome of those debates."[104] The literature that refers to these rulers, however, was not as widespread in Spain as it was in France during the seventeenth century; their public representation in Spain was limited to a characterization of them as submissive women. In fact, as Sánchez explains, one has to search minor nonofficial writings (chronicles, convent records, and private correspondence) to be able to appreciate the power exercised by these women.

Well informed about Spanish history and the participation of women in it, Guevara must have been aware of the royal French figures' threatening power and authoritative voices when she was writing her *Treatise* and *Disenchantments*. Indeed, there are several reasons to think that she was aware of the new feminist current of thought from France regarding the *femme forte*: the fame of the Medici regents (Catherine and Marie), the particular relationship between the Spanish and the French royal families, exemplified in the figure of Anne of Austria, daughter of Philip III, who married the dauphin Louis XIII and was regent queen of France from 1630 to 1650, and also the possible personal connection between Guevara and the French court, which she attended on several occasions in order to plead some titles and properties.[105]

In any case, those characteristics that were associated with the *femme forte* are exactly the ones that are associated with Guevara's women: heroism, nationalism, constancy, fidelity, energy, devoutness, and above all valor. In this sense, the selection of women is not arbitrary. As M. L. West explains

---

*en toute sorte de vertus*, 2 vols. (Paris: Antoine de Sommaville and Augustin Courbé, 1645), and by Pierre Le Moyne, *La gallerie de femmes fortes* (Paris: Antoine de Sommaville, 1647).

103. MacLean, *Woman Triumphant*, 86.

104. Magdalena Sánchez, *Empress*, 10.

105. For example, in the report of her journey to Vitoria, Guevara tells the queen that she would see her again in Paris "as she was planning to litigate the house of Ortubia, which is hers and is in the possession of a nephew of the lord of Agramonte, who was in Madrid" (see appendix B).

in his work on the Hesiodic catalogue, any selection pursues a goal, most of the time a political goal.[106] Therefore, it is not by chance that Guevara chooses not to highlight in her women those characteristics advocated by the conduct books of her time; that is, as Isabel Barbeito Pita says, charity and compassion, chastity and moderation, maternal virtues, contentment in the private sphere.[107] On the contrary, the women chosen by Guevara relate more to the *femme forte* and to the models of women presented in the thirteenth-century Spanish tradition. For example, the *Crónica Adefonsi Imperatoris* included norms of conduct for queens Doña Sancha and Doña Berenguela, norms according to which women should be warrior-protectors, able to fight and participate in government tasks at the same level as men.[108] Guevara is presenting a genealogy of women that legitimates a new Spain of Amazons, capable of restoring honor to the country through the use of arms and letters.

As M. L. West explains, catalogues "largely composed of names that are famous or significant, and designed to support the nation's historical traditions" are not simply lists of names but rather are "interlaced with narrative[s] explaining what people did or where their descendants settled."[109] In the second chapter of *Disenchantments*, Guevara tells the reader of particular deeds done by valorous women and entwines each story with a personal commentary that responds to a feminist ideology in agreement with the French *femme forte* and the Spanish warrior-protector: governments by women are often better than those by men; it is more than plausible for women to go to war and fight (Guevara complains that if a woman wants to go to war, people call her "virile" as well as criticize and laugh at her); women of wit and valor should be active participants in councils because their advice is as good as the best given by men, if not better; women should be feared; women would be able to surpass men if they were allowed to make use of letters; women who are dishonored should not kill themselves but rather kill the men who violated them; and so on. Women should participate in the politics of their time by fighting, advising, and ruling. Thus, women should be at the head of the state, replacing a masculine head whose dynasty, significantly, during the 1660s was dying because of the lack of succession. From the Queen of

---

106. M. L. West, *The Hesiodic Catalogue of Women: Its Nature, Structure, and Origins* (Oxford: Clarendon Press, 1985), 11.

107. "Modelos de conducta y programas educativos para la aristocracia femenina (siglos XII–XV)," in *De la Edad Media a la Moderna: Mujeres, educación y familia en el ámbito rural y urbano*, ed. María Teresa López Beltrán (Malaga: University of Malaga, 1999), 47–63.

108. Ibid., 42–43.

109. *Hesiodic Catalogue*, 29.

Angels, whose strength pushed her to accompany her husband instead of "excus[ing] herself for being so heavy with child," to Queen Isabella who, "being valiant," decided to ride alongside her husband, "on horseback, encouraging the people" to fight and clean Spain of Moors, the list of valorous women exemplifies not an ideal but a real model of womanhood that in Guevara could give birth to a new country led by women.

But Guevara is not only proposing a new female model for Spain. She is also defining herself in relation to such a model. As previously explained, in the *Treatise* she insists on participating in the war against Portugal and organizing—along with some of her female servants—an army of valorous women very different from the cowardly soldiers fighting that war. This personal participation reaches its height when she directly attacks the king and figuratively takes his place as the head of Spain by establishing a correlation between herself and the queen regent of Portugal, Luisa de Gusmão. The presence of women throughout her writings (in particular, the chapter "Concerning Valorous Women" from *Disenchantments*) authorizes this removal of the king. Like Sor Juana Inés de la Cruz in her *Respuesta*,[110] Guevara composes "a gallery of mirrors that reflected many of her own aspirations,"[111] and places herself in a position that challenges the king's power and the power of a misogynist society. In the solitude of her house, her three husbands having died in battle in the service of the king, Guevara legitimates herself as the head of her house and of Spain, of which her house is a microcosm.

These are the terms in which Guevara is portrayed in the "Report on the Day's Journey That the Countess of Escalante Made to the City of Vitoria to Kiss Her Majesty's Hand" (appendix B). As the title says, this is a report about a stopover made by the royal family in Vitoria in 1660, on the way to the French border for the betrothal of the Princess María Teresa and the duke of Anjou, future Louis XIV of France. Significantly, there is an official version of this trip by the royal family and the consequent signing of the Treaty of the Pyrenees between France and Spain.[112] The two versions are completely different, and this difference is established from the title itself: the countess has supplanted the king as protagonist of the report; it is no longer the king's trip but rather the journey of the countess. Her story is

---

110. Sor Juana Inés de la Cruz, *La Respuesta/Answer*, ed. and trans. Electa Arenal and Amanda Powell (New York: Feminist Press, 1994).

111. Scott, "La gran turba," 213.

112. Don Leonardo del Castillo (vassal of the king and officer of the Spanish Department of State), *Viage del Rey nuestro señor Don Felipe IV el Grande, a la frontera de Francia. Funciones reales del desposorio y entregas de la Serenísima Señora Infanta de España Doña María Teresa de Austria* (Madrid: Imprenta Real, 1667).

as important as that of the king. One could think that such a report was ordered by Guevara with the intention (maybe fulfilled) of sending it to "your Majesty." As the historian Fernando Bouza says, it was unusual for a high-ranking noble not to have his own bureau, in which he kept important documents about his estate and properties along with documents that served to extol his family and house, among which one could find this type of writing.[113] The report obviously fulfills that objective. With Guevara as the protagonist, the report is organized around her different encounters between with members of the court, in particular with the queen and her ladies-in-waiting. However, while the official report focuses on the figure of the king and the male courtiers, Guevara's report centers of course on herself—her beauty, wit, and wealth, as well as her power, much superior to that of the king and his suite. There is a clear gendered point of view in the way both accounts of the same trip are presented. So, for example, when on the fourth of May the inhabitants of Vitoria go to kiss the king's hands in a royal audience, the official report does not mention the queen. In the countess's report, however, the town of Vitoria goes to kiss the queen's hand, which takes place while Guevara is having an "entertaining" conversation with the queen. The scene of the encounter between the queen, her ladies, and Guevara occupies the center of the report and brings to the reader's mind a female court similar to the French ones, with regent queens as heads of state. The entire journey of the royal family is supplanted by the movements and activities of the countess, María de Guevara, who, as some soldiers claim, "is worth two men."

María de Guevara has challenged the king's power and the masculine way of ruling Spain. With her original catalogue of valorous women, Guevara creates a model for Spain that breaks from the masculine tradition of making history. Guevara as the leader and head of Spain pleads for a national "matriotism" that will help to restore Spanish honor. The community of women formed by queens, aristocrats, and vassals that Guevara proposes will impose a new political and cultural order in Spain, and Spanish history will be rewritten accordingly.

### Placing Men in This New Spain

In this community of women, in this Spain of Amazons, men are called to rethink and renegotiate their position in order to maintain a cultural balance. Guevara does not advocate for a Spain with no men; she wants women to have their own space and men to adapt to new needs and conditions.

113. *Corre manuscrito*, 241–48.

What Guevara proposes is that men remove themselves from the state of decadence in which they are embedded politically, socially, and sexually. For this, Guevara develops a discourse that ranges from generality (regarding men in their civil state as husbands) to specificity (regarding men's class and function in society, particularly soldiers, courtiers, and advisors to the king).

As husbands, Guevara claims that "men are all the same," and she dedicates the third chapter of her *Disenchantments* to them. Significantly, this chapter comes after the one on valorous women. Guevara understands that in order to rewrite the history of Spain and make women the core of its well-being, men must change. She blames men for using women to their advantage, for treating women as objects, and for believing their beauty and dowry to be their most important components. She also criticizes men's infidelity and lack of confidence in women, mainly in comparison to the faithful conduct of women which she has exemplified in the previous chapter. Guevara emphasizes that husbands should look to their wives for valor and intelligence since their advice and words are as good as those of men. To authorize herself, Guevara insists on the fact that the main reason why men have relegated women to an inferior status is fear—fear of being surpassed by women's good judgment and strength. As she says, "men made the laws and knew that many women could become their equals." And God is her main source of authority, so her threats are supported by God's possible action against men: "Married men, respect your wives, because God gave them to you as companions, and do not throw them to the den of lions, as was done to Daniel. For God shows tolerance, but not forever." Guevara pleads for a society of equality between men and women in the private sphere of the home.

But she also pleads for this equality in the public sphere of politics and war. Indeed, as has been said previously, Guevara emphasizes the presence of women on the battlefield (she being the first to go, if necessary), a presence that should be celebrated instead of criticized. Part of the reason for this emphasis was that noblemen had renounced going to war. As Maravall explains, the military tradition had been displaced by a new, more courtly way of life, supported practically by the absolute monarchy of the last three Habsburg kings. Seventeenth-century Spanish noblemen preferred to discuss the politics and diplomacy of war rather than fighting directly on the battlefield; the techniques had been modernized and the personal valor associated with the warrior-noble had been lost.[114] In general, and from a

114. José Antonio Maravall, *Poder, honor y élites en el siglo XVII* (Madrid: Siglo XXI, 1980), 201–14.

social perspective, the military tradition had been devalued to the point that many noblemen paid in order not to go to war so that the army was formed for the most part of members of popular groups, forced to go to war and not rewarded once they returned. Following mostly the military treatises of her time, Guevara's words carry a sense of nostalgia for the military past. From her aristocratic and conservative position, Guevara discusses the who, why, how, and when of going to war, as she did a year earlier in her *Treatise*. She again insists on finding an explanation for the defeats in Portugal. She distinguishes between new and old soldiers, bad and good soldiers, and she blames money and rewards for the distinctions. Older, more experienced, and better trained soldiers are not being rewarded for their actions in war, nor are their wives and children in case of death; in consequence, they refuse to go to war. New bad soldiers, traitors and cowards, are sent to fight for a country for which they have no respect, and they are recruited and led by traitors and cowards as well. However, these are the ones rewarded with money and posts at the court when they return. As Guevara says, old good soldiers are, instead, "set aside in a corner," just as women have been placed in a corner by men throughout history.

At court, then, it is not surprising to encounter counselors and advisors who are vain, greedy, and incompetent, particularly in councils as important as war and finance, both of which are fundamental for the victory over Portugal and for the hoped-for economic recovery of Spain. Her recommendations go so far as to specify the following:

> On the Council of War there should be men who have experience in sailing, and two lawyers to take care of litigation, and not men who, without having sailed, are leading the navy. . . . It is also important that there be men on the Council of War who have been soldiers, for without having known war they will lead the army badly, nor will they know what the soldiers deserve. And in wartime, the paymasters and those who manage the money should be reliable, with an accounting taken of their affairs, because when they do not pay the soldiers, the soldiers leave at the first opportunity. (*Disenchantments* IV)

The solution to this situation is that the king should use good judgment in handing out the posts. In Guevara's effort to educate her king, the topic of assigning posts to the appropriate men is continually raised throughout her texts. In chapter IV of *Disenchantments*, after having expressed her opinion regarding valorous women and ideal husbands, Guevara turns to the topic "On How Kings Should Act in Assigning Government Posts." The authorities upon whom Guevara bases her discourse are the Emperor Marcus Aurelius

on earth and God in heaven, along with some well-known philosophers of classical Greek antiquity. Given that one can never completely trust a foreigner, it is wiser for the king—almost an obligation—to be familiar with those to whom he gives the posts, who should be those who are virtuous and who, because of their experience and knowledge, can advise properly. For that, the king must know his subjects personally, along with their stories and chronicles, and must also know his kingdom. For this reason, the king has to actively participate in the court he is ruling over, since without a ruling king there is chaos, and this, according to Guevara, is what is happening in Spain. "Justice" and "mercy" are required in this good king: mercy to reward, justice to punish those who deserve it. And as Guevara has chosen the ideal female models for the new Spain of Amazons, she also presents the king-to-be—Charles II, to whom *Disenchantments* is dedicated—a list of examples of men who, throughout history, have demonstrated wise and prudent governmental skills. At the top of her list is Philip II, the Prudent (r. 1556–98), the last king of the Habsburg line to keep the empire in place. Then there are heroic figures such as Ruy Díaz de Vivar, the Cid, and Bernardo del Carpio. On that list, and more important for her own self-empowerment, are royal or aristocratic members related to the Navarre family, who are also related to her own houses and lineages: Don Juan Labrit and Queen Catalina, the duke of Nájera, Don Uño (lord of Vizcaya), and an unnamed lord from the house of Gamboa. Finally, there are vassals and servants, such as Juan Velázquez de Cuellar. By using those models and after expelling the foreigners who are ruining the welfare of the state, the king will be able to exercise his power adequately. Guevara, though, does not stop here. She insists that courtiers return to their estates. If the king must be personally familiar with his vassals, the noblemen should be even more so with their subjects. With Antonio de Guevara's words quite present in her mind, Guevara explores the importance of leaving the court and retiring to the countryside.

"The court is harmful to one's soul, one's health, and one's wealth," says Guevara. Since all the dangerous vices and deviances at the court cannot be eliminated, the only solution is to leave. Her complaints are against "dishonorable conversations" and "gossips"; wasteful spending in "games," "finery," and "superfluities" (instead of using the money to pay servants adequately); the undue importance given to appearance (e.g., "new carriages," "jewels"); "filthy illnesses" provoked by sex and alcohol that are ruining families; the poor administration of money and properties, and so on. Her criticisms are reminiscent of those of Antonio de Guevara, in his expressed contempt for wealth, although the countess prefers the effect of specific examples. For instance, while Antonio de Guevara says that "in the court, a courtier does

many things because many others do them and not because he wants to,"[115] María de Guevara explicitly talks about two men: when one of them "adds some feature to a new carriage, another man, who has had his carriage for only a year, will dismantle it in order to make it like the other's, even though his could have lasted for four more years" (*Disenchantments* I). With the use of particular examples, María de Guevara is able to bring the court to life, as if she were speaking of specific cases that everyone could relate to. Her intentions are not philosophical but rather practical. As a woman who is in direct contact with daily life and activities, she has the authority to make a frontal attack, appealing to her personal knowledge and experience. In fact, it is here that she differs most from Antonio de Guevara. Guevara is a courtier himself, leaving the court for his own well-being. Other courtiers can follow his example but he prefers not to "advise" or "recommend" that they leave the court since "it is great recklessness and frivolity to advise";[116] it is better if everyone chooses what is best for his soul and body. María de Guevara, instead, has never been a courtier. From the information compiled about her life, it is known that she probably visited the court on several occasions but spent most of her life residing on and taking care of her estates in Extremadura and the north of Spain (i.e., Álava, Navarre, Cantabria), where she maintained an excellent relationship with her vassals. The countess appreciates what it means to live outside the court and from her own experience declares that "it is safest for them [the lords] to retire to their properties and flee from possible hazards," while the only people who stay with the king are those who really need to ("those who serve the royal house . . . , as well as the councilors, lawyers, contractors, merchants, traders, plaintiffs," *Disenchantments* I).

In contrast to the court, the village is presented as the perfect space for noblemen to live and to exercise their authority without having any conflict of power. Echoing Antonio de Guevara's positive view of the village,[117] María de Guevara praises it as a place where a lord will avoid idleness, have time to read and learn from his ancestors, honor his wife and family, avoid spending on superfluities, go to mass, practice charity, penance, patience and humility, be generous, marry his daughters with their equals, and, most important, have direct contact with his vassals in good times (e.g., to celebrate holidays and festivities) and in bad (e.g., to exercise justice). In other words, the lord will exercise mercy and justice just as the king should do.

---

115. Antonio de Guevara, *Menosprecio de corte*, 195.
116. Ibid., 137.
117. Ibid., 155 ff.

Significantly, the model spaces Guevara uses as contrasting examples to the corrupted court are the "Republic of Vitoria," "Extremadura," and "Pamplona," all of which are places in which she normally resides. Her discourse of contempt for the court and praise for the village is not a general one that simply opposes two lifestyles. Guevara has put herself once again at the same level as her king, transforming the humanist topos of disapproval of the court and praise for the village into the disapproval of Philip IV's court and praise for María de Guevara's estates. In Guevara's "matriotic" Spain, there is nothing else for the king to do than follow her advice.

In the final chapter of *Disenchantments*, however, María de Guevara reshapes her discourse by giving it a religious slant, so that her attacks on the court and the king are softened. Virtue becomes the closing subject of her text, virtue that a lord can acquire by living in the village but that can be passed on to those living at the court; in particular, to the king and to those occupying important posts. Religious models, from Saint Isabel of Hungary to Saint Onofre of Egypt, will help everyone (in the court and the village) to live as Christians, which, in the end, is what will unite every Spaniard against the heretic Portuguese, English, French, and so on.

In Guevara's plan, men—whether they be kings, noblemen, or lords, either at the court or in the village—have much to learn from women. The basic lesson: men need to change. In her texts, Guevara presents a lesson on good government and good citizenship. In the struggle to recover Spain's honor, women will fight with pen and sword, and men will follow women's advice and example so as to aid in this recovery.

### The Other Texts

The final texts to be included in this edition differ in nature and authorship from the preceding two, though they are no less important in understanding María de Guevara's prominent position in late-seventeenth-century Spain. The first appendix is from the *Memorial of the House of Escalante and of Its Services to the King*, written by María de Guevara herself in 1654. Only the last part of the memorial, the summary of Guevara's lineage and her petitions to the king, has been translated in this edition. The second appendix is the "Report on the Day's Journey That the Countess of Escalante Made to the City of Vitoria to Kiss Her Majesty's Hand," written probably by order of María de Guevara in 1660.

As I have mentioned previously in the sections on Guevara's life and the analysis of her works, these two texts are fundamental to Guevara's attempt to position herself in the history of Spain. Genealogical treatises were a very popular genre during the sixteenth and seventeenth centuries. Aristocratic

families and those aspiring to be part of the nobility had to demonstrate that their ancestors were worthy of their name and that they had no blood ties to Jews, Muslims, or New Christians. The genealogical memorials attempted to prove that the family's origin went as far back as Adam and Eve, and each family was often shown to be related to a royal family member from Spanish history.

The objectives of these memorials varied, but on many occasions they were followed by certain political and socioeconomic requests to the king. Such is the case in Guevara's *Memorial*. She traces her origins to the fathers of the Spanish *Reconquista* and relates them directly to Castile and Navarre royal blood lines: "The Countess of Escalante and Tahalú says that she is obliged to remind your Majesty of her ancestors' continuous services to these crowns for more than nine hundred years."[118] Women occupy a central role in this memorial since the line of succession and lineage affects their estate and name as much as men's. In fact, it is significant that the main beneficiaries of the request made to the king are María de Guevara herself (in the name of her lineage) and her mother. At the end of the memorial, the countess twice insists that her mother's finances be repaired. Mother and daughter thus become the final link in the chain of an honorable family, and the requests will enable this family to continue being productive, which in turn will benefit the kingdom and its future. This is the reason Guevara's discourse results in a mix of pride and humility. That is, Guevara can prove her lineage through the many chronicles and history books she has read as well as through the archival documents she owns, valuable pieces of cultural property that authorize her to confront the king with pride and make the appropriate requests.[119] Thus she reminds Philip IV of everything her family has done throughout history and challenges him for having taken posts, properties, and privileges away from her family. However, her threats to the king contrast with the way in which she places herself, "at the royal feet of your Majesty as your humble servant."[120] It should be noted that it is not until this text has been written and published that María de Guevara reappears on the scene in 1663 with her *Treatise* to the king. This memorial becomes her public letter of introduction to the royal sphere, from which she attempts to get not only the specific economic and social rewards she is requesting, but also the political recognition and authority she needs in

---

118. *Memorial*, 2v.

119. *Memorial*, 19r.

120. *Memorial*, 20v.

order to give advice to the king and put herself in his place—at least at the
level of discourse.

María de Guevara's intention to replace the king is very explicit in her
"Report." As stated in previous sections, this report runs parallel to an official
one in which the king, Philip IV, is the protagonist. In her report, however, Guevara becomes the center of attention. When she is not admired
and praised by powerful male members of the court (such as Don Luis de
Haro and his sons), she is portrayed next to the queen and her ladies-in-
waiting. While the *Memorial* emphasizes women's place in Guevara's lineage
and culminates in the mother-daughter connection, the "Report" centers on
the queen and Guevara, surrounded by women at the court. The "masked"
woman in the royal family's suite who provokes the curiosity and entertainment of the queen and her ladies is María de Guevara, who uses her power
to position herself subtly at the same level as the king and queen. Not only
is she "worth two men," she can also compete with the king politically,
socially, and economically. Guevara has her own territory of authority, she
does not need the court, and she is the queen in her own space. Guevara
might miss having a husband.[121] But not having him means that she is the
head of her houses, microcosmos of the court of Philip IV, and as its head, a
model lord for her vassals. Could it also be that Guevara is putting forward
an idea of nationalism for the provinces of Basque origin with her as its
leader? Perhaps. But Guevara certainly places those territories at the center
of Spanish history. And Guevara becomes the one head that can lead the
country to a safer and more successful future.

## FUTURE AND FORTUNE OF THE TEXTS: THIS EDITION

María de Guevara's life and works have lain in oblivion for more than three
hundred years. As with many other women of her time, there was little room
for her voice and ideas to be heard. Society maintained that women were to
sit in the corner, limited to the private sphere. It is the task of this edition
to bring her out of that dark corner and into the light of history where they
belong. Guevara's words are valuable, not only because she was a woman
who made her voice heard but also because she did so with regard to issues
of state, challenging the king and his ruling policies.

---

121. She says in the same report: "And what grieved the countess most on this occasion was
not having a husband of the rank required by the situation, one who could come out to greet
your Majesty, as . . . the head of the Ganboyno house, which is made up of three provinces,
Álava, Vizcaya, and Guipúzcoa."

María de Guevara's silence endured until the beginning of the twentieth century. At that time, bibliographer and historian Manuel de Serrano y Sanz rescued her from the archives.[122] In the few pages dedicated to Guevara, Serrano y Sanz includes a biographical sketch and, more important, reproduces three texts (the *Treatise*, the "Report," and a letter to Don Juan José of Austria which is accompanied by a gazette). He also indicates where to find the *Memorial* and *Disenchantments*, which the biographer summarizes very briefly.

More recently, María de Guevara is included in a bibliographical catalogue compiled by Isabel Barbeito Carneiro as part of her doctoral thesis.[123] It is surprising to find Guevara in this catalogue since Barbeito devotes it only to women from Madrid. It is probable that Barbeito is assuming that Guevara was born in Madrid, but there is no reliable data to indicate that. In fact, as has been shown in this introduction, it is more likely that Guevara spent most of her life outside of the court governing her estates, since her husbands were usually either away in the war or deceased. Barbeito does not provide additional information regarding Guevara's life. However, she does update and bibliographically organize Guevara's autographed writings and printed texts and includes short sections from each one. Less bibliographical is Barbeito's article, in which she summarizes Guevara's main ideas according to three main issues: her origins, her feminism, and her sociopolitical positioning.[124]

In addition to these bio-bibliographical entries on María de Guevara, only a few cases of critical approaches can be found. One example is Teresa Langle de Paz's article, which analyzes the utopian feminism of María de Guevara's *Disenchantments* with special emphasis placed on the question of authority.[125] Another is Lisa Vollendorf's chapter on the history of women's education, which dedicates some words to Guevara and her *Disenchantments of the Court and Valorous Women*, reinforcing the vision of Guevara as a strong woman who affirms "women's superior intellectual abilities" while instructing aristocratic men to be "respectable citizen[s]."[126] Guevara's persona is also scrutinized by Nieves Baranda, who treats Guevara as a reader, by

122. He included her in his *Apuntes de una Biblioteca de Autoras Españolas*, 474–80.

123. *Escritoras madrileñas del siglo XVII. Estudio bibliográfico-crítico*, 297–307.

124. "María de Guevara, *son politikon*," in *Estudios sobre escritoras hispánicas en honor de Georgina Sabat-Rivers*, ed. Lou Charnon-Deutsch (Madrid: Castalia, 1992), 62–78.

125. "En busca."

126. Lisa Vollendorf, *The Lives of Women: A New History of Inquisitional Spain* (Nashville, TN: Vanderbilt University Press, 2005), 181, 182. See the chapter entitled "Toward a History of Women's Education," 169–86.

imagining the library Guevara might have possessed in order to write all her texts.[127] Finally, Guevara's writings are briefly referred to in *Historia de las mujeres en España y América Latina. El mundo moderno* (2005), where historians Fernando Bouza and María Victoria López-Cordón present her as an important example of the female culture of the time.[128] This growing academic interest in María de Guevara demonstrates the importance of recovering her voice and words for the modern reader.

With the exception of Serrano y Sanz's reproduction of the *Treatise* and the "Report," most of María de Guevara's texts are still in archives of libraries such as the National Library in Madrid. Fortunately, the *Memorial* has been microfilmed and can also be found in Simón Palmer's catalogue.[129] For *Disenchantments*, though, the researcher still has to go to the library to be able to read it. In other words, this is not only the first time that Guevara's texts have been translated into English but also the first time they have been edited for a contemporary audience, Hispanist or otherwise. In the case of the *Treatise*, I have followed the nonautographed manuscript 12.270, pages 401–32, from the National Library in Madrid. For *Disenchantments*, I have used the printed document R/4.496, also found at the National Library. For the summary of Guevara's origins, that is, the final pages of her *Memorial*, I have translated from National Library, V-C 57-13, and for the "Report," I have followed Serrano y Sanz's reproduction, since the nonautographed copy at the National Library (MSS. 13.185) has ink stains that make the document difficult to read.

For the translation, I have tried to be as faithful as possible to the original, but for the sake of clarity and readability, I have modified Guevara's punctuation according to modern criteria. Also, whenever possible, I have translated proper names into English. I have attempted to maintain Guevara's tone and style, as well as her sometimes confusing syntax. For this reason, certain ambiguities in the original text have been left unresolved.

---

127. Nieves Baranda, *Cortejo a lo prohibido. Lectoras y escritoras en la España moderna* (Madrid: Arco/ Libros, 2005), 51–62.

128. Fernando Bouza, "Memorias de la lectura y escritura de las mujeres en el Siglo de Oro," and María Victoria López-Cordón, "La fortuna de escribir: escritoras de los siglos XVII y XVII," in *Historia de las mujeres en España y América Latina*, ed. Isabel Morant, vol. 2: *El mundo moderno*, ed. M. Ortega, A. Lavrin, and P. Pérez Cantó (Madrid: Cátedra, 2005), 169–91 and 193–234, respectively.

129. *Escritoras*.

# VOLUME EDITOR'S
# BIBLIOGRAPHY

## PRIMARY SOURCES

Alvares da Cunha, Don Antonio. *Campanha de Portugal: Pella provincia do Alentejo.* Lisbon: Henrique Valente de Oliveira, 1663.

Austria, Don Juan José of. *Carta a Felipe IV, 11 de Julio de 1661.* MSS 2.388. National Library of Madrid.

Cabrera de Córdoba, Luis. *De historia, para entenderla y escribirla.* Madrid: Luis Sánchez, 1611.

Castillo, Don Leonardo del. *Viaje del Rey nuestro señor don Felipe IV el Grande a la frontera de Francia. Funciones reales del desposorio y entregas de la Serenísima Señora Infanta de España Doña María Teresa de Austria.* Madrid: Imprenta Real, 1667.

Cerda, Father Juan de la. *Vida política de todos los estados de mugeres; en el qual se dan muy provechosos y christianos documentos y avisos, para criarse y conservarse debidamente las mujeres en sus estados.* Alcalá de Henares: Juan Gracián, 1599.

Du Bosc, Jacques. *La femme heroique, ou les heroines comparées avec les heros en toute sorte de vertus.* 2 vols. Paris: Antoine de Sommaville and Augustin Courbé, 1645.

Guevara, Antonio de. *Menosprecio de corte y alabanza de aldea. Arte de Marear.* Ed. Asunción Ralló. Madrid: Cátedra, 1987.

———. *Relox de Príncipes.* Ed. Emilio Blanco. 2 vols. N.p. : ABL/Conferencia de Ministros Provinciales Franciscanos de España, 1994.

Guevara, María de. *Carta a Don Juan de Austria, acompañada de una gaceta, 9 de Julio de 1668.* MSS 18.655, box 26, no. 26. National Library of Madrid.

———. *Desengaños de la Corte y Mujeres Valerosas* (1664). R/4.496. National Library of Madrid.

———. *Ejecutoria ganada a pedimento de la Condesa de Escalante, del pleito que en esta Real Audiencia ha tratado con Antonio Abad de Arizaga y Bartolomé de Gárate y otros consortes, vecinos de la villa de Elgoibar.* Valladolid, 1669. MSS 19.085. National Library of Madrid.

———. *Memorial de la casa de Escalante y servicios de ella al Rey Nuestro Señor.* Valladolid, 1654. V-C 57-13. National Library of Madrid.

———. *Tratado y advertencias hechas por una mujer celosa del bien de su Rey y corrida de parte de España* (1663). MSS 12.270. National Library of Madrid.

Le Moyne, Pierre. *La gallerie de femmes fortes.* Paris: Antoine de Sommaville, 1647.

Luna, Álvaro de. *Libro de las virtuosas y claras mujeres* (1446). Madrid: Sociedad de Bibliofilos Españoles, 1891.

Mendoza, Bernardino de. *Teoría y práctica de guerra* (1595). Ed. Juan Saavedra and Juan Sánchez Belén. Madrid: Ministerio de Defensa, 1998.

"Relación de la jornada que la Condesa de Escalante hizo a la ciudad de Vitoria a besar la mano a su Magestad." In *Apuntes de una Biblioteca de Autoras Españolas desde el año 1401 al 1833,* ed. Manuel Serrano y Sanz, 1: 474–76. Madrid: Atlas, 1975.

Zayas y Sotomayor, María. *The Enchantments of Love: Amorous and Exemplary Novels.* Trans. H. Patsy Boyer. Berkeley: University of California Press, 1990.

Zeballos, Gerónimo de. *Arte real para el buen gobierno de los Reyes, y Príncipes, y de sus vasallos.* Toledo: By the author, 1623.

## SECONDARY SOURCES

Ballesteros Robles, Luis. *Diccionario biográfico matritense.* Madrid: Ayuntamiento, 1912.

Baranda, Nieves. *Cortejo a lo prohibido. Lectoras y escritoras en la España moderna.* Madrid: Arco/Libros, 2005.

Barbeito Carneiro, María Isabel. "María de Guevara." In *Escritoras madrileñas del siglo XVII. Estudio bibliográfico-crítico,* 2: 297–307. Ph.D. diss., Universidad Complutense de Madrid, 1986.

———. "María de Guevara, son politikon." In *Estudios sobre escritoras hispánicas en honor de Georgina Sabat-Rivers,* ed. Lou Charnon-Deutsch, 62–78. Madrid: Castalia, 1992.

Barbeito Pita, Isabel. "Modelos de conducta y programas educativos para la aristocracia femenina (siglos XII –XV)." In *De la Edad Media a la Moderna: Mujeres, educación y familia en el ámbito rural y urbano,* ed. María Teresa López Beltrán, 37–72. Malaga: University of Malaga, 1999.

Bouza, Fernando. *Corre manuscrito: Una historia cultural del Siglo de Oro.* Madrid: Marcial Pons, 2001.

———. "Memorias de la lectura y escritura de las mujeres en el Siglo de Oro." In *Historia de las mujeres en España y América Latina,* ed. Isabel Morant, vol. 2: *El mundo moderno,* ed. M. Ortega, A. Lavrin, and P. Pérez Cantó, 169–191. Madrid: Cátedra, 2005.

Boyajian, James. *Portuguese Bankers at the Court of Spain, 1626–1650.* New Brunswick, NJ: Rutgers University Press, 1983.

Calvo Poyato, José. *Juan José de Austria.* Barcelona: Mondadori, 2003.

Cortés Cortés, Fernando. *Militares y guerra en una tierra de frontera. Extremadura a mediados del siglo XVII.* Mérida: Junta de Extremadura, 1991.

Covarrubias, Sebastián de. *Tesoro de la lengua castellana* (1611). Madrid: Castalia, 1994.

Curtius, Ernst. *European Literature and the Latin Middle Ages.* Trans. Willard Trask. New York: Harper and Row, 1963.

*Diccionario de Autoridades* (1726). Facsimile ed. Madrid: Gredos, 1984.

*Diccionario Enciclopédico Espasa-Calpe.* Madrid: Espasa-Calpe, 1998.

Dobson, Michael. *England's Elizabeth: An After Life in Fame and Fantasy.* Oxford: Oxford University Press, 2002.

Domínguez Ortiz, Antonio. *Política y hacienda de Felipe IV.* Madrid: Derecho Financiero, 1960.

————. *La sociedad española del siglo XVII. El estamento nobiliario.* Facsimile ed. 1963; Granada: University of Granada, 1992.

Doran, Susan. *Queen Elizabeth I.* New York: New York University Press, 2003.

Elliott, John H. *The Count-Duke of Olivares: The Statesman in an Age of Decline.* New Haven: Yale University Press, 1986.

Estébanez Calderón, Don Serafín. "Fragmentos de la Historia de la Infantería Española." In *Obras Completas,* ed. Jorge Campos. Vol. 2. Madrid: Atlas, 1955.

Fernández Santamaría, J. A. *Reason of State and Stagecraft in Spanish Political Thought, 1595–1640.* Lanham, MD: University Press of America, 1983.

————. *The State, War, and Peace: Spanish Political Thought in the Renaissance, 1516–1559.* Cambridge: Cambridge University Press, 1977.

Galino Carrillo, María Angeles. *Los tratados sobre educación de príncipes (Siglos XVI y XVII).* Madrid: CSIC, 1948.

Herrero García, Miguel. *Ideas de los españoles del siglo XVII.* Madrid: Gredos, 1966.

Jordan, Constance. *Renaissance Feminism: Literary Texts and Political Models.* Ithaca, NY: Cornell University Press, 1990.

Kagan, Richard. "Clio and the Crown: Writing History in Habsburg Spain." In *Spain, Europe, and the Atlantic World: Essays in Honor of John Elliott,* ed. Richard Kagan and Geoffrey Parker, 73–99. Cambridge: Cambridge University Press, 1995.

Kagan, Richard, and Abigail Dyer, eds. and trans. *Inquisitorial Inquiries: Brief Lives of Secret Jews and Other Heretics.* Baltimore: John Hopkins University Press, 2004.

Kamen, Henry. *Spain, 1469–1714: A Society of Conflict.* London: Longman, 1983.

Keinbaum, Abby Wettan. *The War against the Amazons.* New York: New Press/McGraw-Hill, 1983.

King, Margaret. *Women of the Renaissance.* Chicago: University of Chicago Press, 1991.

Langle de Paz, Teresa. "En busca del paraíso ausente: 'mujer varonil' y 'autor femenil' en una utopía feminista inédita del siglo XVII español." In *Hispania* 86.3 (2003): 463–73.

López-Cordón, María Victoria. "La fortuna de escribir: escritoras de los siglos XVII y XVII." In *Historia de las mujeres en España y América Latina,* ed. Isabel Morant, vol. 2: *El mundo moderno,* ed. M. Ortega, A. Lavrin, and P. Pérez Cantó, 196–234. Madrid: Cátedra, 2005.

MacLean, Ian. *Woman Triumphant: Feminism in French Literature, 1610–1652.* Oxford: Clarendon Press, 1977.

Maravall, José Antonio. *Poder, honor y élites en el siglo XVII.* Madrid: Siglo XXI, 1980.

————. *Teoría del estado en España en el siglo XVII.* Madrid: Centro de Estudios Constitucionales, 1997.

Nader, Helen. Introduction. In *Power and Gender in Renaissance Spain: Eight Women of the Mendoza Family, 1450–1650,* ed. Helen Nader, 1–26. Urbana: University of Illinois Press, 2004.

Ortega López, Margarita. "El período Barroco (1565–1700)." In *Historia de las mujeres en España,* ed. Elisa Garrido González, 253–344. Madrid: Síntesis, 1997.

*Oxford Classical Dictionary, The.* Ed. Simon Hornblower and Antony Spawforth. 3rd rev. ed. Oxford: Oxford University Press, 2003.

Ralló, Asunción. Introduction. In Antonio de Guevara, *Menosprecio de corte y alabanza de aldea. Arte de marear,* 15–94. Madrid: Cátedra, 1987.

Romero-Díaz, Nieves. *Nueva nobleza, nueva novela: Rescribiendo la cultura urbana del Barroco.* Newark: Juan de la Cuesta, 2002.

Saavedra, Juan, and Juan Sánchez Belén. Introduction. In Bernardino de Mendoza, *Teoría y práctica de guerra* (1595). Madrid: Ministerio de Defensa, 1998.

Sánchez, Magdalena. *The Empress, the Queen, and the Nun: Women and Power at the Court of Philip III of Spain.* Baltimore: John Hopkins University Press, 1998.

Sánchez Rubio, Carlos M., et al. *Coreographia y descripción del territorio de la plaza de Badaxos y fronteras del Reyno de Portugal confinantes a ella.* Mérida: Junta de Extremadura, 2003.

Schutte, Anne Jacobson, Thomas Kuehn, and Silvana Seidel Menchi. Introduction. In *Time, Space, and Women's Lives in Early Modern Europe,* ed. Schutte, Kuehn, and Menchi, vii–xvii. Sixteenth Century Essays and Studies, vol. 57. Kirksville, MO: Truman State University Press, 2001.

Scott, Nina. "Los espíritus tutelares de la Avellaneda." In *Mujeres latinoamericanas: Historia y Cultura, siglos XVI al XIX,* ed. Luisa Campuzano, 2: 187–93. Mexico City: Casa de las Américas, 1997.

———. "'La gran turba de las que merecieron nombres': Sor Juana's Foremothers in *La Respuesta a Sor Filotea.*" In *Coded Encounters: Writing, Gender, and Ethnicity in Colonial Latin America,* ed. Francisco Javier Cevallos et al., 206–23. Amherst: University of Massachusetts Press, 1996.

Serrano y Sanz, Manuel. "María de Guevara." In *Apuntes de una Biblioteca de Autoras Españolas desde el año 1401 al 1833,* 1: 474–80. Facsimile ed. 1903; Madrid: Atlas, 1975.

Simón Palmer, María del Carmen. *Escritoras españolas, 1500–1900: Catálogo. Biblioteca Nacional de Madrid.* 2 vols. Madrid: Chadwyck-Healy España, 1992–93.

Sonnino, Lee A. *A Handbook to Sixteenth-Century Rhetoric.* New York: Barnes and Noble, 1968.

Valladares, Rafael. *Portugal y la Monarquía hispánica, 1580–1668.* Madrid: Arco Libros, 2000.

———. *La rebelión de Portugal. Guerra, conflicto y poderes en la Monarquía Hispánica (1640–1680).* Valladolid: Junta de Castilla y León, 1998.

Vollendorf, Lisa. *The Lives of Women: A New History of Inquisitional Spain.* Nashville: Vanderbilt University Press, 2005.

Weber, Alison. *Teresa of Ávila and the Rhetoric of Femininity.* Princeton: Princeton University Press, 1990.

Weissberger, Barbara. *Isabel Rules: Constructing Queenship, Wielding Power.* Minneapolis: University of Minnesota Press, 2004.

West, M. L. *The Hesiodic Catalogue of Women: Its Nature, Structure, and Origins.* Oxford: Clarendon Press, 1985.

Whinnom, Keith. "The Problem of the Best-Seller in Spanish Golden Age Literature." *Bulletin of Hispanic Studies* 57 (1980): 189–98.

Wiesner-Hanks, Merry. "Women's Authority in the State and Household in Early Modern Europe." In *Women Who Ruled: Queens, Goddesses, Amazons in Renaissance and Baroque Art,* ed. Annette Dixon, 27–60. Michigan and London: Merrel/University of Michigan Museum of Art, 2002.

# I. TRATADO Y ADVERTENCIAS HECHAS POR UNA MUJER CELOSA DEL BIEN DE SU REY Y CORRIDA¹ DE PARTE DE ESPAÑA (1663)

Señor,

Si a vuestra Majestad le dijesen lo que pasa,² cierto que procurara remediarlo y no tuviéramos tan malos sucesos; la batalla pasada del cerco de Yelbes,³ el vulgo hecha la culpa a un hombre, y [a] los que gobiernan las armas de Vuestra Majestad; y [de] ésta que ha sucedido este año del 63,⁴ se hecha la culpa al mismo; Señor, la voz del pueblo suelen llamar voz de Dios; mas cuando este hombre no lo haga con malicia, es desgraciado y fuera bien quitarle de allí.

Dirá Vuestra Majestad: ¿quién mete a una mujer en esto? A que respondo que harta lástima es que lo lleguemos a entender las mujeres tan bien como los hombres y a sentirlo mejor.

En otros tiempos vemos en las historias que iban los soldados por su voluntad y no forzados como ahora; los hombres de importancia empeñaban los estados y llevaban a su costa más gente que podían; ahora, estos nietos de aquellos, no tienen fuerzas para sustentar sus casas, porque les quitan sus haciendas y se van disminuyendo casa y lustres, y ensalzadas otras que se levantan del polvo de la tierra, comprando lugares y estados y recreos; dígalo Extremadura y Andalucía y otras partes que están rabiando.

Cierto, Señor, que para que los Reyes conozcan lo que es cada casa y lo que le han servido los dueños de ellas y el grado en que se debe estimar cada uno, conviene que desde que comienzan a hablar los Príncipes los enseñen a leer historias y crónicas, pues conocerán la estimación que se debe hacer de cada uno; perdone Vuestra Majestad, que como yo he leído tanto, preciándome de esta curiosidad, me atrevo a decirlo así.

## I. TREATISE AND WARNINGS BY A WOMAN, CONCERNED FOR THE GOOD OF HER KING, AND AFFRONTED[1] BY PART OF SPAIN (1663)

My Lord:

If someone would tell your Majesty what is taking place,[2] you would certainly try to prevent it and we would not have such a poor outcome. For the last battle at the siege of Yelbes,[3] the common people blame one man as well as those who lead your Majesty's troops. And as for that which has taken place this year of 1663,[4] the same man is blamed. My Lord, the voice of the people is usually called the voice of God; since this man's actions are not with evil intention, he is unfortunate, and it would be better to remove him.

Your Majesty may say: who is a woman to meddle in this? To which I respond: how sad that we women come to understand what is happening as well as men do, but feel it even more.

We see in the histories that in other ages soldiers went to war willingly and were not forced to do so as they are now. Men of importance pledged their estates and at their own expense took with them all the people they could. Now the grandchildren of those people no longer have the strength to sustain their houses because their properties are being taken, and illustrious lineages are disappearing while others who rise from nothing are being praised, are buying villages, estates, and recreational houses—as is seen in Extremadura and Andalusia and other places that are suffering so terribly.

It is true, dear Lord, that in order for kings to know what each house is worth and how well their owners have served you and how much value to place upon each, it is well that from the moment princes begin to talk, they should be taught to read histories and chronicles, so that they may know what level of esteem to bestow upon each one. Forgive me, your Majesty, but since I have read so much, I pride myself on being curious, and I dare speak to you in this manner.

Señor, el soldado que vuelve pobre de la guerra y empeñó su casa para irse, ése es buen soldado, digno de puestos, mercedes y honras que Vuestra Majestad le haga, pues los buenos soldados son los que tienen a su Rey la corona en su cabeza; mas el que comenzó a servir descalzo y hace casa y estados sin dárselos a Vuestra Majestad, mal soldado, porque hace verdadero al vulgo; que o bien es traidor, recibiendo cohechos, o se queda con las pagas de los soldados; y esto no puede faltar, porque el sueldo no alcanza a tanto, y el buen soldado, si le cobra, lo gasta con los demás por tenerles contentos para la ocasión; y así lo atribuimos a lo peor, según los malos sucesos que vemos.

En las historias vemos que hombres muy humildes han valido tanto por la guerra, que de hombres humildes se han hecho insignes; y sus reyes los han honrado tanto como hoy vemos en sus nietos, títulos y grandes, bien merecido a sus hechos; y en este tiempo vemos lo contrario: que la gente particular que va a servir es la más baja e inferior que hay en el reino, porque la componen de hombres que están sentenciados a galeras y muchos a horca;[5] pues si esta gente no tiene honra en su tierra, ¿cómo la tendrá en el ejército y se les fía la de Vuestra Majestad y la de todos, pues los ponemos a que nos afrenten?; y si en las aldeas se pide un soldado, dicen los labradores que no quieren ir a venir mancos y andar pidiendo limosna, como andan muchos hombres honrados; que en ley de Dios y en justicia se les debía dar de comer a cada uno conforme a su esfera; y así se juntan los consejos y buscan un mozuelo perdido y holgazán, que no se pueden averiguar con él, y le ponen en la cárcel y le llevan por fuerza por soldado, y en su vida tomó espada en la mano y sabe mejor correr que reñir; y de estos tales se forman escuadrones. Pues, Señor, gente tal, ¿qué ha de hacer sino huir en la ocasión y luego, con el ejemplar de los que los gobiernan, que son los primeros que huyen; y así lo escriben del ejército y lo dicen algunos que han venido aquí, que dice[n]: "si sale dando voces el que nos gobierna, y diciendo 'cada uno escape la vida, que somos perdidos,' ¿qué hemos de hacer?;" estos tales hombres se habían de poner en presidios cerrados, que se disciplinen y enseñen allí y sacarlos soldados viejos para la ocasión, y muchos que andan aquí pretendiendo y no los despachan, estando hartos de servir; y deben advertir a Vuestra Majestad que los llame con agasajo y les mande que vayan a esta guerra, y que en viniendo los premiará muy bien, y si murieren se les hará merced a sus mujeres e hijos.

My Lord, the soldier who returns poor from war and who has mortgaged his house in order to go—that is a good soldier, worthy of any posts, rewards, and honors that your Majesty may bestow upon him, for the good soldiers are those who keep the crown on their king's head. But the one who began his service shoeless and who accrues houses and estates without giving them to your Majesty—a bad soldier is he, because he confirms what the common people say: either that he is a traitor for taking bribes or that he keeps the soldiers' wages for himself. And this is something that must not happen, because the salary does not go far enough. The good soldier, if he gets paid, will spend it on the other soldiers in order to keep them happy when the occasion arises. Thus we attribute all this to the worst, based on the bad outcomes we are witnessing.

In the histories we see that very humble men have served well in war, that humble men have become distinguished, and that their kings have honored them in such a way that today we see these honors in their offspring, who are now titled noblemen and grandees, honors well deserved because of their grandparents' deeds. However, in this day and age, we see the opposite: that the individuals who go to serve are the lowest and the most inferior men in the kingdom, men who are sentenced to the galleys and many to the gallows.[5] So, if these people have no honor in their estates, how are they to have it while in the army? And how are they to be entrusted with your Majesty's honor and that of us all, since we sent them there to dishonor us? If in the villages a soldier is requested, the peasants say they do not want to go so as not to return crippled and have to beg, as do many honest men. Under the law of God and as justice states, each should be fed according to his status. But the councils meet and look for a lost and lazy young man, one who cannot be controlled, and they jail him and force him to be a soldier, although never in his life has he taken up a sword, and he is better at running than at fighting. And of these people the troops are formed. So, my Lord, what are such people as these to do except run away at the first chance they get, following, after all, the example of those who command them, who are the first to flee? And so it is written of the army and so say some of those who have returned: "If he who commands us runs away screaming and saying, 'Everyone run for his life, we are lost,' what are we to do?" Such men as these should be put in prisons, to be disciplined and trained there, and taken out as old soldiers once they are needed. And to those who go around here waiting to be rewarded with a title but who are not given an audience—though they have been serving for a long time—your Majesty should be advised to summon them with lavishness and order them to go to this war and, on

Señor, no hay mercedes más bien empleadas que en los soldados que sirven bien y aventuran sus vidas y honras, porque van al degolladero fiados en los que viven sin honra y los dejan, como lo hemos visto, solo[s] con la gente honrada, aunque unos muertos y otros prisioneros, como ha sucedido ahora. Aquí, Señor, tiene Vuestra Majestad, obligación de honrar mucho a éstos que cumplieron con su obligación, haciéndolos mucha merced y agasajo, procurando honrar las casas de los muertos; libertar los prisioneros y hacerles merced, pues hemos visto en esta ocasión que se les puede fiar la lealtad de la Corona; ¿qué razón halla Vuestra Majestad a lo que le aconsejan, para que un caballero, dueño de unas casas muy ilustres y que a doce años que sirve en guerra viva, y que hoy está prisionero por su Rey, no sólo se le ha hecho ninguna merced, pero que se le está quitando sus juros y los de su mujer, con que él dejó a su hacienda empeñada para ir a servir, y ella no puede sustentar su casa con una medianía, teniendo la de sus cuatro abuelos que la sustentaba con mucha ostentación y dieron muchas victoria[s] a España?[6]

Pregúntase, Señor, por qué no van a la guerra muchos soldados viejos que hay, y mucha gente noble que se están en sus casas; y responden:

porque los puestos de la guerra se dan a extranjeros no fieles, y perdemos la reputación y vidas los que seguimos sus órdenes y vemos que cuando el cerco de Yelbes, se hizo merced a muchos que huyeron y no a los hijos de muchos que murieron. Y los puestos de la paz[7] se dan a los que nunca han salido de sus casas y regalos, y esto se hace a vista de los que han servido y están arrinconados, y si nos matan, no hacen caso de nuestras mujeres e hijos, y para quedar un hombre honrado en la campaña, muerto o herido o prisionero, como lo vemos al presente; y estamos viendo que si se muere uno de los que tiene puestos en la paz, les envían las mercedes a sus casas; y así es mejor o servir en la paz o estarnos en nuestras casas.

Señor, esto se debe mirar muy bien y poner en el Consejo de Guerra hombres que hayan sido soldados y sepan lo que merecen los que lo son. Esta guerra de Portugal la hemos de mirar más por reputación que por interés, y yo afirmo que no es contra cristianos, supuesto que vienen los ingleses herejes a darles las victorias;[8] que en todas partes la menos gente es la noble y jamás la plebeya, y en Portugal los plebeyos son judíos que los echó de

their return, to heap great benefits upon them and, if they happen to die, to reward their wives and children.

My Lord, there are no better rewards than those given to soldiers who serve well and risk their lives and honor, for they go to the scaffold, trusting those who live without honor and who abandon them, as we have seen, along with the honorable people, of which some are dead and others imprisoned, and this has now taken place. Here, my Lord, your Majesty has the obligation to honor highly those who carried out their obligation, by providing them with great rewards and lavish treatment, endeavoring to honor the houses of the dead, liberating the prisoners and rewarding them. For we have seen that when they are honorable, their loyalty to the crown can be trusted. How does your Majesty explain the advice you are offered, given that a nobleman, the owner of very illustrious houses, who for twelve years has served in the current war, today finds himself imprisoned for his King, and not only has gone without reward, but has his pensions taken from him, as are those of his wife, with whom he left his property pledged in order to serve? Nor can she maintain her house with a small pension, despite having the one from her four grandparents who supported her with great ostentation, and who brought many victories to Spain.[6]

Ask yourself, my Lord, why so many of the old soldiers and many noble people who stay in their houses do not go to war. They may respond to you:

> Because the war posts are given to faithless foreigners, and those of us who follow their orders lose our reputations and our lives. And we saw, at the siege of Yelbes, favor granted to many of those who fled and not to the children of many who died. And the Council of State positions,[7] as well as rewards, are given to those who have never left their houses. This is done in the presence of those who have served and who are set aside in a corner. If we are killed, they pay no attention to our wives and children, and for a man to be honored on the battlefield, he must be either dead or wounded or a prisoner, as we see nowadays. We also see that if one with a Council of State position dies, rewards are sent to his house; so it is better either to serve the Council of State or to remain in our houses.

My Lord, this must be studied carefully: in the Council of War there must be men who have been soldiers and who know what soldiers deserve. We must understand that this war against Portugal is more for our own prestige than for any interest. And I affirm that it is not against Christians, given that the heretic Englishmen come to bring them victories.[8] And, although everywhere the fewest are the nobles and never the plebeians, in Portugal

Portugese. judaizers

Castilla el señor rey Don Fernando, y los acogieron en Portugal;[9] y como ellos [son] ricos y aquel reino tan pobre, se mezclaron con la gente ordinaria;
con que la consecuencia está clara, de que la guerra no es contra cristianos;
y el permitir Dios estos malos sucesos es por nuestros pecados.

Señor, siempre he oído decir a grandes soldados que para ganar a Lis-
boa es necesario ir por mar y por tierra, y todo lo demás es perdernos; ¿qué
importa que ganemos cuatro plazas si viene por la mar el inglés y nos las
quita, como lo vemos ahora?; el reino de Portugal no se puede defender si no
tuvieran la ayuda de los ingleses; y si no los cerramos el paso, es perdernos,
Ea, Señor, pues allá los alienta una mujer, aliéntelos de aquí otra.[10] Bien sabe
Vuestra Majestad que sé yo hacer libros y memoriales,[11] y así me atrevo a
hacer este, celosa del servicio de Vuestra Majestad y harta de oír decir que
nadie se atreve a decir lo que siente, porque no los traguen los dragones
que todo lo aplican para sí; y es terrible cosa que porque estén encontrados
cuatro hombres que gobiernan, lo paguemos todos;[12] remédiese esto en la
paz y pónganse en la guerra al lado del señor Don Juan, para que le ayuden,
soldados viejos castellanos y antiguos en Flandes,[13] y échese un bando que
[a] toda la gente noble y plebeya que por su voluntad quisiere ir a la guerra
se le harán después mercedes conforme a sus calidades y casas, sin traerlos
arrastrados y por los Consejos, y verá Vuestra Majestad cómo habrá muchos
que vayan; y salgan las cuatro Órdenes militares y sáquense los legos de los
conventos y hasta escuadrones de mujeres, pues esta guerra es contra una
Segunda Cava de España,[14] pues cuando las mujeres no peleemos serviremos
en las fortificaciones de peones, y yo la primera, como harán cuatro de mi
parte, aunque las demás sean inferiores; venguemos este agravio como lo
hicieron las vizcaínas en Fuenterrabía[15] y las de Castilla[16] y doña Blanca de
Guevara, la Barbuda.[17] Señor, averígüese si esta desdichada batalla ha sido
desdicha causada por la gente de pocas obligaciones que llevamos o si [ha]
habido algún traidor, y córtesele la cabeza a quien lo mereciere y que cono-
zca el mundo y Portugal que los castellanos no son todos unos.[18]

Los portugueses nunca serán buenos, porque cuando ningún noble
quiera ser Rey han de levantar al zapatero, y esto se lo oí decir a un portugués, siendo muchacha en Extremadura. Y cuando se dijo que querían enviar
a gobernar al señor Don Carlos,[19] que esté en el cielo, le oí decir a Don Francisco de Mora, portugués, gobernador de la raya,[20] que harto se holgarían
en Portugal para levantarlo por rey; diciendo yo que no lo admitiría respon-

the plebeians are also Jews that King Ferdinand expelled from Castile and that Portugal welcomed.[9] But since they are rich and that kingdom is so poor, they mixed with the common people. The consequence is obvious: the war is not against Christians. And God is allowing the current bad events to take place just because of our sins.

My Lord, I have always heard it said by high-ranking soldiers that in order to win Lisbon we must go by land and by sea, and that anything else means defeat. What good does it do to take a handful of towns, if then the English come by sea and take them from us, such as we see occurring now? The kingdom of Portugal cannot be defended without the aid of the English; if we do not block their path, we shall be lost. So, my Lord, since a woman is encouraging them there, let there be another to encourage our men from here.[10] Your Majesty knows quite well that I can write books and memorials,[11] which is why I dare to write this one, concerned as I am about the service they render your Majesty, and tired of hearing that no one dares express what he feels, for fear of being swallowed by dragons who take everything for themselves. It is terrible that because of conflicts between four rulers we all pay the price.[12] Let this be remedied during times of peace. And in wartime let there be placed at Don Juan José's side, for his aid, old Castilian soldiers who gained experience in Flanders.[13] Let there be a public edict, proclaiming that all people, noble and plebeian, who go to war voluntarily and not forced by the councils shall be rewarded according to their position and their lineage. Your Majesty shall see that many will go. Send out the four military orders, remove the laymen from the convents, and send even troops of women, because this war is against a second Spanish *Cava*.[14] Do this so that when we women are not fighting, we shall remain in the fortress serving as foot soldiers. I shall be the first, as well as four more on my behalf, though they be of inferior rank. Let us avenge this offense as did the Biscayan women in Fuenterrabia,[15] and as did those of Castile,[16] and Doña Blanca de Guevara, the bearded one.[17] My Lord, let it be ascertained whether this unfortunate battle has been lost because of those irresponsible people we have pressed to serve or because of some traitors, and let us then cut off the head of whoever deserves it. Let it be known throughout the world and in Portugal as well that not all Castilians are the same.[18]

The Portuguese people will never be good. For when there is no noble-man who wants to be king, they will lift up a shoemaker, and this I heard from a Portuguese man when I was a young woman in Extremadura. And when it was said that Don Carlos,[19] may he rest in heaven, was to be sent to govern there, I heard from the Portuguese Don Francisco de Mora, governor of the border,[20] that Portugal would be very glad to have him as king. To

dió: "matáranle o prendéranle y levantarán a otro"; y un fraile portugués oí decir que cuervos le sacasen los ojos y se los llevasen a vomitar a Portugal; y así, Señor, esta gente nunca puede ser buena, y no hay que llevarlos con blandura ni piedad, sino ir ganando lugares, que no faltarán castellanos que los pueblen; hacer como cuando los poblaron los moriscos[21] y dárselos a los soldados; que si esto se hubiera hecho ni ellos hubieran robado nuestro bagaje ni los portugueses nos hubieran vuelto a llevar a Évora.[22] Yo afirmo y pongo mi cabeza que si ganáramos a Portugal, que lo han de despoblar e irse a otros reinos, por lo mucho que aborrecen a los castellanos; y no es mucho en los judíos el peregrinar por reinos extraños; y quien aconsejó lo contrario no tuvo razón o no quiso tenerla.

Vamos ahora a los portugueses que aquí tenemos; no son más que espías dobles y solo están esperando a decir "viva quien vence;" y hay quien dice que la noche que vino la mala nueva[23] se juntaron a hacer un banquete; esto no lo vimos; lo oí decir a uno; están esperando el fin para decir después viva quien vence; los más de ellos no tienen allá hacienda y gozan aquí las mesadas que Vuestra Majestad les da quitándonos a los españoles viejos y leales nuestros juros[24] y haciendas para darlos a ellos; y esto es claro, puesto que los hombres de negocios que hay portugueses, vinieron aquí descalzos y se han enriquecido con nuestras haciendas, pues para sacar un real[25] de su poder, de lo poco que Vuestra Majestad nos deja, nos cuesta ir al Consejo muchas veces, y como ellos son quien tienen el dinero, si se ha de llevar al ejército, o no lo hay para llevarlo, lo saben ellos, y es cierto que dan aviso al enemigo, y en fin, Señor, nunca es bueno tener el enemigo dentro de casa, sino que Vuestra Majestad mande que los llamen a todos y les digan que Vuestra Majestad no los puede dar mesadas; que el que quisiere irse a Portugal se vaya, y el que quisiere ir a servir a Vuestra Majestad, que sea en Flandes, que se la dará su sueldo, y después se les hará mercedes; y a los hombres de negocios y demás gente particular que hay aquí enviarlos con Dios y quitarles las haciendas, pues las han ganado aquí, y dejarles solo para el camino, pues no tenemos allá nosotros castellanos con quien hagan otro tanto. Y en los Consejos, ¿por qué se han de sentar portugueses para tener avisos que poder dar si quieren?; y si Vuestra Majestad cree que todos son fieles y que merece se les haga merced, puede hacérsela en parte adonde no nos den qué sospechar; en fin, Señor, hágase esta expulsión como la de los moriscos; y compruebo esto con que se vea cuántos se han huido de beneficiados de Vuestra Majestad: el Conde de Miradel [sic] y don Francisco de

which I said that Portugal would not accept it, but he replied that even if they killed him or arrested him, another would rise in his place. But then I heard a Portuguese friar say that he wished crows would pluck out Don Carlos's eyes and vomit them up in Portugal. So you see, my Lord, those people can never be good. And they should be treated neither gently nor mercifully. We should instead win more and more villages, as there is no lack of Castilians to populate them. Do as was done when towns inhabited by *moriscos* were given to our soldiers.[21] For if this had been done, they would not have stolen our military baggage, nor would the Portuguese have taken Évora from us again.[22] I affirm and stake my life on it, that if we were to defeat Portugal, they would leave and go to other kingdoms, because of how much they hate Castilians. For the Jews it is not too much to wander around foreign kingdoms. Whoever gave other counsel was not right or did not want to be right.

Let us speak now of the Portuguese we have amongst us. They are no more than double agents, waiting only to say "long live the victor," whoever that may be. And there are those who say that on the night the bad news arrived,[23] they gathered to celebrate at a banquet. We did not see this, but I heard it said. They are awaiting the end in order to cry "long live the victor," whoever that may be. Most of them have no property there, but here they enjoy the monthly payments that your Majesty gives them, along with the *juros*[24] and properties you take from us, old and faithful Spaniards, and give to them. And this is true: consider the Portuguese businessmen who came here shoeless and who have become rich on our wealth. Meanwhile, in order to obtain even one *real*[25] from your government—of the little that your Majesty allows us—we must go to the council many times. And since the Portuguese are the ones who have the money, they are the ones who know if money needs to be taken to the army or if there is no money at all. Then it is certain that they tell the enemy. So, my Lord, it is never good to have the enemy inside one's house! And so your Majesty should order that all be summoned and told that your Majesty cannot give them monthly payments, that all who wish to return to Portugal should leave, and that those who wish to serve your Majesty should do so in Flanders, where they will be given wages and later rewarded. And as for the Portuguese businessmen and other commoners here, bid them farewell and take their properties away—since they all were acquired here—and give them enough only for the return journey. After all, we have no Castilians in Portugal to whom they could do the same. And why are there Portuguese in all the council offices? To let them send warnings if they like? If your Majesty believes that they are all faithful and that they deserve to be rewarded, then you may do so in

Acevedo pidieron ayuda de costa para ir a Flandes y se fueron a Portugal;[26] también se fue don Sancho Manuel y el hermano de Peñalba y otros muchos de gente ordinaria y tesoreros;[27] y estos que están aquí esperan el suceso para hacer lo mismo y llevarnos el dinero.[28]

En fin, Señor, nunca de moro buen cristiano; y repare Vuestra Majestad que los más portugueses que llevan mesadas tienen allá hermanos o hijos que gozan lo de allá y ellos lo de acá, por comer a dos carrillos; y esto lo digo con ansias del corazón y afecto que tengo al servicio de Vuestra Majestad, y nieta de abuelos que tantas victorias han dado a Castilla.

Señor, Vuestra Majestad vea la crónica del señor Emperador, y hallará cómo vino muy niño a España y trajo un valido que la gobernaba e impuso tantos tributos que se levantaron las Comunidades;[29] y ahora son muchos más los que nos echan; Vizcaya estuvo para perderse cuando la sal; Portugal se levantó cuando el papel; si bien éstos poco habían menester; Cataluña ya ve Vuestra Majestad lo que pasó en ella; Andalucía ha estado alterada sobre la variedad de moneda y bajas que cada día tenemos, y esto muchas veces; Valencia ha estado revuelta ahora, porque los querían echar un tributo en la carne; Nápoles estuvo alterada hasta que el Conde de Oñate lo sosegó;[30] y en fin, Señor, con los vasallos es menester piedad, y los que dan estos arbitrios destruyen el mundo y enriquecen ellos; y cuando se dan los oficios mande Vuestra Majestad que se haga inventario de la hacienda con que entran y la que sacan, y se sabrá el que es buen juez; y que se modere la mucha gente que hay en el Consejo de Hacienda comiendo a costa de Vuestra Majestad y de todos, y hoy hay cuatro Presidentes de Hacienda que llevan gajes y todo esto lo pagamos los tristes vasallos[31].

La vanidad está muy en su punto; la señora reina doña Catalina[32] salió a misa de parida en Valladolid en una hacanea;[33] el señor Emperador dormía en el campo en una tienda; y ahora no hay obligado, ni mercader, ni oficial que no ande en coche; y así no hay mulas para los labradores; la cebada vale cara; los que no pueden quie[re]n traer tantas mulas y tantos lacayos como los que pueden, porque no son menos que ellos, aunque lo es la hacienda; y así, Señor, es menester poner punto fijo, señalando lo que ha de traer cada Grande y cada Título y cada caballero[34] y cada Oidor, y a la gente particular

a way that will not seem suspect to us. So, my Lord, order this expulsion as was done with the *moriscos*. I can prove my point; just notice how many have fled after reaping benefits from your Majesty: Count Miradel [*sic*] and Don Francisco de Azevedo asked for financial assistance to help with Flanders but instead went to Portugal;[26] Don Sancho Manuel also left, as did his brother from Peñalba; and many others who were commoners or treasurers.[27] And those who are here are awaiting the occasion to do the same and to steal our money.[28]

So, my Lord, never can a Moor become a good Christian. And note, your Majesty, that most of the Portuguese who receive monthly payments have siblings or children over there who enjoy what they have there, while these people enjoy what they have here; thus they dine at two tables. I say this with concern in my heart and fondness for serving your Majesty, as a granddaughter of men who brought so many victories to Castile.

Your Majesty, read the chronicle of our emperor, and you will find that he came as a child to Spain, and brought with him a *valido* (prime minister) who ruled here and who imposed so many taxes that the *Comunidades* revolted;[29] and now we have even more taxes. Biscay almost rebelled because of the salt issue; Portugal rose up because of the paper situation, although it had little need to do so; Catalonia—your Majesty can see what happened there; Andalusia has been upset about the changes in money and its daily decreases in value, which occur more and more often; Valencia is up in arms because of a proposed meat tax; Naples was agitated until Count Oñate calmed it down.[30] So, my Lord, pity is necessary with your vassals. Those who impose these taxes destroy the world and enrich themselves; and when offices are assigned, your Majesty should order that an inventory be taken of the property with which the officials arrive and of what they have when they leave, and it will be clear which of them are just. Let there be a limit upon the number of people in the Council of Finance, because they dine at the expense of your Majesty and of all of us, for today there are four presidents of Finance who receive salaries, and we, unhappy vassals, are the ones who pay for all this.[31]

Vanity has reached its peak: the lady queen Catalina[32] went to her first postpartum mass in Valladolid riding upon a palfrey,[33] and the emperor slept in the countryside in a tent; but now there is no city supplier, merchant, or craftsman who does not ride around in a carriage. As a result, there are no mules for the peasants; barley is expensive; those who cannot afford it would like to bring as many mules and footmen as those who can, so as not to be considered lesser, even though their wealth is. Thus, my Lord, we must bring this to a halt by clarifying what is to be used by each grandee

quitarles los coches y que anden a caballo, y con eso habrá mulas para los labradores, y lacayos para la guerra, que andan aquí unos mocetones vagamundos que es lástima; ahora me acabaron de contar que los comisarios que van a hacer gente a los lugares, conciertan muchos soldados a dinero y se los echan en las faldriqueras; pues si ellos hacen estas cosas, ¿cómo no han de dejar solo a un hijo de Vuestra Majestad en la ocasión, como lo han hecho ahora? Señor, hallo es preciso buscar dos buenas cabezas: una que gobierne la paz y otra que disponga y gobierne desde aquí la gente que ha de ir a la guerra; que muchos gobernadores lo descomponen todo, y se habla mal de algunos y se dice que se hizo un navío y que tardaron tanto en ponerle las velas y garfios que solo de guardas se gastaron cuarenta mil ducados y yo me [he] escandalizado de oírlo; y cuando una cosa tarda se dice comúnmente: "es el socorro de España que siempre viene tarde." Todo esto, Señor, conviene que se mire muy bien; y yo digo lo que dice el pueblo y lo que se me alcanza como buena vasalla y deseo de servir a Vuestra Majestad, a quien le suplico me perdone y reciba el buen celo, que en esta ocasión quisiera ser una amazona y que todos fuesen en España para volver por la honra de ella y la de mi Rey, a quien guarde Dios mil siglos con mucha sucesión y amparo de estos reinos.

and each titled noble, each *caballero*[34] and each judge, and the commoners must be relieved of their carriages and made to go about on horseback. If we do this there will be mules for the peasants and footmen for the war, for it is sad to see that some young men around here are idle. I have just been told that the officers who go from town to town recruiting people for war get them to agree to serve and promise to pay them but then put the money in their own pockets. So if they are doing these things, why would they not abandon a son of your Majesty the first chance they get, as they have done on this occasion? My Lord, I find it necessary to look for two good leaders: one to manage the affairs of the Council of State and the other to organize and govern, from here, those who must go to war. For many governors disturb everything, and some of these governors are spoken ill of. It is said that a ship was built and that it took so long to add the sails and hooks that forty thousand ducats were spent on guards alone, and this offended me when I heard about it. When something takes a long time, it is often said: "Aid from Spain is always late in coming." My Lord, it would be a good idea to look at all this very carefully, for I am repeating what people are saying and what reaches my ears as a good vassal who wishes to serve your Majesty, whom I beseech to forgive me and accept my genuine concern. Would that I were an Amazon at this moment, and that everyone in Spain were an Amazon, to return her honor and the honor of my king. May God watch over you for a thousand centuries and grant you a long succession and protection for these kingdoms.

## II. DESENGAÑOS DE LA CORTE,
## Y MUJERES VALEROSAS (1664)

*Compuesto por un autor moderno,[1] poca experiencia, y grande celo. Dedicado al Príncipe Nuestro Señor que Dios guarde, Don Carlos José.*

Gran Príncipe de España, a quien San Diego de Alcalá[2] trajo a estos Reinos, porque debamos más a este Santo, y le pidamos interceda con Dios nos guarde a V.A. para amparo de ellos, y su restauración; y cuando después de los largos días de su Majestad Don Felipe IV llegue V.A. a heredar estos Reinos, permita Dios, que todos estén restaurados, y vueltos a la obediencia de tan gran Monarca, y que se cumpla la profecía de ganar la casa Santa en V.A. yo lo espero en Dios, y en un general tan alentado, como el Señor Don Juan de Austria, en quien hierve la sangre de tan gran parentesco, y deseo de servir a su Rey.

Un Autor moderno pone a los pies de V.A. esta corta obra, aunque Gigante en deseos, y la dedica a tan gran Príncipe, como el de España, y le suplica mande a su Maestro, que después de el Cristos enseñe a V.A. a leer en esta pigmea obra, para que sea Gigante en el deseo;[3] y por ser el asunto, de que pienso tratar, de *mujeres valerosas,* suplico a V.A. ampare a las que lo fueren en estos tiempos, y reciba el buen celo, y le guarde Dios a V.A. como hemos menester, y esperamos lo ha de alcanzar de su Divina Majestad San Diego, y el Príncipe,[4] que nos llevó a poner en el trono de los Ángeles, para que lo ayude a pedir a Dios, el cual nos lo conceda, como hemos menester.

El Príncipe, que hoy tenemos,
Para darnos luz al mundo,

## II.  DISENCHANTMENTS AT THE COURT
## AND VALOROUS WOMEN (1664)

*Written by a modern author[1] with little experience and great concern. Dedicated to the Prince our Lord; may God be with you, Don Charles Joseph.*

Great Prince of Spain, whom Saint Diego of Alcalá[2] brought to these kingdoms, for which we are in debt to this saint. We ask Saint Diego to intercede with God on your behalf, to watch over your Highness and protect and restore the kingdoms. And when the long days of our Majesty Philip IV have come to an end and your Highness inherits these kingdoms, God willing, may they all be restored and turned once again to proper obedience of such a great monarch, and may the prophecy be fulfilled, which says that your Highness will reach the holy house. I hold this hope in God and in a general as brave as is Don Juan José of Austria, within whom runs such grand family blood as well as the desire to serve his king.

A modern author places at the feet of your Highness this work which is short, yet giant in intentions, and dedicates it to a prince as great as is that of Spain, and implores that once you learn the alphabet, you order your tutor to use this small work to teach your Highness to read, so you may become giant in intentions.[3] Also, because the subject with which I am going to deal is *valorous women,* I implore your Highness to protect those who may be valorous nowadays, and be aware of my concern, and may God be with your Highness, for the good of all of us. And we hope you achieve this thanks to his holy Majesty Saint Diego and to the prince,[4] whom Saint Diego placed upon the throne of angels in order to help him intercede with God on our behalf, may He grant that to us, for the good of us all.

> The Prince we have today
> to bring our world the splendor of the sun,

Es un Don José Primero,
Sexto Carlos sin Segundo

### CAPÍTULO 1

*Desengaños de la corte, y mujeres valerosas*

La malicia, la envidia, y la avaricia todo reina en estos tiempos; y adonde más hace su asiento, es en las Cortes de los Reyes, los Monarcas, en donde todos tiran para sí, y ninguno para su Rey; no hay padre para hijo, y esto lo vemos hoy patente, y se pudieran señalar algunos, si mi intención fuera agraviarlos, mas no es ése mi intento; y así solo diré aquí lo que fuere enderezado al servicio de Dios, y de mi Rey, y bien de las Almas, pues para ellas no podemos desear más que salvarnos, y la vida eterna, que con esto la conseguiremos; y cierto, que en la Corte lo pongo por dudoso, porque aunque hay buenas almas, y las confesiones se frecuentan mucho, hay que reparar en que no todos, ni todas, pueden estarse en sus casas; porque más triste vida, que la de la aldea, y así es preciso juntarse en las conversaciones, de las cuales las más son perjudiciales, y las que menos lo son, si en ellas no se quitan las honras, como en otras, por lo menos se murmura, y se echan juicios temerarios, y de allí se vienta en otras partes, añadiendo más, y de esta suerte corriendo, hasta que llega a ser perjudicial.

La felicidad se pone en los juegos, y galas, destruyendo sus casas, y haciendo indecencias; las mujeres traen tantas galas, que no les alcanza la hacienda. Las plebeyas lo buscan con mal modo: los nobles dejan de pagar a sus criados, con que cada día los tiene nuevos; porque son pobres, y de pocas obligaciones, y no tienen espera.

Pues Señor, mejor fuera dejar los juegos, y las superfluidades, y pagar a vuestros criados, y con esto no conocerían otros amos, y sirvieran con ley; que muchos ha habido, que la han tenido, como los de Ruy López de Ávalos, que gastaron sus haciendas en defensa de su amo;[5] y en estos tiempos conocí una criada, que llevó por su ama muchos tormentos, hasta quedar manca, por haber muchos años que la servía, pero los que entran hoy, y salen mañana, qué ley pueden tener, sino deshonrar las casa, y esto por las malas pagas.

Si el otro saca una inventiva de un coche nuevo, y ha un año que otro señor tiene otro, le deshace por hacerle como aquél, pudiendo durarle cuatro años.

is one Don Joseph the First,
Charles the Sixth, second to none.

### CHAPTER 1

*Disenchantments at the Court and Valorous Women*

Viciousness, envy, and avarice all reign over these days, and have settled heaviest upon the courts of kings and monarchs, where everyone looks out for himself and not for his king. There are no fathers for sons, and this we see clearly today. Examples could be given, if I wished to offend everyone, but that is not my intention. So here I will say only that which is directed toward service to God, and to my king, and to the good of souls, since for them we can wish nothing more than to save ourselves and have eternal life, and so we shall attain it. True, I doubt this could happen at the court because, though there are good souls and confessions are very frequent, it must be noted that not all men nor all women can afford to maintain their houses, so that life there is more miserable than that of the village. So it is necessary to gather in conversations, though most of it be harmful, and that which is less so (even when it is not slanderous—as it is in some cases), at the very least contains gossip, and rash judgments are formed; and from there, comments are aired in other places, and are added to, and so in this vein become harmful.

Happiness is staked upon games and finery which ruin their houses and make them commit indecent acts. Women wear so much finery that their wealth does not go far enough. The common women look for that finery in a bad way. Noblemen stop paying their servants, whereupon they have new ones every day, since they are poor and have few obligations and have no patience.

So my Lord, it would be better to set aside the games and superfluities, and pay your servants; in this way they would not seek out other masters and would serve with loyalty. Many servants have there been who have had this loyalty, like those of Ruy López Dávalos, who spent their wealth to defend their master.[5] And recently I met a female servant who, for the good of her lady, suffered many torments, to the point of losing the use of one hand, for having served for so many years. It is quite the contrary with those who begin their service today and end it tomorrow; what honor will they have except the honor of dishonoring the houses where they serve? And all because of poor wages.

If a neighbor adds some feature to a new carriage, another man, who has had his carriage for only a year, will dismantle it in order to make it like the other's, even though his could have lasted for four more years.

Si la otra señora tiene una joya rica, que pudiera durar a sus bisnietos, la deshace para comprar otra, que vino de otro Reino, lo más de ello falso, y que no dura cuatro días. Si se quitan las puntas de plata, porque no se gaste, vienen de otro Reino puntas de hilo, y seda, con que nos llevan la plata, y viene a ser peor.

En los oficios no hay tasa, ni cuenta en los despachos, con que nos quitan las capas. En las plazas están los Alguaciles convenidos con los que venden, y así nos cuesta todo más, y todos son ladrones en sus oficios, sin que los que lo han de gobernar lo reparen, ni castiguen, y en fin la Corte es perjudicial para el alma, para la salud, y para la hacienda.

No digo yo, que todos nos podemos ir de ella, porque los que sirven en la Casa Real es preciso que estén, los Consejeros, Letrados, Asentistas, mercaderes, tratantes, pleiteantes, y pretendientes, aunque estos mejor fuera que no estuvieran; porque hay hombres, que pueden gobernar un Reino, y vienen a pretender, y gastar su hacienda; y porque no tuvo favores, o dineros para pagar el oficio se vuelve empeñado para muchos años, y de estos tales hombres, hay grandes sujetos en los lugares, y no son conocidos, porque no asisten en la Corte viviendo con la lisonja, y el Monarca no conoce mas de los que le andan alrededor, que algunos tienen buena maña, y otros no saben más que la bachillería, y en apurándolos no tienen cabeza.

Muchos andan perdidos, y echan a perder sus mujeres, con enfermedades sucias, con que pierden la sucesión, y el que la tiene, nacen los hijos tan enfermos, que al primer aire que les da se les mueren, y con la vida que traen viven muy poco, y hay muy pocos que lleguen a viejos, y han introducido unas bebidas, y se envician tanto en ellas, que los matan más aprisa. Las ofensas de Dios son grandes, y se vive muy aprisa, y de la misma suerte se mueren sin decirles una Misa; y esto lo he visto en grandes personas, porque no alcanzan a pagar las deudas, que hicieron para cosas excusadas, haciendo de la noche el día y del día la noche.

Las casas mal gobernadas, y las haciendas peores porque no las ven sus dueños, y así están todos pobres, y el que está rico no se lo envidio, porque o lo gana en puestos o en tratos, esto en todo género de gente, que no les falta para dar a bufones, y lisonjeros, y no a pobres vergonzantes que están en sus casas pereciendo, y se vieron en bien.

If a woman has an expensive jewel, one that could last long enough to be passed on to her great-grandchildren, she gets rid of it to buy another from some other kingdom, usually counterfeit, and that lasts a few days at best. If silver lace trim is forbidden in order to save money, linen and silk lace trims are brought from another kingdom, whereupon they take our money, and it turns out worse.

In the trades there are no standards, nor careful accounting in transactions, so they are taking the clothes from our backs. In the marketplaces, the constables are in league with the sellers, so everything is more expensive, and everybody is a thief at his trade, while those who rule do nothing to mend or punish it. This is why the court is harmful to one's soul, one's health, and one's wealth.

I am not saying that all of us can leave the court, because it is essential that those who serve the royal house remain there, the councilors, lawyers, contractors, merchants, traders, plaintiffs, and aspirants, although it would be better that the latter not be there. For there are men who can govern a kingdom but who come to court to seek a position at the court and spend their wealth; and when they receive no rewards or money to pay for their expenses, they return home, in debt for many years to come. Of this sort of men some are great names in the villages, but they are not well known at the court because they do not attend the king or live with flattery, and the monarch knows only those who surround him closely; some are skilled, but others know only how to engage in idle talk, and when pressed they are without the foggiest notion.

Many men are lost and ruin their wives with filthy illnesses, then can no longer have offspring; or if one of them does, the children are born so sickly that they die upon taking their first breath. With the life they lead, they live a very short time, and very few reach old age. Men have become so dependent upon new types of drinks that they are dying faster. Great are the offenses committed against God, and such people live with great haste and die in the same way, without first having Mass said for them. This I have seen in important people, all because they do not manage to pay their debts, debts which were shouldered for unnecessary things, and whose lives, as a consequence, changed overnight.

Houses are poorly governed and wealth is even more poorly managed, because the owners do not look after them, and so everyone is poor. He who is rich is not one I envy, because whether he earns the money from his post or from trading, it's the same with all types of people: they have enough to give to buffoons and flatterers but not to the poor who, out of shame, are now perishing in their homes—although they were fine in the past.

No hay regla sin excepción, en medio de esto las personas que viven en la Corte ajustadas, hay más que estimarles, pues no se llevan mal ejemplo, que vemos, mas lo más seguro es el retiro a los lugares propios, y huir las ocasiones. Hay mucha gente en la Corte, que no se sabe de qué viven: y comen y visten, como los que tienen hacienda, quién duda que algunos son espías de otros Reinos, y aún de nosotros mismos, pues no estamos unidos como lo manda Dios, y como debemos estar para servir a nuestro Rey, y otros son ladrones. No se guardan contrabandos, que por dinero dejan entrar de Portugal cuanto hay, y nos llevan la plata para hacernos guerra; y en fin la Corte es peligrosa y no es buena para los que no tenemos qué hacer en ella. Véase un libro, que hizo un grande hombre, que fue Fr. Antonio de Guevara Obispo de Mondañedo, Cronista del señor Emperador, que se titula *Menosprecio de la Corte, y alabanzas de la aldea*,[6] de cuya vida trataremos en otro capítulo, y ahora de nuestras mujeres valerosas.

## CAPÍTULO 2

### De mujeres valerosas

Muchas mujeres ha habido valerosas, y atentas, de las cuales nombraremos algunas; y quien nos da el ejemplo, es la Reina de los Ángeles, que aunque mi pluma no sabrá explicarlo, pondré aquí un ejemplo suyo, para adornar esta obra llevando tan buen principio, pues para darnos ejemplo de lo que debemos hacer, acompañó a su marido S. José, cuando fue al llamamiento del rey Herodes, y pudiendo excusarse por estar tan preñada, no lo hizo, sino parió en un portal al Salvador del mundo,[7] aquí tenemos mucho, que meditar los Cristianos, que para decirlo yo, había de ser un San Agustín.[8] Síguese a este ejemplo otro de una Antecesora suya, que fue la Reina Micol:[9] cayó su marido David de la gracia de Saúl, envió a prenderle; y ella olvidando el que Saúl era su padre, y su rey, solo se acordó de lo que dice Dios, "dejarás a tu padre, y madre por tu marido," valióse de su entendimiento, echando en la cama una estatua, y mandó que entrasen los Ministros, y viesen, que David estaba malo, durmiendo, y en el ínterin se escapó por una ventana, quedando ella en peligro, de que Saúl vengase en ella su indignación si quisiese. Fr. Antonio de Guevara trata en sus escritos del valor de la Reina Cenobia,[10] que sustentó mucho tiempo guerra contra Roma, y la Reina Madre gobernó en Francia;[11] y la Reina doña Catalina en España,[12] que el gobierno de las mujeres a veces suele ser mejor, que el de muchos hombres.

There is no rule without an exception, and in the midst of this we must respect even more those who live carefully at the court, because they do not follow the bad example that we see. It is safest for them to retire to their properties and flee from possible hazards. There are many people at the court of whom no one knows on what they live; they eat and dress like the wealthy. Undoubtedly some of them are spies from other kingdoms or even from amongst ourselves—seeing how we are not united as God wishes and as we should be to serve our king—and others of them are thieves. Smuggling cannot be prevented, since for a fee everything in Portugal is allowed through, and they take our money to wage war against us. In short, the court is harmful, and it is not good for those of us who have no reason for being in it. I recommend a book written by a great man, Father Antonio de Guevara, bishop of Mondañedo, chronicler of his lord the Emperor, entitled *The Disparagement of the Life of a Courtier and the Praise of the Life of the Village*,[6] whose life we shall discuss in another chapter. But now, on to our valorous women.

### CHAPTER 2

#### *Concerning Valorous Women*

Many valorous and thoughtful women have there been, a few of whom we shall name. The one who sets the example for all is the Queen of Angels. Though my pen may not know how to explain it, I shall include here an example from her life, to embellish this work with a fine beginning. In order to set an example for us of what we should do, she went with her husband, Saint Joseph, to answer the call of King Herod. And though she could have excused herself for being so heavy with child, she did not. Rather, she gave birth in a manger to the Savior of the world.[7] Here we Christians have much to meditate upon (I would have to be Saint Augustine to tell it all).[8] Following this example is that of one of her forebears: Queen Michal.[9] Her husband David fell into disfavor with Saul, who ordered that he be captured; and she, forgetting that Saul was her father and king, remembered only what God has said: "You shall leave your father and mother for your husband." Using her wit, she placed a statue in the bed, then ordered the ministers of justice to enter and see that David was sick and sleeping. In the meantime, he escaped through a window, while she remained behind, although Saul could take revenge on her if he so desired. Father Antonio de Guevara deals in his works with the valor of Queen Zenobia,[10] who for a long time waged war against Rome; and the queen mother who ruled in France;[11] and Queen Catalina in Spain:[12] a government of women is at times better than that of many men.

Mató el Conde Fernán González en batalla al Rey de Navarra, y su hijo trata la venganza con mal modo, concertándole de casar con su hermana doña Sancha: va el Conde muy lozano a las bodas, y lo que hizo fue meterle en una prisión; y doña Sancha, que le miraba como a un marido (y en el sentir de todos lo era) dice: "el Conde mató a mi padre en campaña; mate mi hermano al Conde, y no me ponga a mi por broquel para hacer una traición." Vístese de valor, falséale las llaves, sácale de la prisión, y viénese con él a Castilla. Visto esto el Rey de Navarra concierta con la Reina de León, que también era su hermana, que llamen al Conde a Cortes, y le pongan en prisión, ejecutose así; y luego la Infanta su mujer, finge que va a Santiago en hábito de peregrina, pasa por León, pide licencia para verle en la prisión, vistiole sus vestidos, y echole fuera con buena maña, y quedose ella en la prisión: la fama de estas mujeres vive eterna.[13]

Muere el Rey de Nápoles, deja mandado que su hija Juana heredera del Reino se case con el Rey Andrés (como si los padres pudieran forzar las voluntades, que Dios nos deja en nuestro libre albedrío) viene el Rey Andrés, pone la guerra, y obliga a que se case por fuerza, y en teniéndola sujeta hace lo que los malos maridos; ella como valerosa y Reina propietaria cuélgale el día de San Andrés, y fue la cuelga de veras, pues le envió a que le enviase nuevas del otro mundo.[14] Si hubiera algunas que la imitaran, vivieran los hombres a raya, y no que ellos hicieron las leyes y todas fueron en su favor, queriendo que ellas se contenten con las armas de la rueca, y de almohadilla; pues a fe, que si usasen las mujeres de las letras, que les sobrepujaran a los hombres; pero esto temen ellos, y no quieren que sean Amazonas, sino tenerles las manos atadas, con que no parece bien, que las mujeres salgan de su rincón; pues ¿cómo en las historias se extiende la fama de las mujeres, que han sido valerosas?

Marco Aurelio dice en sus escritos mucho de las mujeres, que han sido valerosas por las letras; y añade que si se diesen a los estudios, fueran más agudas que los hombres, y que ellos deben sufrirles mucho, y tolerarlas,[15] y que los Romanos las tienen por sentencias, y los Bárbaros por esclavas. Cásase la hija del Conde Lozano con el Cid, por vengar la muerte de su Padre, mírale dormido, saca un cuchillo para matarle, acuérdase que es su marido, arroja el cuchillo, y con lágrimas le despierta, y le pide perdón, y él la estima más desde aquel día, porque vio junto el valor y el cariño.[16]

Count Fernán González kills the king of Navarre in battle, and his son plots a devious vengeance by agreeing to marry his sister Sancha to the count. The count attends the wedding ceremony with much self-assurance. But what does the king do but imprison him? And Doña Sancha who considers him her husband (as everyone believes him to be) says: "The count killed my father in battle; my brother should kill the count but not use me as a shield to carry out a deception." She arms herself with courage, copies the keys, removes him from prison, and goes with him to Castile. On seeing this, the king of Navarre arranges for the queen of León, who is another of his sisters, to summon the count to court and, once there, to imprison him. And so it is carried out. Then his wife, the princess, pretends to go to Santiago dressed as a pilgrim. She stops by León, requests permission to visit him in prison, dresses him in her clothes, gets him out with great skill, while she herself remains behind in prison. The reputation of these women lives eternally.[13]

When the king of Naples dies, he has left orders that his daughter Giovanna, inheritor of the kingdom, shall marry King Andrew (as if parents could force the free will granted us by God). King Andrew arrives, declares war, and forces her to marry him. He, as many bad husbands do, keeps her subject to his control. She, as a valorous woman and proper queen, has him hanged on the Saint Andrew's Day. The hanging was certainly real, as she asked him to bring her news from the other world.[14] If there were women to follow her lead, men would be held in check; but since men made the laws, all are written in their favor, requiring women to be satisfied with the arms of the distaff and the pincushion. For by my faith, if women made use of letters, they would surpass men, which is just what men fear; they do not want women to be Amazons but rather to have their hands tied, making it unbecoming for a woman to leave her corner. So how is it, then, that the reputation of women who have been valorous has been spreading throughout history?

Marcus Aurelius in his writings speaks at length about women who have been valorous for their learning. He adds that if women were educated they would be sharper than men and that men should permit them a great deal and tolerate them,[15] given that the Romans consider them wise and that the barbarians consider them slaves. Count Lozano's daughter marries the Cid to avenge her father's death. She watches him as he sleeps, takes out a knife to kill him, remembers that he is her husband, tosses away the knife, and with tears awakens him and asks for his forgiveness. From that day forward he holds her in higher esteem, having seen in her both valor and tenderness.[16]

Anda David por las montañas huyendo de Saúl, sin tener qué dar a sus soldados; envíale un recado a Nabal, aquel ganadero rico, que le envíe un socorro, y no solo no lo hace, pero que le responde con desabrimiento (que esto es lo que más se siente, cuando una persona se avergüenza a otra), viene David con sus soldados a destruir el lugar; sale Abigail mujer de Nabal, que era entendida, prudente, y caritativa, a la defensa con todos sus criados; oblígase David en ver, que aquella mujer enmendó la rustiquez del marido bruto, y vuélvese muy agradecido.[17]

Viene Marfidio Rey moro a pedir la Infanta de Navarra doña Urraca, no se la dan, cerca Pamplona, vese el Rey don García apretado, y determina de dársela, y ella pone los ojos en el camino de Francia, y la esperanza en Dios, y empieza a entretener al hermano; y en este ínterin permite Dios, que es el verdadero socorro, que llegue con el de Francia, y con sus dos hijos, doña Blanca de Guevara, hija del Conde de Oñate, y viuda de Ortuño de Lara, como General, prende a Marfidio, y liberta Navarra;[18] y si ahora una mujer quisiera hacer esto, y es varonil, se rieran de ella, malos tiempos hemos alcanzado.

Salen todos los hombres de Ávila en una guerra, reconocen los Moros que la Ciudad está sola con mujeres, y vienen sobre ella, júntanse todas, y con buena maña, y gran valor cierran las puertas, y pónense en las murallas con sombreros, y arcabuces, espantan a los Moros, y vuélvense.[19] Es sin duda, que si algunas mujeres que se conocen de ánimo, y valor las entraran en los Consejos, y juntas, los dieran tan buenos, como los más acertados Consejeros.

Van los Moros a entrar en una Ciudad nuestra, y sale una hornera, que se llamaba Antona García, y con la pala del horno defiende la Ciudad, hasta que llegue el socorro;[20] es verdad, que entonces no había armas ofensivas, con que se conocía el que era valiente, que ahora con estas voces de fuego no se conoce la valentía, y el más gallina puede matar al más valiente.

Al Rey don Alonso estando en Burgos le pareció bien una señora de estos Reinos,[21] y no pudiendo conseguir su deseo, buscó la ocasión de prender a su marido, y le envió a decir, que había de morir en la prisión, si no concedía con su gusto; y ella que era entendida, honrada, y noble, puso en una balanza el amor de su marido, y en otra su honra, y el corazón en Dios, con que se salió bien de todo, valiéndose de una industria; tomó una vela, y quémase todo un brazo, y pónele una unturas; envía a llamar al Rey, y dícele, que está llena de fuego de san Antón,[22] y que por eso se defiende;

David is in the mountains fleeing from Saul, with nothing to offer his soldiers. He dispatches a message to Nabal, the rich stockbreeder, asking him to send help. Not only does he not do it, but his response to David is cutting (and this is what stings the most, when one person shames another). David goes with his soldiers to destroy the place, but Abigail, Nabal's wife, who was learned, wise, and charitable, comes to his defense and appears with all her servants carrying gifts. David is compelled to see that the woman has mended her uncouth husband's lack of manners, and he goes on his way most grateful.[17]

The Moorish king Marfidio comes to ask for the princess of Navarre, Doña Urraca, in marriage. He is refused and as a result lays siege to Pamplona. Her father, King García, sees himself in dire straits and determines to grant him her hand. She fixes her gaze on the road to France and her hope in God, and sets about distracting her brother. In the interim, God, who is our real help, allows Doña Blanca de Guevara, daughter of Count Don Pedro de Oñate and widow of Ortuño de Lara, to arrive with the king of France and her two sons. Like a general, she captures Marfidio and liberates Navarre.[18] If a woman wants to do such a thing today, and if she is manly, she will be laughed at. Bad are the times which are upon us.

All the men of Ávila set out to war, and the Moors, knowing that there are only women in the city, rush upon it. The women gather together and with great skill and valor close the gates. Then, positioning themselves on the walls with men's hats and harquebuses, they frighten off the Moors.[19] There is no doubt that if women who were known for their spirit and valor were allowed on councils and in offices, they would give as much good advice as the keenest councilors.

The Moors are about to enter one of our cities, and a baker named Antona García comes along with a wooden shovel used for lifting bread from the oven and uses it to defend the city until help arrives.[20] For in that age there were no offensive weapons, and therefore it was clear who was valiant. But nowadays with these mouths of fire we do not know what courage is; the greatest coward can kill the bravest.

While King Alonso was in Burgos, he took a liking to a woman from those kingdoms.[21] But since he could not fulfill his desires, he looked for the opportunity to arrest her husband. He then sent her word that her husband would die in prison if she did not satisfy his pleasures. She, who was learned, honorable, and noble, weighed the love of her husband on one hand and her honor on the other, placed her heart in God and made use of her wit, so that everything turned out well. She took a candle, burnt her entire arm, rubbed on some ointments, then sent for the king. She tells him that she is

óyela el Rey, y estímaselo en mucho, suelta a su marido, y hácele merced: llegó a oídos de la Reina la visita, pero no las circunstancias, y otro día va a Palacio, y hácele la Reina un desaire, ella descubre su brazo; y cuenta el caso a la Reina, con que quedó muy obligada; esto puede una buena maña, y una mujer honrada, y fina con su marido.

Sale el Rey don Fernando a las guerras de Granada, y la Reina doña Isabel como le quería bien, y era valerosa, no le quiso dejar solo; va a su lado a caballo alentando la gente, ganan a Granada, y otras muchas Ciudades, con que limpiaron a España de Moros;[23] y si en estos tiempos fuera una mujer con su marido a la guerra, la murmuraran, en lugar de aplaudirla.

Qué más valor, que el de aquellas siete doncellas, que estaban escogidas para entregar a los Moros, cuando España estaba tan desventurada, que daba las cien Doncellas de parias, y habiendo de ser todas sanas; éstas siete se mancaron ellas mismas por no ir, y llaman hoy el lugar Simancas, por este hecho tan heroico.[24] Y llevando otro año las cien Doncellas, entre ellas iba una, que galanteaba un Caballero Figueroa,[25] el cual salió, y se las quitó a los Moros, y libertó a España de este feudo tan desdichado por librar a su dama, que no era mujer propia, que a serlo quizás no lo hiciera.

La Reina Penélope se vio cercada de su enemigo, pidiole de término para entregar la Ciudad, que le dejase acabar de tejer una tela, que ella misma tejía (que entonces hasta las reinas trabajaban, y en estos tiempos, ni aún las mujeres ordinarias lo hacen), concedióselo su enemigo, púsole guardas de vista, tejía todo el día, mas con su buena maña, e industria lo destejía de noche, con que dio lugar a que le viniese socorro, y le derrotase a su enemigo.[26] Y en estos tiempos hubo una señora valerosa (que por tener a sus nietos vivos no la nombro) que estando en una cacería de campo suya, fue la Justicia a prenderle un Hijo, y le dio de palos al Juez, y fue otro de una chancillería, y ella, y sus criados le mataron y le enterraron delante de la puerta en pie con medio cuerpo de fuera, y la vara en la mano, y todos la temblaban, que también es menester que haya mujeres que se den a temer.

Va el Almirante de Castilla a Fuenterrabía, y porque los hombres no dejen de acudir a la defensa del Francés, acuden las Vizcaínas, y trabajan como unos Roldanes.[27] El Emperador Marco Aurelio, dice mucho de las mujeres y las Matronas Romanas, y que pudiese tener cada una dos ropas ricas con

full of Saint Anthony's fire and that this is her reason for resisting him.[22] The king listens to her and esteems her greatly. He then frees her husband and rewards her. The queen gets word of the visit but not of the reasons behind it. So on another day, when the woman visits the palace, the queen slights her; she uncovers her arm and explains the situation to the queen, who then felt greatly obliged. This can be accomplished by a good trick, and by a woman who is honorable and good to her husband.

King Ferdinand goes to war against Granada, and Queen Isabella, loving him so and being valiant, refuses to let him go alone. She rides alongside him, on horseback, encouraging the people. They gain Granada and many other cities and thereby cleanse Spain of Moors.[23] But in these times if a woman were to go to war with her husband, she would be criticized rather than applauded.

What greater valor is there than that of the seven maidens who were chosen to be delivered to the Moors, when Spain was so unfortunate that it had to give one hundred maidens as tribute, all of whom had to be whole and healthy. These seven each cut off one of their own hands so as not to have to go, and today the place is called Simancas for this heroic act.[24] And another year, when the one hundred maidens were being delivered, among them was one who was being courted by the nobleman Figueroa.[25] He went and took her from the Moors and liberated Spain from such a wretched agreement by freeing his lady, who was not even his wife; if she had been, he perhaps would not have done what he did.

Queen Penelope was besieged by her enemy, and she requested terms for the city's surrender: that she be allowed to finish a cloth she herself was weaving (in those days even queens worked, whereas nowadays not even common women do). Her enemy agreed, and guards were set to watch while she wove all day long. But with her great wit and skill she unwove it at night, thus making time for help to arrive in order to defeat her enemy.[26] And in our times there was a valorous lady (whose grandchildren are still living and whose name, therefore, I will not mention) whose son was arrested by bailiffs while she was out hunting in her fields. And what a mighty beating she gave the judge! When someone else from the chancellery came, she and her servants killed him and buried him up to his waist in front of the door, with his staff in his hand, and everyone trembled before her. For there must also be women who make themselves feared.

The admiral of Castile goes to defend Fuenterrabia, but in order to keep the men fighting against the French, the women of Biscay come and set to work as brave as Rolands.[27] Emperor Marcus Aurelius says much about women and about Roman matrons: each should have two expensive dresses

licencia del Senado, y la que sacaba alguna más era delito,[28] qué de delitos
hubiera en estos tiempos si se usara esto.

La Reina Dido se mató, porque la burló un Príncipe de Troya,[29] lo
mismo hizo Lucrecia,[30] ellas fueron grandísimas majaderas, que mejor fuera
matarlos a ellos, que no matarse ellas:[31] Mejor lo hizo la Cava, aunque nos
costó tan caro a España,[32] y la hermosa Judit cortó la cabeza al Capitán
Holofernes, y la colgó en la muralla.[33] Los Predicadores nos dicen cada día
el ejemplo de las Siete Vírgenes prudentes, y las siete locas; qué dichosas
serán las que imitaren a las prudentes, y que desdichadas las que imitaren a
las locas, porque aunque después se enmienden, nunca pueden dejar de ser
lo que fueron;[34] y Aristóteles decía, que Dios hacer no podía no haber sido lo
que fue;[35] dejemos ahora estas sentencias, pensando cuál es mejor seguir a las
Prudentes, o a las Locas, y pasemos a decir de los hombres alguna cosa.

## CAPÍTULO 3

### *De las desantenciones que tienen los hombres con las mujeres propias*

Los hombres todos son una misma *faula* [sic],[36] y así empezaremos este capítulo con ella: el marido más firme llaman a Orfeo, porque fue por su mujer
al infierno; queden ellos que van allá por sus mujeres, no por finezas, como
Orfeo, sino por lo mal que proceden con ellas.[37] Cría la otra madre a su hija
con mucho regalo, y delicadeza, de tal manera, que un confite le hace mal,
no quiere que la den ninguna pesadumbre, y entrégala después a un hombre,
que le da tantas; lo primero le lleva todo Antón Martín a casa,[38] y luego se la
llena de hijos de ganancia (que estas ganancias son las que dan a las mujeres
propias) y juégale la dote, y las joyas, y si habla una palabra, oye dos mil
desaires, y si lo defiende, hace una jornada larga, y tiene la culpa la mala
condición de ella, que ellos nunca la tienen en nada; sucédeles un trabajo, y
vuelven como el hijo pródigo a casa.

El Emperador Marco Aurelio aconseja cómo se han de portar los maridos con sus mujeres para vivir en paz;[39] mas como ahora tratan poco de las
letras, no lo saben, o no quieren saberlo. También aconseja, que los Príncipes
sean liberales, y procuren la paz, y yo digo lo mismo; mas también es fuerza
que se defiendan si les ponen guerra.[40] También dice que el más entendido es
el que piensa que sabe menos, y el más simple, el que piensa que sabe más;[41]
Dios consiente pero no para siempre, y permite que haya traidores para cas-

with the license of the Senate, and she who had more than that would be committing a crime.[28] How many crimes there would be these days if this rule were in effect.

Queen Dido killed herself because a Trojan prince deceived her.[29] Lucretia did likewise.[30] They were enormously stupid, as it would have been better for them to kill the men than themselves.[31] *La Cava* did it better, though she cost us Spaniards dearly.[32] And the beautiful Judith chopped off Captain Holofernes' head and hung it on the wall.[33] Preachers every day give us the example of the seven wise virgins and the seven foolish ones: how happy will be those who imitate the wise virgins and how unhappy those who imitate the foolish, because even if the latter eventually mend their ways, they never cease to be what they were.[34] As Aristotle said, God could not have done what He did if He were not what He was.[35] Let us set aside these maxims and ponder whether it is better to follow the wise virgins or the foolish ones, and let us go on to say a little something about men.

## CHAPTER 3

### On Men's Discourtesy toward Their Own Wives

Men are all the same,[36] and with this we shall begin the chapter. People call Orpheus the most steadfast of husbands, because he went to hell to get his wife. Those who go there for their wives, not out of signs of love like Orpheus, but out of wickedness, should remain with them.[37] A mother raises her daughter with great tenderness and refinement, so nothing more than a little candy can harm her. She wants her daughter never to suffer grief; and then she goes and gives her to a man who causes her so much. The first thing that happens is he brings everything from Antón Martín[38] home and then fills the house with children of his mistress (these are the profits that they give to their own wives), and he gambles away her dowry and her jewels, and if she speaks a single word, she will hear two thousand affronts; and if she defends him, it makes for a long journey. And at fault is her bad nature, while they are never blamed for anything. If they run into any sort of hardship, they return home like the prodigal son.

Emperor Marcus Aurelius gives advice about how husbands are to behave with their wives in order to live in peace.[39] But since men nowadays deal little with learning, they either do not know this, or do not wish to know. He also advises that princes be liberal and that they secure peace, and I say the same; but he also encourages them to defend themselves if war is waged against them.[40] He says, too, that the most learned person is he who thinks he knows the least, and the most foolish, he who thinks he knows the

tigar pecados, como lo permitió cuando Bellido de Olfos mató al Rey don Sancho en el cerco de Zamora, porque perseguía a una mujer, que aunque no lo era propia, era su hermana.[42] Pecan aquellas malditas Ciudades, y no habiendo en ellas más que un justo, que estaba unido con su mujer, mándales Dios que salga con su familia, y castígalas, y dice que si hubiere cinco justos les perdonara:[43] luego entre nosotros no hay cinco justos pues nos vienen los castigos por muchas partes, y así conviene que vivamos ajustados como lo manda Dios, y se cumplirá en nosotros el verso del *Magníficat* que dice: *Dios ensalza al que se humilla, y Dios humilla al que se ensalza,*[44] y no tengamos tanta soberbia, que la abatirá Dios.


Aristóteles con ser Gentil, dijo: *causa causarum miserere mei;*[45] pues si un Gentil con su sabiduría conoció a Dios, luego los Cristianos debemos conocer que nos mira Dios, y vivir con atención, y con eso nos dará buenos sucesos, y la vida eterna y no que como ellos hacían las Leyes, y conocieron que muchas mujeres los podrían igualar procuraron aniquilarlas.

Sueña el Rey de Egipto con siete vacas gordas, y siete flacas. Declárale José el sueño, y dice que las siete gordas son siete años abundantes, las siete flacas, siete años estériles, nómbrale por su Gobernador, sacándole para esto de la prisión, guarda de los años buenos, para los malos, queda el Reino contento, y bien gobernado.[46] Cómo habíamos menester ahora un José, que ayude a nuestro Monarca; porque en este tiempo vemos que las flacas somos los Vasallos, que nos enflaquecen con tributos, y decretos, y las vacas gordas son los que lo manejan, sin reparar en el daño, que se nos sigue, con que derraman la harina, y recogen la ceniza.

En la antigüedad se cuenta que un árbol sudó sangre, y que fueron a ver las raíces para saber de qué procedía, y hallaron enterrado al pie un hombre eminente, a quien las raíces tenían agarrado, hecho carne y sangre: y así los que manejan la hacienda de los Monarcas la tienen hecha carne y sangre, y nosotros somos el árbol, que la sudamos para cobrar nuestras haciendas. Anda el infante Don Pedro[47] por el mundo, topa un hombre de mal arte, y preguntándole de qué nación era, le responde, "yo soy con el Moro, moro, y con el Cristiano, cristiano." Esto mismo se usa en las Cortes de los Reyes, y así anda todo de mala data; qué de ejemplares tenemos que poner, pero basta lo que vemos.

Abrasan a Troya por Elena; no era mujer propia, que quizás no lo hicieran si lo fuera:[48] sale huyendo Eneas con su padre a cuestas, y su hijo en brazos, y su mujer asida del cinto, y con el tumulto de la gente piérdese, y

most.[41] God consents and allows—but not forever—that there be traitors, so that sins may be punished, as He allowed when Bellido de Orfos killed King Sancho in the siege of Zamora for harassing a woman who, though not his wife, was his sister.[42] Those accursed cities commit sins, and when in those cities there is no more than a single righteous man united with his wife, God orders him to leave with his family and then punishes the cities, saying that if there were five righteous men, he would forgive them.[43] It must be that there are not five righteous men among us, since punishments come to us from many directions. And so it is advantageous that we live rightly as God wishes, and may that verse from the *Magnificat* be fulfilled in us, the one which says: "God praises him who humbles himself and humbles him who praises himself."[44] And let us not have so much pride, because God will knock it down.

Aristotle, a pagan, said: *causa causarum miserere mei.*[45] If a pagan with his wisdom knew God, then we Christians should know Him, for He watches us; and we should live carefully so that He will reward us with fortunate events and eternal life. But men made the laws and knew that many women could become their equals, so they attempted to annihilate them.

The king of Egypt has a dream about seven fat cows and seven thin ones. He tells Joseph of his dream, who says that the seven fat cows mean seven plentiful years, and the seven thin cows, seven lean years. The king appoints him governor, removing him from prison. During the good years he sets aside provisions for the bad ones; the kingdom is content and well governed.[46] How badly we need a Joseph now to help our monarch! Because nowadays we see that the thin cows are we vassals who are weakened with taxes and decrees, and the fat cows are those who rule without taking heed of the harm that befalls us, whereupon they spill the flour and gather the ash.

It is said that in antiquity a tree once sweated blood, and that people went to see its roots to find out from where the blood flowed. And they found, buried at the base of the trunk and held fast by the roots, a prominent man, whose blood and flesh were decomposing. And those who manage the monarch's finances have them in a similar state of decomposition; meanwhile we are the tree that sweats blood to earn our wealth. Prince Don Pedro[47] is traveling about the world; he comes across a trickster who, when asked his nationality, replies, "With the Moors I am a Moor and with Christians, a Christian." This very same thing is used in the royal courts, and for that reason, everything is being ruined. There are so many examples we could use, but what we see suffices.

They set fire to Troy because of Helen; she was not theirs; perhaps if she had been, they would not have done so.[48] Aeneas flees with his father on his shoulders, his son in his arms, and his wife clinging to his belt, but in all the

quémase;[49] por cuánto dejara de ser mujer propia la que fuese en peor lugar, y pereciera.

Ofrece Abraham a Dios sacrificar lo primero que viese en su casa, cierto es que no había ningún criado, porque eso no fuera mortificación, y entonces no estaban los zaguanes llenos de vagamundos jugando, y esto tienen muchos por autoridad en estos tiempos, más valiera sustentarlos en la guerra en servicio de Dios, y de su rey. Tampoco pensó que fuese el ganado, que estaría en el campo: topó a su hijo y como era santo, manda Dios a un Ángel, que baje, y se le quite:[50] lo más cierto es que las mujeres son las primeras, que salen a recibir a los maridos; pero Dios libró a ésta, que si acierta a salir, sin duda, que se olvida de que es santo, y la sacrifica; y si no mírese a David, que con ser santo, y deber tanto a su mujer Micol (pues le libró del rigor de Saúl) se olvidó de esto, y no le guardó lealtad, sino que se enamoró de Betsabé:[51] los más hacen ahora esto mismo, y aquellos que hablan halagüeños a sus mujeres suelen ser peores.

El rey de Inglaterra casó con una Infanta de Castilla, que no hay más que poder ser, y teniendo una hija en ella la repudió por casarse con Ana Bolena, una hereje de pocas obligaciones, y porque el Papa no vino en ello, le negó la obediencia, y metió la herejía en Inglaterra; y teniendo escritos muchos libros en aumento de la Fe, volvió la pluma, y escribió otros en contra,[52] que los que escriben son como los Letrados que defienden un mismo pleito cada uno diferente, y hallan autores para todo; y así el que escribe, si vuelve la pluma, halla autores, y ejemplares, y moralidades, y alegorías para escribir diferente como las halló Enrique para perdición de aquel Reino.

El Rey Chico de Granada tenía encontrados a sus vasallos Zegríes, y Abencerrajes,[53] y pareciéndoles a los Zegríes que favorecía más a los Abencerrajes, levantaron un testimonio a uno de ellos con la Reina Sultana, y como el Rey no debía saber estas opiniones, cerró con la primera nueva, y degolló a los Abencerrajes, prendió a la Reina, echole la ley a cuestas; y aunque era Mora volvió Dios por su ignorancia, y permitió que cuatro Caballeros Cristianos volviesen por su honra: era entendida y conoció que nuestra ley era la buena, bautizose, y recogiola Dios en su rebaño, que a veces toma este camino para que no se pierda un alma: crecieron las guerras civiles entre los Moros, perdieron a Granada, y la ganó el Rey Don Fernando, y la Reina Doña Isabel. Este Rey Chico obró mal como marido en creer fácilmente la maldad contra su mujer, y como Rey en no conocer los bandos de aquellos linajes.[54] Los hombres deben mirar el sujeto, y valor de las mujeres, que es

turmoil she gets lost and dies in a fire.[49] Hence the worse the spot, the more likely she would be abandoned if she was their own woman.

Abraham offers as a sacrifice to God the first thing he sees in his house. (Of course a servant did not count, for that would be no real hardship. Back then the vestibules were not full of idle gamblers; so many agree nowadays that it would be better if those gamblers were at war serving God and their king). Nor did he think the sacrifice would be the livestock in his fields: he came across his son, but because he was a holy man, God sent down an angel to take his son away from him.[50] It is certainly true that women are the first to go out and greet their husbands; but God spared Abraham's wife, because if she had happened to appear, Abraham would undoubtedly have forgotten he was holy and would have sacrificed her. Indeed, look at David who, though he was such a holy man and owed so much to his wife Michal (because she spared him from Saul's severity), forgot all of this and did not stay faithful to her but instead fell in love with Bathsheba.[51] Most men today do exactly the same, and those who flatter their wives are usually the worst.

King Henry of England married a princess of Castile, the highest rank a woman can be, and after having a daughter with her, disavowed her in order to marry Anne Boleyn, a heretic of few obligations. Since the pope was not in agreement with that, the king refused to obey him and brought heresy to England. And having written many books in appreciation of the faith, he reversed his pen and wrote many other books against it.[52] For those who write are like lawyers who defend the same case in different ways and find an authority for any position. And so if he who writes reverses his pen, he will find authorities, examples, morals, and allegories in order to write differently, like those found by Henry to bring his kingdom to ruin.

King Chico of Granada had certain vassals, the Zegríes, who opposed another group of vassals, the Abencerrajes.[53] Since it seemed to the Zegríes that the king favored the Abencerrajes, they falsely accused one of them of being with the queen Sultana, and since the king must not have known about their discord, he refused to hear more after receiving the first report, and he beheaded the Abencerrajes, arrested the queen, and brought the full weight of the law to bear against her. Yet although she was a Moor and therefore ignorant, God came to her aid and allowed four Christian knights to restore her honor. She was wise and recognized that our law was the right one. She had herself baptized, and God took her into His flock; He sometimes acts in this way, so that a soul may be saved. The civil wars between the Moors increased, and they lost Granada to King Ferdinand and Queen Isabella. This King Chico acted poorly—first as a husband, so easily believ-

lo que no se acaba, si no es con la vida, que el dote, y la buena cara, se acaba muy aprisa con el tiempo, y se hallan con una simple en casa.

Qué gracias puede dar a Dios un hombre, que le sucede un trabajo, y halla en casa una mujer con quien poder comunicarse, y tomar consejo; porque aunque el de la mujer es poco, el que no le tome es loco; y qué desgraciado es, el que halla lo contrario. Señores casados, estimad a vuestras mujeres, pues os las dio Dios por compañeras, y no las arrojéis, como Daniel, en el lago de los Leones,[55] que Dios consiente, y no para siempre: y pues presumir los hombres, que sabéis más, y tomáis para vosotros los gobiernos, y puestos, tolerad, y llevad con prudencia las condiciones de vuestras mujeres, pues quien más sabe, más ha de sufrir; y si una mujer tiene mala condición, llevadla con prudencia; y si la tiene buena estimadla, y mostradla mucho cariño, que con esto viviremos en paz; Dios nos la dé, gracia y acierto para proseguir este libro.

## CAPÍTULO 4

*Que trata cómo se han de portar los Reyes, para dar los puestos*

El Emperador Marco Aurelio, llora la perdición de Roma, y dice, que cuando estaba poblada de Romanos antiguos, estaba fértil, y como debía estar, y que ahora tiene la mala ventura de estar poblada de hijos espurios y extranjeros, y que esa es su perdición.[56] Lo mismo podemos llorar de España, pues todas las llaves, así de la paz, como de la guerra, tienen hoy los extranjeros; Dios dice que la caridad bien ordenada empieza de sí mismo; y así un Rey ha de tener por sí mismo a sus Vasallos, y darles los puestos más honrados, y las llaves de su Reino, porque en efecto la lealtad de los que tienen buena sangre, no puede faltar. También digo que es justo ser liberal con los extranjeros, que vienen a servirle, y hacerles mucha merced pero no fiarles las llaves, y los secretos; porque hemos visto en nuestro tiempo muchas cosas en contrario, de lo que debían ser cuando se les fiaba esto. Tiene obligación un Rey de saber, y conocer, a quién da los puestos grandes, y no gobernarse solo por lo que le dicen, porque a veces llega uno y le dice, que fulano es a propósito para tal puesto, y es porque se lo paga, o tiene otras dependencias de amistad, o parentesco; dale el Rey el puesto, vase a servir, y gobernarle, quiere sanear lo que le costó, y mucho más, con que recibe cohechos, y vende los puestos menores a hombres, que por no tener méritos no se los dieran, si no

ing the gossip against his wife, and then as a king, being unfamiliar with the factions dividing those particular lineages.[54] Men should study this topic as well as the valor of women, something that never ends except in death. For time brings the dowry and a pretty face quickly to an end, and men find themselves at home with a simpleminded woman.

Great thanks can be given to God by a man who undergoes some hardship and who has a woman at home with whom he can talk about it and from whom he can receive advice. For though a woman gives little advice, he who does not follow it is mad; and how unfortunate is he who does the opposite. Married men, respect your wives, because God gave them to you as companions, and do not throw them to the den of lions, as was done to Daniel.[55] For God shows tolerance, but not forever. And since you men presume to know better and take for yourselves the reins of government and its offices, tolerate and handle your wives' dispositions with prudence; because he who knows the most will suffer the most. And if a woman is of bad temper, handle her prudently; but if she is good-natured, esteem her and show her great love, and in this way we shall live in peace. May God grant us this peace, as well as the grace and wisdom to proceed with this book.

CHAPTER 4

*On How Kings Should Act in Assigning Government Posts*

Emperor Marcus Aurelius grieves for the fall of Rome and says that when it was populated by ancient Romans it was fertile and that all was as it should be; and now that it has the misfortune of being populated by illegitimate children and foreigners, this is its undoing.[56] In the same way we can grieve for Spain, for all the keys—both to peace and to war—are held by foreigners. God says that proper charity begins at home; thus a king should look after his vassals and give them the most honorable positions and the keys to his kingdom because, truth be told, the loyalty of those of good blood can never be found wanting. Also I say that it is right to be generous with the foreigners who come to serve him, and to give them many rewards, but not to entrust them with those keys or with his secrets. For in our time we have seen that when people are entrusted with those things, much goes contrary to what should occur. A king is obliged to know and be familiar with those to whom he gives the important positions and not to govern solely on what he is told; because sometimes a person comes along and tells him that so-and-so is appropriate for such and such a position—saying it because he has been paid to do so, or because of some connection by friendship or kinship. The king grants the man that position, and he begins serving the king and

los pagaran; destruyen la Provincias, y Reinos, encúbrenselo al Rey; porque como no trata con nadie, no puede saberlo. Si este Monarca tratara con más de los que le andan al lado, y hablara, y examinara a los que da los puestos, conociera los sujetos.

En Roma, dice Marco Aurelio, que eligieron un Gobernador, que es como ahora Presidente, que se llama Aurelio, solo porque era virtuoso; y gobernó tan bien, que después le eligieron por Emperador:[57] pues si un Monarca tiene un vasallo en gran puesto de gran cabeza, cristiandad, y ley, y sujeto, por qué le han de quitar, solo porque digan, que a temporadas le da la gota teniendo buena la cabeza: hay pocos hombres como ellos; y así debe un Monarca estimar a hombres semejantes, y cuando no puedan andar traerlos junto a sí en una silla, para que le den consejos. El Cid venció muchas batallas después de muerto,[58] pero en este tiempo no sucederá esto, pues apenas hubiera uno muerto, cuando se supiera en otros Reinos, que estamos llenos de espías: y así el Monarca tiene gran trabajo, y ha menester gran consejo, y conocimiento, y no tratando con muchos, no puede conocerlos.

Yo conozco persona, que da vuelta a sus Estados en diferentes tiempos; y conoce cuáles son mejores sujetos de sus vasallos, y da los puestos a quien los merece, con que todos quedan contentos, su hacienda aumentada, y hecho el servicio a Dios:[59] pues si un Monarca hubiera hecho otro tanto, y dado vuelta a sus Reinos, y hubiera estado en cada uno un año, todos le cobraran más cariño, y le importara harto; y no dijera el vulgo, que se mueve esta rueda sin ver por donde le viene el agua; que aunque no lo ven no lo ignoran, pero lo creen como fe, pues ven que se dan los puestos, a quien nunca se pensó; y en lugar de castigar se premia, piedad es, pero mal ejemplo para los que sirven bien, que habrá algunos, que digan, si se premia con igualdad al que sirve bien, como al que sirve mal; no nos matemos mucho, si bien esta no es razón para el que tiene buena sangre, aunque tenga sentimientos; pero hay muchas que la tienen buena con mal natural, o la pasión los ciega, que es lo mismo. El Monarca que tenemos es de lindas entrañas, cree lo que le dicen, y cada uno tira para sí; todos tiran la piedra, y esconden la mano.

governing. Then the man wishes to recover his costs, and much more, and so he accepts bribes and sells lesser positions to men who, for lack of merits, would never have received them without paying for them. Thus they destroy provinces and kingdoms and conceal the fact from the king who, since he speaks directly with none of them, cannot know all this. If this monarch spoke directly with more of those at his side, and inquired of those to whom he gives the posts, he would know his subjects better.

In Rome, says Marcus Aurelius, people chose a governor (who is like our current president) whose name was Aurelius, only because he was virtuous. And he governed so well that those people later chose him as emperor.[57] So if a monarch has a vassal in an important office, one who is wise, a good Christian and loyal, as well as a good subject, why remove him? Only because some say that from time to time he suffers from gout, even though his mind is sound? There are few such men, and thus a monarch should hold them in high esteem, and when they are unable to walk, they should be brought in on a chair to give you advice. The Cid triumphed in many battles after he was dead,[58] but nowadays no such thing can happen, since the moment someone dies, other kingdoms find out about it, plagued as we are by spies. Thus the monarch endures great hardships and needs great counsel and wisdom; and without dealing with many people, he cannot know who they are.

I know a person who makes his/her rounds of the estates at different seasons and knows which of his/her vassals are the best subjects, and assigns posts to those who deserve them.[59] In that way all are happy, their wealth increases, and God is well served. So if a monarch were to do likewise and make the rounds of his kingdoms, and had spend a year in each one, everyone would be more fond of him and would care for him greatly. And the common people would not say that the wheel is moving but no one knows where the water comes from. For though they do not see it, they are not ignorant of it but take it on faith, since they see that posts are given to those whom one would never have imagined. And instead of being punished, they are rewarded, which is merciful, but a bad example for those who serve well. For there will be those who say, "If the same rewards are given to those who serve well as to those who serve poorly, let us not work ourselves to death." However, this is no excuse for the one who is naturally of good blood, even though such a person may be resentful; but there are many who are of good blood but bad-natured, or blinded by passion, which is the same thing. The monarch we have has a good heart and believes what people tell him, but everyone tries to benefit himself. And everyone throws a stone and later hides his hand.

Dios pone a los Reyes dos Ángeles de guarda, en una mano la Justicia, y en otra la misericordia; que sean de buenas entrañas es muy bueno, mas también han menester tener un poco de hiel, que conociéndolos de cera, los hacen pabilo. Felipe Segundo fue un gran Monarca, y el santo Fr. Julián estando en Paracuellos tuvo revelación de la hora, y día en que la alma de este Monarca subió al Cielo; y lo dijo delante de cinco testigos.[60] Andaba este Rey adquiriendo noticias, conociendo sujetos, íbase al Escorial, salía solo al campo, preguntaba a los labradores que no le conocían, qué se decía del Rey, con que nada ignoraba, y con esto sabía a quién había de dar los puestos, y con una palabra mataba a un hombre, daba vuelta a muchas partes de su Reino, y cuando su padre le dejó el Reino, bien conoció le sabría gobernar; hacía lo que santo Tomás, ver, y creer, con que nadie se atrevía a hablarle más que la verdad, fue hombre muy trabajador, y cuando fue a Portugal hizo nueve títulos, confirmó otros siete, y les hizo otras mercedes,[61] aunque ahora nos dan el pago que se ve, queriendo más obedecer a un vasallo igual suyo, que a un tan gran Monarca, como el que hoy tenemos.

Muchos Reyes se han visto de diferentes genios, como se ve en las historias, mas este Monarca puede dar ejemplo a todos: y su Nieto, que hoy tenemos, no es menos en entendimiento, y cristiandad, mas importara mucho que le imitase en procurar conocer sujetos como lo hacía su Abuelo, porque no conoce más que a cuatro hombres, que andan al lado, y hay grandes sujetos arrinconados.

En el Consejo de Guerra había de haber hombres, que hubiesen navegado, y dos Letrados para los Pleitos, y no hombres, que sin haber navegado gobiernan las Armadas. Cuéntase, que en una ocasión llegaron a decir al Consejo, que se había perdido una Nao por culpa del Guardián de ella, y un Consejero pensó, que era algún Fraile; y dijo "¿quién le mete al Guardián en eso? Estese en su Convento." Y así lo que no ha visto una persona mal lo puede gobernar de lejos, de que se originan tantos malos sucesos. También importara, que en el Consejo de Guerra hubiera hombres que hayan sido soldados, pues sin haber visto la guerra mal podrán gobernar los ejércitos, ni saber lo que merecen los soldados. Y en la guerra conviene, que los pagadores, y los que manejan el dinero, sean de toda satisfacción, y que se les tome cuentas, porque no pagando a los soldados se van en la mejor ocasión.

God gives every king two guardian angels: Justice on the one hand, and Mercy on the other. That they be of good heart is very good, but it is also necessary that they have a bit of gall, because if they are known to be overly gentle, they will be ignored. Philip II was a great monarch, and Saint Julian, while in Paracuellos, had a revelation of the very day and hour in which this monarch's soul would ascend to heaven, and he said so in front of five witnesses.[60] This king would gather news, get to know his subjects, go to the Escorial, set out alone through the countryside, and ask the peasants, who did not recognize him, what was being said about the king. In this manner, there was nothing he was unaware of, and he knew to whom he should give the government posts, and with a single word he could have a man killed. He would make his way through many parts of his kingdom, and when his father left him the kingdom, he knew very well that his son would know how to govern. Philip II did as Saint Thomas did: he saw in order to believe, and because he did so, no one dared speak anything other than the truth to him. He was very hard-working, and when he went to Portugal, he named nine new titles, confirmed another seven, and gave out other rewards;[61] but now we see how the Portuguese are repaying us, by preferring to obey a vassal of their own instead of such a great monarch as the one we have today.

As we have seen in the histories, there have been many kings of different sorts of character, but this monarch, Philip II, sets the example for all of them. And his grandson, whom we have today, is of no lesser wisdom and Christianity, but it is of great importance that he imitate his grandfather in attempting to get to know his subjects, because today he knows only a handful of men, all of whom accompany him, while in the meantime there are great vassals pushed aside in some corner.

On the Council of War there should be men who have been at sea, and two lawyers to take care of litigation, and not men who, without having been at sea, are leading the navy. It is said that on one occasion the council was told that a ship had been lost through the negligence of its guardian officer, and one of the councilors thought it was a guardian friar that was being spoken of, and he said, "What has a convent guardian got to do with this? He should stay at his monastery." And so that which a person has not seen can only be governed badly, and that has given rise to many bad outcomes. It is also important that there be men on the Council of War who have been soldiers, for without having known war they will lead the army badly, nor will they know what the soldiers deserve. And in wartime, the paymasters and those who manage the money should be reliable, with an accounting taken of their affairs, because when they do not pay the soldiers, the soldiers leave at the first opportunity.

Decía un soldado muy entendido, que por un clavo se perdía un Reino: falta el clavo, cáese la herradura, máncase el caballo, matan al caballero, piérdese la plaza, y tras ella el Reino; y así es necesario grande cuidado con las guerras, y que aquí haya quién gobierne, y escoja la gente que va, y allá quién lo ejecute y disponga; y si en los puestos de paz se necesita experimentar, a quién se dan, mucho más importa que se haga en los de la guerra, pues son las llaves de nuestra defensa. No se han de dar los puestos a un mozo bisoño, porque tenga buena sangre, sino a un soldado antiguo, aunque sea de fortuna.

*Semínides* [sic] el Filósofo, puso la felicidad del hombre en ser bien quisto en su pueblo;[62] diciendo que los hombres que son mal acondicionados, los habían de echar a las Montañas a morar con los brutos; porque no hay igual felicidad en esta vida, como que un hombre vea que todos le aman en su República; y así conviene que todos los que tienen puestos, así en la paz como en la guerra, tengan agrado con los pretendientes, y litigantes, y no sean ásperos de condición, como algunos que yo conozco; que no solo no despachan, pero responden con dos piedras en la mano, que quisiera más una persona perder su hacienda que andar tras de ellos.

Gorgias el Filósofo puso la felicidad en oír cosas que aplacen; diciendo que no siente tanto la carne una grave herida, cuanto siente el alma una mala palabra;[63] porque a la verdad no hay música más dulce a las orejas, como son sabrosas al corazón las buenas palabras: y así señores, ya que no despacháis a cada uno como quiere, por lo menos salgan gustosos de vuestras casas, con buenas razones, supuesto que no os cuesta nada.

Arquitas el Filósofo puso la felicidad en vencer batallas;[64] diciendo que naturalmente el hombre es tan amigo de sí, y de salir con su apetito, que aun en muy pequeñas cosas, y burlando no querría ser vencido; porque a la verdad liberalmente, el corazón humano sufre todos los trabajos de esta vida, solo con pensar, que algún día alcanzará la victoria. Cuando se ve un General con su gente cerca del enemigo, ha de prevenir todos los lances, para que no le cojan descuidado; y como un Predicador se pone en un púlpito a predicar a los Fieles, o un Catedrático en una cátedra a enseñar a sus discípulos; así él ha de mandar juntar toda su gente todos los días, o por lo menos cada semana, y mandar que cada vez se ponga un soldado de los más diestros, y les haga una plática, previniéndoles todo lo que puede suceder; y diciéndoles si el enemigo acomete por tal parte, hemos de hacer esto, y si por esta otra, estar prevenidos, para tomar los puestos.

A wise soldier used to say that because of a nail, a kingdom could be lost: the nail goes missing, the horseshoe falls off, the horse is crippled, the knight gets killed, his fortress is lost, and after that the kingdom. Thus it is necessary that much care be taken in wartime, with a leader who chooses which people will go, and that there be someone to execute and carry out the leader's orders. And if we need to examine those to whom the Council of State posts are given, it is that much more important to do the same with the Council of War posts, as they are the key to our defense. These posts should not be given to a green recruit only because of his noble blood, but rather to an old soldier, though he be a soldier of fortune.

Seminides [*sic*] the philosopher said that man's happiness was to be found in being well liked in his village.[62] He said that bad-tempered men should be thrown out into the mountains to dwell with the beasts, because for a man there is no happiness in this life like that of seeing he is loved by everyone in his republic. And so it is best that whoever has a post, at the Councils of State as well as of War, be affable with aspirants and litigants, and not be of a sour disposition, like some I know, who not only do not do business well but do it with two stones in their hand. A person would rather lose all his wealth than to depend on such people.

Gorgias the philosopher said that happiness was to be found in hearing pleasurable things, that the flesh does not feel a deep wound so much as the soul a harsh word.[63] Because, truth be told, there is no music sweeter to the ears or more warming to the heart than kind words. So, gentlemen, since you do not serve all people as they wish, at least let them leave your house with gladness for having heard the right phrases, inasmuch as this costs you nothing.

Archytas the philosopher said that happiness lies in being victorious in battle.[64] He said that man is naturally so fond of himself and of fulfilling his own desires that even in the smallest matters and in jokes he refuses to be defeated. Certainly, the human heart is able to bear the hardships of this life just by thinking that someday it will achieve victory. When a general with his troops is near the enemy, he should anticipate all moves, so as not to be caught unawares. And just as a preacher stands in his pulpit to preach to the faithful, or a professor sits in his chair to teach his students, the general orders his troops to gather every day or at least every week, and each time orders one soldier from among the most skilled to give a talk, and to make the rest aware of all that can happen, and he tells them: "If the enemy attacks from this side, we will do this, and if the attack comes from that side, be ready to take up your positions."

También ha de tener cuidado que los soldados que están alojados en diferentes partes se junten, y hacerles la misma plática: porque si ahora entraran a decir que un toro entraba en una casa, todos se previnieran, pero si el toro se entrara de repente, y los cogiera de susto, todos perecieran. Y así fue la batalla de Yelbes, que los cogieron descuidados.[65] Tampoco es bien, que los Generales estén esperando las órdenes de los Consejos, porque siempre llegan tarde, como los socorros mal dispuestos; y es bien experimentar a los cabos, antes de ponerse en ocasión. Aquí viene bien el cuento de su padre del Cid; diéronle la bofetada, vino a su casa afrentado, llamó a sus hijos, y para saber cuál tenía más valor para encomendarle la venganza; a cada uno de por sí les fue apretando la mano, y todos se quejaron, con que conoció su poco valor de ellos; llamó al Cid, y apretándole la mano como a los demás, no se quejó, con que reconoció el gran valor, y le fió su honra, y el Cid la vengó, y fue tan grande hombre por la guerra como se sabe; y vino a casar sus hijas con Reyes, lo cual no hicieron los demás sus hermanos.[66]

Bernardo del Carpio conoció que su tío el Rey don Alonso tenía pocos bríos y que el Rey de Francia se nos iba entrando. Alentó su gente, salió a la defensa, y libertó a España.[67] Y así el vasallo, que está rico con los puestos que le dio su Rey, tiene obligación, viéndole con guerras, y necesidad, a ponerlo todo a sus pies; y el que no lo hiciere será mal vasallo, indigno de que su Rey le honre, ni dé puestos.

D. Juan de Labrit, marido de la Reina doña Catalina de Navarra, estaba un día melancólico, y un vasallo suyo, que se llamaba D. Francés de Beamonte, señor de Arazuri y Montalbán, le preguntó qué tenía, y le respondió: "está la Reina para parir, y véome sin dineros"[68] fuese a su casa, y trájole un bolsillo con diez mil escudos,[69] que para aquellos tiempos, y la pobreza de aquel Reino era mucho; pero en estos tiempos todo se va en vanidad, galas, lacayos, y juegos, lo que no había en otros tiempos; pues en el Archivo de Salvatierra de Álava, hay una carta del Condestable de Castilla para el Duque de Nájera, dándole cuenta de que casa una hija; y le dice, "Vendréis a la boda, traeréis el vestido de las fiestas, y comeremos gallina":[70] en aquel tiempo se comía gallina en las bodas, pero en éste cada día.

En la Crónica del Rey Don Pedro de Castilla, en el capit. 9 folio 11 se dice, que cuando dicho Rey Don Pedro de Castilla iba contra Don Uño, Señor de Vizcaya, que era niño, le llevó huyendo a Navarra don Juan de Av-

A general should also be sure to gather together those soldiers who are quartered in different places and give them the same talk. Because if someone came in saying that a bull was to enter a house, everyone would prepare himself, but if the bull came in suddenly and caught them by surprise, all would perish. And that was the case at the battle of Yelbes, where they were taken unawares.[65] Nor is it good for generals to await the councils' orders, which always come late, like badly disposed relief troops; and it is good to make sure the corporals gain experience before they face a serious occasion. Here the story of the Cid's father speaks to our point. He received a slap in the face, came home dishonored, called his sons together, and in order to find out which of them was valiant enough to be trusted to avenge him, he gripped the hand of each one individually. All of them cried out, whereupon he knew of their cowardice. He called the Cid, and though his hand was gripped like the others, he did not complain, whereupon the father recognized his great valor. He entrusted him with his honor, and the Cid avenged it. And, as we know, he was a very great man in war, and he married his daughters to kings, something his brothers did not do.[66]

Bernardo del Carpio knew that his uncle, King Alonso, was a man of little spirit, and that the king of France was coming. Bernardo encouraged the people, came to the defense of the kingdom, and liberated Spain.[67] And so the vassal who is rich from the posts given him by the king has the obligation and duty, in time of war, to place all he has at the king's service, and he who does not do so is a bad vassal, unworthy of the king's honor or government posts.

Don Juan de Labrit, husband of Queen Catalina of Navarre, was feeling sad one day. One of his vassals, Don Francés de Beamonte, lord of Arazuri and Montalbán, asked him what was wrong, and he responded: "The queen is about to give birth and I have no money."[68] Don Francés went to his own house and returned with a bag filled with ten thousand *escudos*,[69] which for that time and the poverty of that kingdom was a large sum. But nowadays everything goes for vanity, adornments, footmen, and gambling, things we did not have in the past. In the archives of Salvatierra of Álava, there is a letter from the constable of Castile to the duke of Nájera, telling how one of his daughters was to be wed, where he says: "Thou shalt come to the wedding, and thou shalt wear the celebration garment, and we shall feast on chicken."[70] In those ages hen was eaten at weddings, but in this age, daily.

In the chronicle of King Pedro of Castile, in chapter 9, page 11, it states that when the aforementioned king, Don Pedro of Castile, was going against Don Uño, lord of Vizcaya, the latter was a child, and was taken by

endaño, y doña Mencía su Madre;[71] que así tenemos obligación los vasallos a defender nuestros dueños, y tener ley, y amor con ellos. Y un Señor de la Casa de Gamboa, fue ayo de un Príncipe; y porque cayó una teja, y le mató, y tenía la banda de sus armas coloradas, la tiñó negra, y hoy la traen así.[72] Juan Velázquez de Cuéllar fue Ayo, y testamentario del Príncipe D. Juan;[73] y fue tanto el sentimiento que hizo de su muerte, que trajo capuz perpetuo, como lo dice Felipe de Cominis en sus memorias, Memoria 71.[74] Y Sandoval en el capit. 72 dice, que en el Bautismo del Señor Infante D. Fernando, que después fue Emperador año de mil quinientos y tres,[75] iba Juan Velázquez con su capuz negro, y gorra de terciopelo,[76] ésta es la lealtad de Vasallos, y siendo Maestre de Sala de la Señora Reina Católica, y Contador mayor de Castilla, y teniendo otros puestos grandes, no tenía más gajes, que cien mil maravedís,[77] que muy diferentes son los que se dan en estos tiempos.

Antístenes Filósofo, puso la felicidad después de muerto;[78] diciendo que con verdad no se ha de llamar pérdida, sino aquella donde se pierde la fama, porque el hombre cuerdo en muy poco ha de temer la muerte, si por virtudes, y hazañas deja la fama viva. Y si alguno preguntare cómo se gana esta fama digo que de muchas maneras; lo primero siendo santos, y esta fama la celebra el Cielo y la tierra; lo segundo siendo tan grandes guerreros, que se llenen las historias de sus hechos; lo tercero teniendo buen entendimiento, y escribiendo mucho para que quede en el mundo memoria de ellos.

Palemón el Filósofo, puso la felicidad en ser el hombre elocuente,[79] diciendo, y jurando que el hombre que no sabe hablar en todas cosas, no es tan pariente de los hombres, como de las bestias; porque al parecer de muchos no hay igual bienaventuranza en esta triste vida, como ser el hombre de dulce lengua, y honesta vida. Y este Filósofo dice muy bien; porque hay personas que no saben hablar más que en una cosa, y cada día hablan lo mismo, y en sacándolas de aquello no saben responder; y todos los que no leyeron no sabrán más que otro. Las crueldades de Nerón todos las saben, y así no es necesario repetirlas, sino solo decir, que tenemos muchos Nerones, que nos matan con cuchillo de palo; Dios se acuerde de nosotros, y nos ponga en la guerra grandes Nerones, que es adonde los hemos menester. Muchos ejemplares pudiera dar de éstos, mas no quiero molestar al Lector, sino dejarlo a su curiosidad.

Don Juan de Avendaño and his mother, Doña Mencía, who fled with him to Navarre.[71] Such is the obligation we vassals have to defend our masters and to show them loyalty and love. A certain nobleman of the house of Gamboa was the tutor of a prince for whom, because his prince was killed by a falling roof tile, he dyed his red military band black. And so they wear it today.[72] Juan Velázquez of Cuéllar was tutor and executor to Prince Juan.[73] So saddened was he by the prince's death that he wore a perpetual mourning cowl, as Philippe de Commynes says in his memoirs, memoir 71.[74] And Sandoval, in chapter 72, says that at the baptism of Lord Prince Don Ferdinand, who later was emperor in the year 1503,[75] Juan Velázquez was still wearing his black mourning cowl and velvet hat;[76] that is the loyalty proper to a vassal. And though he was chamberlain to the Catholic Queen and chief accountant of Castile, and though he held other important positions, his perquisites were no more than one hundred thousand *maravedíes*,[77] a far lesser sum than that which is given today.

The philosopher Antisthenes stated that happiness is to be found in being well-known after death.[78] He said that, truth be told, one may not consider a life to have been wasted unless one's reputation is lost, because a sensible man should hardly be afraid of death if by virtue and deeds his reputation lives on. And if someone were to ask how this reputation might be earned, I would say that there are many ways; first, by being holy, a reputation which heaven and earth would celebrate; and second, by being a soldier so great that the histories are filled with his deeds; third, by being a learned person and writing copiously, so that there remains in the world a memory of the holy men and soldiers.

Palemon [*sic*] the philosopher said that happiness is to be found in being a man of eloquence.[79] He said and swore that the man who knows not how to speak of all things is a relative not so much of men as of the beasts, because many hold the opinion that there is no greater happiness in this sad life than in being a sweet-tongued man of honest living. And this philosopher has spoken well; for there are those who can talk of one thing only, and every day they repeat that, and when another subject arises, they do not know how to respond. And all those who never read will know no more than anyone else. Everyone knows of Nero's cruelties, and so there is no need to repeat them, except to say that we have many Neros who are killing us with a very blunt dagger. May God remember us and give us great Neros for the war, which is where we need them most. Many are the examples I could give like these; however, I do not wish to bother the reader, but would rather leave him to his curiosity.

*① Life is a dream*

## CAPÍTULO 5

*Que trata de los desengaños de la corte, y vida quieta de la aldea*

La más segura vida para el alma, y para el cuerpo, es retirarse de tantas ocasiones como hay en la Corte, y lo más acomodado, es la Aldea, y más si es propia. Entra un señor en sus lugares, recíbenlo sus Vasallos con grande alegría, y regalo, apenas llega a sus manos la trucha, la perdiz, el gazapo, la fruta, y otro cualquier regalo, cuando va a las manos del señor con grande alegría: el vasallo, y todos los demás viven a raya, viendo que los mira el señor; y qué bien fuera si todos viviésemos así, viendo que nos mira Dios; de que tan obligados estamos.

Conoce el señor los sujetos, y da los oficios a quien los merece; lo cual no hiciera si no estuviera allí, porque el Gobernador los diera a quien se los pagara, y a sus parientes, y amigos, que no son a propósito, esto mismo se hace en todas partes. Viene el día de la fiesta, y los mozos y mozas festejan a los señores con su gaita y tamboril, llega el buen día, van a cazar y pescar, o a una Romería, o fiesta a otro lugar, acompáñale toda la gente, hombres y mujeres, que parecen escuadrones de soldados, salen de los lugares circun-vecinos propios y ajenos, y hacen la misma fiesta; viene un día festivo, y los señores hacen la fiesta en la Iglesia, convócase la comarca, y échanles mil bendiciones, y si hace mal día se están en la chimenea leyendo y haciéndose capaces para conocer lo que es el mundo y el pago que da: hallan tantos validos que han caído de la privanza por envidia, y otros por ambición, y no saberse gobernar, viéneles una carta de la Corte, dándoles cuenta cómo se ha perdido una Armada o una batalla, y como buenos vasallos lo sienten aquel día y otro día se van a cazar y desechan melancolías, y no hay quien les traiga a la memoria cosa que lo sea.

Pónense a leer unas Crónicas, conocen lo que han servido sus Abuelos para poder hablar gordo en las ocasiones, hallan allí lo que es cada casa, y con quiénes pueden casar sus hijos, lo que no se hace en la Corte, que no se mira más de quién tenga más dote, y se recate a los casamientos, como si se vendieran, y así bajan muchas casas, como lo vemos al presente, porque el dinero se gasta en vanidades, y la poca calidad se queda en casa, herencia que les dejan a sus hijos los cortesanos, lo que no hacen los que están en sus lugares, que aumentan las haciendas y dejan a sus hijos acomodados, y salen a servir a su Rey en las ocasiones, como lo han hecho muchos que se hallarán

CHAPTER 5

*On the Disenchantments at the Court and the Quiet Life in the Village*

The safest life for soul and body is to retire from the dangers that abound at the court, and the most suitable place is the village; better yet if it is one's own. A lord returns to his estates and is received by his vassals with great joy and pleasure. No sooner do they gather trout, partridge, young rabbit, fruits, and many other gifts than they give it all to their lord with great joy. The vassal and all the others go trembling, knowing that their lord is watching them. And how wonderful it would be if we all lived that way, knowing that we are watched by God, to whom we are so obliged.

The lord knows his subjects and assigns positions to those who deserve them; something that could not be done if he were not there. On the contrary, the governor (the lord's assigned representative) would give them to whoever paid for them, and to their relatives, and friends who are unsuitable. This very thing happens everywhere. A holiday arrives and the young men and women entertain their lords with flag pipes and small drums. The great day arrives, they go hunting or fishing or on a pilgrimage, or to a festival in another village. All the men and women accompany him, such that they resemble squadrons of soldiers. They come from nearby villages that do or do not belong to him and have the same celebration. When a holiday arrives, the lords celebrate it at church. They call together people from all over the region and shower them with their blessings; or if the weather is poor that day, they stay inside by the hearth, reading, trying to learn what the world is about and how it can harm one. In contrast, there are so many *validos* (prime ministers) who have fallen from favor, some out of envy, others out of ambition, for not knowing how to govern themselves. A letter arrives for them from the court, reporting that a fleet has been lost, or a battle, and like good vassals they feel remorse on that day, but the next day they go hunting and cast aside their melancholy, and there is no one to remind them of things that might sadden them.

The lords sit down to read some chronicles. They learn how well their grandparents have served and thus are able to speak splendidly at the right moment. They find out what every house is worth and to whom they should marry their children, something which is not done at court, where the only concern is who has the largest dowry, and they haggle over marriage as if it were to be sold. And thus many houses fall, as we are seeing at present, because money is spent on vanities, and one finds only bad-quality things in their homes—which is the only inheritance that the courtiers leave to their children. This is not done by those who remain on their estates, who

en las Historias; y hoy estamos viendo que todos los señores que están en sus lugares, están muy bien acomodados; y los que están en la Corte están pereciendo, si no es aquellos, que tiene dicha de que les den algún puesto.

Heráclito puso la felicidad en tener tesoros;[80] diciendo que el hombre pródigo y desperdiciador, por mucho que tenga, siempre será a todos importuno; que a la verdad respeto tiene de hombre cuerdo, el que para las necesidades futuras guarda algún secreto tesoro. Este Filósofo aconseja muy bien: que un señor sea generoso es muy bueno, y parece bien en los grandes Príncipes, y señores; pero no que sea perdido, ni pródigo, que si después se le ofrece una ocasión grande, aún en su padre no lo hallara, y se avergüenza a todos, y al cabo vende su hacienda y siempre se halla atrasado. La República más bien gobernada, que hay, es la de Vitoria, donde no se consienten coches ni sillas; porque hay Caballeros pobres y Mercaderes ricos, que los sobrepujaran. Todo lo que traen a vender de afuera, hasta que pasan tres días y se abastecen los vecinos, no compran los revendones, que poco se hace de esto en la Corte, pues salen a los caminos a quitarlo, para venderlo al doble, todo se permite, y nada se castiga. En cada barrio de Vitoria, hay una centinela de noche para que ni se que quemen las casas ni las roben; que no hay mayor desdicha que el fuego. Y en Extremadura, si un pastor enciende lumbre en una dehesa, y por descuido de no matarla viene un aire adverso y se quema, cogen al pastor y le ahorcan luego. En Pamplona eligen en cada barrio un Prior y una Priora de la gente más honrada, y todos les van a dar cuenta de los que viven mal, y ellos los castigan sin ser necesario acudir a la Justicia. De esta suerte deben los señores tener buen gobierno en sus lugares y más cuando viven en ellos; porque si el señor es virtuoso, da ejemplo a todos en gran realeza. Dejemos ahora a estos señores en sus lugares con su quietud, comodidades, y regalos y digamos lo que ellos deben hacer.

## CAPÍTULO 6

*De cómo se han de portar los señores que viven en sus lugares*

Señores míos, no todo ha de ser buscar la quietud del cuerpo, que también hemos menester buscar la del alma; en primer lugar debe un señor dar

increase their wealth and leave their children well-off. They go to serve their king when necessary, like many who can be found in the histories. And today we see that all the nobles who are at their estates are very well off, and those who are at court are perishing—except for those who have the good fortune to be given some sort of position.

Heraclitus said that happiness is to be found in having treasures.[80] He said that the prodigal, spendthrift man, no matter how much he has, will always prove bothersome to everyone; whereas truly we respect the wise man who keeps a treasure hidden away for future needs. This philosopher gives excellent advice: it is very good for a man to be generous, something which is looked on favorably in great princes and lords, but not for him to be a libertine or prodigal, because if later a great opportunity arises to be generous, not even with his own father can he be so, and he brings shame on everyone. And in the end he must sell his properties, and he is always behind with payments. The best-governed republic is Vitoria, where neither carriages nor chairs are allowed, because there are poor noblemen and rich merchants who surpass them. All that which is brought from outside to be sold must first be held three days and used to supply the local residents before the merchandise can be bought by the middlemen. Little of this is done at the court since the middlemen go out on the roads to steal and then later resell at twice the price. Everything is allowed and nothing is punished. In every neighborhood in Vitoria there is a night watchman, so that houses are neither burned nor robbed, since there is no greater misfortune than a fire. And in Extremadura, if a shepherd lights a fire in the meadow and if, because he mistakenly does not put it out, a strong wind comes and the fire spreads, the shepherd is caught and later hanged. In Pamplona, each neighborhood chooses a prior and a prioress from among the most honorable people, and everyone reports to them on those who are living wrongly, and the latter are punished, so that it is not necessary to turn to justice. This is the manner in which nobles should govern their estates, more so when they are living there. Because if the lord is virtuous, he sets the example for everyone with great splendor. For now, let us leave these lords at their estates with their peace and quiet, their comforts, and their gifts, and let us speak on what they should do.

## CHAPTER 6

### On How Lords Who Live on Their Estates Should Behave

Dear gentlemen, life is not only a matter of looking for peace of body; we must also seek peace for the soul. In the first place, a lord must set a good

buen ejemplo a sus vasallos, y aunque cada día comulgue en su Oratorio, comulgue en la Iglesia algunas veces por el ejemplo; y si ha tenido alguna travesura, tenerla encubierta hasta que el hijo sea grande; y entonces es preciso descubrirla en conciencia; que a veces estos tales hijos son de provecho, y aumentan las casas, como hemos visto Obispos, Presidentes, y Consejeros, y han hecho mucho por los hermanos legítimos. Tiene obligación un señor a gobernar su Estado con prudencia, conociendo los sujetos, a quienes da los puestos, porque lo demás es perder la República; tomar la residencia por castigar pecados públicos, no consentir juegos, pues de allí redundan muertes, juramentos, y afrentas, en que se ofende a Dios, que es el principal fin; y así se debe mirar mucho en no destruir los vasallos.

Cuenta Marco Aurelio que un villano vino al Senado y les dijo a los jueces muchas pesadumbres, y que si ellos tenían espanto en oírlas, él no tendría miedo en decirlas, pues ellos tenían vergüenza en hacerlas, y les enviaban unos jueces ignorantes y bobos, que ni sus leyes sabían declararlo, ni las de ellos entenderlo; y que el daño procedía de no enviar los más hábiles para administrar justicia, sino a los que tenían muchos amigos en Roma; éstas y otras muchas pesadumbres dijo un villano al Senado, que la razón tiene gran fuerza, y así lo escribe Marco Aurelio, libro tercero, capit. quinto.[81] Y así conviene poner buenos jueces, y entendidos, para que no venga un villano como vino al Senado a decir verdades; sobrellevar los vasallos, no digo yo perder el derecho, ni pechos, y vasallajes[82] que pagan, que esto fuera en perjuicio del heredero; lo que digo es que si los años vienen malos se les espere por la renta, se le preste el trigo, y a los pobres se les haga limosna que es la escalera principal para subir al Cielo; y si se le arrimasen los puntales de la penitencia, paciencia, y humildad, qué aprisa llegáramos arriba, sin temer que nos quiebre ningún escalón.

Tiene también obligación un señor, a mirar por las iglesias, y el culto divino, y en las fiestas grandes, y Cuaresma, si no hay Conventos en el lugar, traer predicadores de afuera, porque aquella gente oiga la palabra de Dios, que como ellos son pobres, no los pueden traer a su costa; tener buen Maestro para sus hijos, enseñarles la Gramática, y los Artes militares, y hacerles que lean buenos libros divinos, y humanos, enseñarles a que sean cazadores, que es un entretenimiento sin perjuicio: remediar las doncellas pobres, porque no se pierdan, amparar los huérfanos, tener los que pudiere en su casa, y los demás ponerlos a oficio, porque no se críen vagamundos,

example for his vassals, and though he may take communion every day in his chapel, it is good to do so in the church sometimes in order to set an example. And if he has had some sort of love affair, he should keep it hidden until the child is grown, and then he must reveal it in good conscience. Sometimes these children are worthy and enrich the houses, as we have seen with bishops, presidents, and councilors, and they have done a great deal for their legitimate siblings. A lord has the obligation to govern his estate wisely by knowing well those subjects to whom he grants positions (because anything else will mean losing the republic); he must reside at his estate to punish wrongdoing (and not only out of self-interest); to punish public sins; to forbid gambling, because it gives rise to deaths, oaths, and assaults (in which the insulted one is God, to whom in the end all such are directed). And thus great care should be taken not to let one's vassal go to ruin.

Marcus Aurelius tells of how a villager came before the Senate and told them of his many griefs against the judges, asking if they were shocked to hear them, because he had no fear in saying them, for they should be ashamed of causing them, of sending ignorant and stupid judges who could neither expound on their laws nor understand them. And the harm came from sending not those who were most capable of administering justice, but rather those who had many friends in Rome. These and many other woes and troubles did a villager relate to the Senate, for there is great strength in justice, and thus writes Marcus Aurelius, in his third book, fifth chapter.[81] And so it is advisable to name good, knowledgeable judges so that no villager will come along like that one who came before the Senate, and reveal so many truths. As for dealing with vassals, I do not say that the rights, taxes, and *vasallages*[82] they pay should be eliminated, as this would be detrimental to the heirs. What I am saying is that if bad years arrive, the nobles should await their payment, that wheat should be lent out to the peasants, and charity given to the poor, which is our main stairway to heaven. And if that were bolstered by the supports of penance, patience, and humility, how quickly we would arrive at the top, without fear of a step giving way beneath us.

A lord also has the obligation to look after his churches and the worship performed there, and during important holidays and Lent, if there are no convents on his estate, he must also bring preachers from outside so that the people may hear the word of God, for they are poor and cannot afford to bring them themselves. He should have a good teacher for his children, to teach them Latin and the military arts, and should make them read good books, on both sacred and humane subjects, and should teach them to hunt, which is a harmless pastime. He must help maidens from poor families so that they do not go astray, and he must shelter orphans, keeping as many

O life's a Dream

ladrones, y hacer cuenta un señor, que lo que había de gastar en la Corte en superfluidades, lo gasta en estas buenas obras, para hallar las de gloria; que son los aposentadores del alma en el Cielo.

También tiene obligación a no dejar perder el estado, porque si un Palacio se puede aderezar este año con cien ducados, y no se aderaza, el año que viene ha menester dos mil; y se deja perder, y hay algunos que dicen "no tengo hijos, no quiero gastar:" no gastéis en hacer aumentos, ni lo quitéis de vuestras personas, pero no dejéis menos cabos, que de esa suerte se acaban las casas, sino aquello que en vuestro tiempo se va perdiendo, irlo aderezando, y conservando, y no tratar solo de destruirlo, y que el que entra lo halle perdido.

Tiene el señor dos criados, y están opuestos, y lo que el uno hace, deshace el otro, ¿qué es lo que debe hace el señor en este caso?; mirar cuál de los dos es de más provecho, y despedir al otro, porque de otra manera nunca estará la casa bien gobernada, y habrá bandos en ella entre los demás criados; y no es buena política, ni gobierno; que estén juntos. Gran cuenta tenemos que dar a Dios, cada uno de lo que ha recibido de su mano, pues solo nos hizo mayordomos de por vida, y nos ha de tomar las cuentas en la otra; y no han de ser como las cuentas que aquí se toman al Consejo de Hacienda, que se remiten a uno, que mañana tendrá el mismo puesto, y lo sucederá otro tanto.

Mayor cuenta tendrá que dar el Pontífice, el Obispo, el Monarca, el Potentado, el señor, y aquellos a quien Dios ha dado mucho de qué darla, que no el pobrecito que no tiene más que una casa, y un poquillo de hacienda, que con dos peones la cultiva; aquí hay mucho que considerar, dejémoslo al buen lector, y tratemos de otra cosa, que este libro, aunque pequeño es el Arca de Noé, y así empezaremos con ella el siguiente capítulo.

## CAPÍTULO 7

*De lo que importa la virtud, y de lo que nos hemos de valer para tenerla*

Envió Dios el diluvio al mundo y mandole a Noé, que hiciese una Arca, y metiese en ella su familia para volver a formar el mundo, porque le halló entre todos el más a propósito:[83] la Corte también es una arca de Noé, donde se encierra todo, mas la diferencia que tiene es que de la Arca salió la paloma a buscar el ramo de paz. Y en la Corte predomina el cuervo, que las espías,

as he can in his home while setting the rest up in a trade so that they are not raised as idlers and thieves. A lord must realize that all the money he would have spent at the court on excesses, he is now spending on these good works, and so he may reach glory, which gives lodging to the soul in heaven.

He also has the obligation not to let his estate fall into ruin, because if a palace can be repaired this year with a hundred ducats, yet goes untended, next year it will cost two thousand, and after that it will go to ruin. There are some who say: "I have no children, I do not want to spend my money." Do not spend to enlarge the estate, or take money from your people, but do not neglect any damages, because that is how houses come to an end. Rather, whatever is falling into ruin during your time, keep it well repaired and maintained, and try to do more than just enjoy it so that whoever comes next will not find it lost and gone.

A lord has two servants and the two are in conflict, so that what one does the other undoes; what is the lord to do in this case? Look to see which of the two is worthier and let the other go. Otherwise the house will never be well governed, and the other servants will take sides; and that is neither good policy nor good government, which go together. We all have to give account closely to God for what each of us has received from His hand, for He only made us stewards in this life. In the next, He will call us to account; and the accounting will not be like that one at the Council of Finance, taken by a person who, whatever he does, will still have the same position tomorrow and will be succeeded by another just like him.

An even more careful account will be asked of the pope, a bishop, a monarch, a potentate, a lord, and those to whom God has given so much to account for, than of the poor man who has no more than a house and a small piece of land he works along with two laborers. There is much to consider here, so we will leave that to the good reader. Let us discuss yet another matter, since this book, though small, is a Noah's ark. And with that, in fact, we will begin the next chapter.

## CHAPTER 7

*On the Importance of Virtue and What We Must Do to Deserve It*

God set loose the Flood upon the world and commanded Noah to build an ark and put his family inside it so as to repopulate the world, because He found him to be, of all His people, the most suitable.[8] The court, too, is a Noah's ark, which holds everything, but the difference is that it was a dove that flew from the ark in search of the olive branch, while at court the crows

y enemigos que tenemos encubiertos, aunque hay otros peores, que son los que con capa de amistad, engañan a una persona; y se fía de ellos, y le venden.

No son pequeños enemigos los que aconsejan, que cada día se echan nuevos tributos, y nos quitan las haciendas; pues con eso se va perdiendo la Monarquía, y vienen a ser enemigos del Rey, y de los Vasallos, solo por aprovecharse ellos, olvidándose de la virtud, que si la tuviéramos no erráramos nada, y Dios nos asistiera.

No importa que un Rey sea virtuoso, si no pone a su lado, y en los puestos quien lo sea; esto importa mucho, y así para ser una persona virtuosa, primeramente, ha de tener caridad, paciencia, y humildad, y penitencia,[84] imitando en la caridad a muchos, que la han tenido, como una S. Isabel Reina de Hungría, que eran tantas las limosnas que hacía, que se las moderaron, (que aún hasta la virtud es perseguida), y cuando no podía más, se quitaba el vestido, para darle a pobres, quedándose desnuda:[85] y un S. Diego, que mandándole el Guardián, que no diese tantas limosnas; y topándole un día con los pedazos de pan en el hábito; y preguntándole qué era lo que traía, respondió que eran rosas, y se volvió el pan rosas. Y otros muchos limosneros que sabemos que han ganado el Cielo por las limosnas. Y en estos tiempos hay muchos también, que las hacen. Y yo conocí un Caballero Ilustre que vivía en una Ciudad, y daba limosnas, que parecía sustentar su hacienda, y tenía su casa con grande lucimiento; y cuando murió se vió una cometa en el cielo, sin ser Pontífice, ni Rey, aunque era nieto de Reyes: y hay hoy personas vivas que la vieron.

También conocí a un Religioso, que de dos huevos, que le daba la Comunidad, dejaba el uno a los pobres; y de la limosna de las Misas hacía los mismo; y siendo mi huésped dejaba el mejor bocado en el plato; y me contó que una Imagen de Nuestra Señora, que está en el lugar adonde estábamos, habló a una persona, y aunque no me dijo a quién, yo luego imaginé, que era a él, y dentro de un mes murió el tal Religioso, y publicó su confesor cómo le había hablado aquella Imagen; este Santo era muy caritativo, y siempre me aconsejaba que hiciese limosnas, y que cuidase de las Iglesias; y es cierto que por la caridad, está gozando de Dios, y en su convento lo dicen así; y yo aconsejo a todos tengan la que pudieren, y hagan muchas limosnas; y el que no tuviere con qué, hágalas con el deseo, y reparen, en que la Orden de N.P.S. Francisco vive de limosna, y hace limosnas, y nunca le falta.[86] Segundo escalón para el Cielo es la paciencia; mírese la que tuvo el santo Job, y la que han tenido otros muchos Santos, y muchas personas que hoy viven

hold sway, which is to say spies and hidden enemies, although there are others even worse, who—behind the mask of friendship—cheat the person who trusts them and then betray him for money.

No small enemies are those advisors who impose new taxes every day and so take our properties from us; in this way the monarchy is being lost, and they become enemies of the king and of his vassals, all for their own benefit, forgetting about virtue; because if we were virtuous, we would not go astray at all, and God would come to our aid.

It does not matter that a king is virtuous if he does not place at his side and in his government posts people who are so; this is very important. And thus, in order to be a virtuous person, one must, first of all, have charity, patience, and humility, and do penance.[84] In charity, one must imitate those who have had it, such as a certain Saint Isabel, queen of Hungary, whose alms were so great that she had to be restrained (for virtue is persecuted); and when she could give no more, she took off her dress to give it to the poor, leaving herself naked.[85] And then there was Saint Diego of Alcalá, ordered by the Guardian not to give so many alms. And one day, happening upon him with pieces of bread wrapped in his friar's habit, he asked him what it was that he was carrying. He responded that they were roses, and the bread turned into roses. And many others who give alms, we all know, have gained heaven by all they gave. And nowadays as well there are many who give them: I met an illustrious nobleman who lived in a city and gave away more in alms than it seemed his wealth allowed, while keeping his house with great ostentation. And when he died, a comet was seen in the sky, and he was neither pope nor king, though he was the grandson of kings. And today there are people still alive who saw that comet.

I also met a friar who, of the two eggs that his community gave him, always gave one to the poor, and with the alms from Mass he would do the same. And when he was my guest, he always left the best morsel on his plate, and told me that an image of Our Lady, which is in the town where we were staying, had spoken to someone and, though he did not say to whom, I later imagined it was him. And within a month, the friar died and his confessor made known that the image had spoken to him. This holy man was very charitable and would always advise me to give alms and to take care of churches. And there is no doubt that because of charity, he is now enjoying the presence of God, and at his monastery they say it is so. I advise that all be as charitable as they can and give many alms; that the person who cannot give much give some, and that one who has nothing have the desire to give. And everybody should take note of how the members of the order of our father Saint Francis live off alms, and give alms, and never go wanting.[86] The

la tienen en sus trabajos, y pues son cruz que Dios nos envía,[87] llevémoslo con paciencia y tendremos este escalón seguro.

La humildad es tercero escalón para el Cielo; véase la que tuvo N.P.S. Francisco, pues por más humildad quiso ser lego;[88] y yendo a pedir al Papa le concediese la fundación de su Religión; y llegando N.P.S. Domingo; le dejó entrar primero solo por humildad, con que viene a ser la Religión de S. Domingo, una hora más antigua que la de S. Francisco.[89] Mírese la humildad de N. Madre S. Clara, que yendo a buscar a San Francisco muchas veces, le mandó que no fuese tan a menudo, quizás temiendo algún testimonio; que hasta los Santos no están libres;[90] y ella preguntó muy afligida; y con grande humildad, que cuándo volvería, y el Santo la respondió, cuando haya higos, y siendo esto en medio del invierno se fue a su casa con gran desconsuelo, y halló un plato de ellos; volvió corriendo al Convento, y el Santo los llevó al refectorio, y publicó este milagro. Todo esto puede la humildad, y obediencia, que esta Santa tuvo, y los que la tuvieron alcanzarán todo cuanto quisieren, y la vida eterna.

Envió Abraham un criado suyo (que en aquellos tiempos se usaban con diferente lealtad, y fidelidad que ahora) a buscar una mujer, que fuese a propósito para casar a su hijo, y diole un cofre de joyas, que le diese; llegó a un lugar adonde no había más de un pozo para beber, iba muerto de sed, topó a muchas mujeres que venían con cántaros de agua; llegó a pedírsela, y ningún tuvo caridad (que en gente ordinaria hay pocos que la tengan), venía la última la hermosa Rebeca, y llegó a pedirle el agua; y ella respondió, "no solo a ti, pero a tus Camellos la daré;" y el mozo reparó en que aquella mujer era a propósito para su amo, porque tenía caridad, y humildad, y así le dio el cofre de joyas, e hizo la elección en ella;[91] todo esto puede la humildad. Y si en estos tiempos enviáramos un criado a tratar una boda para nuestros hijos, y le dieran mil escudos, de la otra parte callara cuántos defectos hubiera, que en estos tiempos está el mundo muy perdido, y en ningún género de cosas puede una persona fiarse de nadie.

Grande escalón es para el Cielo la penitencia; S. Honofre dejó el Imperio, y se fue a hacer penitencia al desierto;[92] S. Jerónimo dejó el Capelo, y se fue al desierto a darse en los pechos con una piedra,[93] desengañado del mundo, tuvo grandes persecuciones, hasta levantarle un testimonio con santa Paula,[94] hasta ponerle unas tocas de viuda en lugar de roquete,[95] y entrar con ellas en Maitines.

second step to heaven is patience. See how much patience that holy man Job had, and how much patience other holy people have had, and many people alive today have it in their trials, since they are the cross God sends us.[87] Let us bear it with patience and this step will be assured to us.

Humility is the third step to heaven. Consider our father Saint Francis who, to be more humble, wanted to be a layman.[88] And as he was on his way to ask the pope that he grant the founding of his religious order, our father Saint Dominic arrived, and out of sheer humility, father Saint Francis let him go in first.[89] For this reason the order of Saint Dominic is one hour older than that of Saint Francis. Look at the humility of our mother Saint Clare who, after going many times to see Saint Francis, was ordered by him not to come so often, perhaps fearing someone would bear false witness (for even saints are not exempt from it).[90] And with great sorrow and great humility she asked when to return, and the saint responded: "When the figs grow." And as this was the middle of winter, she went home quite disconsolate, and discovered there a plate of figs. She went running back to Saint Francis's monastery, and he took them to the refectory and made this miracle public. This is the power of humility and obedience, which this saint had, and those who have it will attain all they could want, and eternal life.

Abraham sent one of his servants (who in those days served with a different sort of loyalty and faithfulness than today) to look for a woman suitable to marry his son, and he gave him a chest of jewels to give to her. He arrived at a place where there was no more than one well to drink from. He was dying of thirst and came across many women who were carrying jugs of water. He asked them for some water but none was charitable (because among common people not many are). The last to come by was the beautiful Rebecca, and he asked her for water. She responded: "I will give not only to you, but to your camels as well." And the young man noticed that this woman was the right one for his master, because she was charitable and humble. And so he gave her the chest of jewels and selected her.[91] This is the power of humility. And if nowadays we were to send a servant to arrange a wedding for our children, and he were given one thousand *escudos* by the other party, he would not reveal any defects the woman might have. For nowadays the world is quite lost, and there is no matter in which a person can trust another.

A major step toward heaven is penitence. Saint Onofre left the empire and went out to the desert to do penance.[92] Saint Jerome left his cardinal's hat and went to the desert to strike his breast with a rock,[93] disillusioned with the world. He was much persecuted to the point that false witness was borne against him and Saint Paula;[94] until she was made to wear widow's weeds instead of a *roquete*,[95] to go to say matins.

S. Luis Rey de Francia dejó el Reino, y tomó el hábito de la Tercera Orden;[96] S. Antonio de Padua, y otros muchos Santos, que sabemos hicieron grandes penitencias.[97] La Magdalena,[98] y S. María Egipciaca,[99] y otras muchas Santas se fueron al desierto; pero en estos tiempos no pudieran hacerlo que está la malicia muy en su punto, y no las dejaran; mas para eso hay Conventos, Aldeas adonde retirarse, y dejar el mundo de veras, y tratar de servir a Dios, que es quien sabe dar el premio: que lo humano todo es aire y viento.

También hemos de conocer, que no todos, ni todas tienen fuerzas, ni salud para hacer penitencia, pero con un dolor de corazón de haber ofendido a Dios, y un deseo de hacerla, lo recibe Dios, que es muy benigno, aunque también es justiciero; y esto mismo han de tener los Reyes de la tierra, pues Dios los puso en su lugar, fiando más de ellos, que de otros: han de castigar a quien lo merece sin tener miedo, ni respeto a nadie, pues no nacieron para tenerle, han de premiar, y estimar a quien lo merece, para pagarles lo que han servido, y que sea ejemplo, para que otros lo hagan, viendo el ejemplar de aquellos. Han de perdonar como lo hace Dios, al que pide misericordia; y pues Dios es la misma piedad, llegarnos a él para todo, que con esto no lo erraremos: S. Pedro negó a Cristo, y con lágrimas alcanzó el perdón, y fue el primer Príncipe de la Iglesia;[100] y si Judas, que vendió a Cristo, no se hubiera desesperado, sino llorado su pecado, le hubiera Cristo perdonado;[101] y así no hemos de desesperar de la misericordia de Dios, que es tan grande, sino pedir con gran contrición el perdón.

Las leyes que dio el Filósofo Bias a los Pirineses; la primera fue de esta manera, "Ordenamos, y mandamos, que ninguno sea elegido por Príncipe de los pueblos, si no hubiere a lo menos cuarenta años, porque de tal edad han de ser los Gobernadores, que ni la poca edad, y la experiencia les haga errar los despachos, y negocios, ni la mucha edad, y flaqueza les estorbe a sufrir los trabajos."[102] Y yo digo, que es muy gran consejo para los Reyes, que dan los puestos porque la edad es la perfecta para el gobierno; pero no es ejemplo esperar a tener esta edad, para tratar del alma, que no sabemos si llegaremos allá.

También importa mucho para la virtud tratar con buena gente, pues Marco Aurelio siendo un Emperador gentil, desterró de su Corte a los truhanes y vagamundos, y los envió a una Isla llamada de Lepanto, a donde era Gobernador un amigo suyo llamado Lasberto, y le escribió una carta diciendo, "Ahí te envío tres Naos cargadas de los maestros, que echan a perder la

Saint Louis, king of France, left the kingdom and became a monk of the Third Order.[96] Saint Anthony of Padua and many other saints we know of did much penance.[97] Saint Mary Magdalene[98] and Saint Mary of Egypt[99] and many other female saints went out to the desert; but nowadays they would be unable to do so since malice is very much at its peak and they would not be permitted. But for this reason there are convents and villages where one may retreat and leave the world behind for good, and try to serve God, who is the One who knows how to truly reward; for all things human are naught but air and wind.

We must also know that not every man or every woman has the strength or health to do penance; but if we go before God with a heart broken for having offended Him and desire to do penance, He will accept it, because He is very kind, though also righteous. And this is the way the kings of the earth should be, since God put them there in His place, and trusted them more than others. They must punish those who deserve it, with neither fear of, nor special consideration for, anyone; this is the way they were born to be. They must reward, and have regard for, those who deserve it, in order to repay them for their service. May that serve as an example for others who, seeing what such rulers have done, may do the same. They must forgive, as God does, the person who asks for mercy, since God is mercy itself. We should go to Him for everything, and in this way we shall not go wrong. Saint Peter denied Christ and, with tears, was forgiven, and he became the first prince of the church.[100] And if Judas, who betrayed Christ, had not lost hope but rather had lamented his sins, Christ would have forgiven him.[101] And so we must not give up hope of God's mercy, which is so great, but rather ask for forgiveness with great contrition.

Of the laws the philosopher Bias gave to the people of Prienes, the first was as follows: "We order and command that no one shall be chosen as prince of the people unless he be at least forty years of age, for that should be the age of governors, such that they neither err in dispatches and business dealings for lack of age and experience, nor find their work hindered by old age and frailty."[102] And I say that this is great advice for kings who grant the posts, for that age is the perfect one for government. But it is not prudent to wait to reach that age to deal with the soul, as we do not know if we will make it that far.

For the sake of virtue it is very important to have dealings with good people. For Marcus Aurelius, being a pagan emperor, banished the rogues and beggars from his court and sent them to an island known as Lepanto, where the governor was a friend of his, named Lasberto, to whom he wrote a letter saying: "Here I send you three vessels laden with the masters who are

República, y si hubiera de enviarte los discípulos no bastaran ciento."[103] Qué bien hicieran los Monarcas si limpiaran sus Cortes de gente de mal vivir, y que de ellos miraran cómo vivían.

David se enamoró de Betsabé, de verla en el baño, e hizo una crueldad, como matar a su marido el Capitán Urías, y después se arrepintió llorando su pecado: y nadie ignora las lágrimas de David, y fue tan grande santo como sabemos, y escribió todos los Salmos que canta la Iglesia;[104] perdonole Dios este pecado como es tan misericordioso, como lo hará a todos los que lloraremos con arrepentimiento nuestros pecados, y huiremos las ocasiones de ofenderle, creyendo que nos mira todo cuanto hacemos, y así cristianos esto encomiendo mucho para que Dios nos perdone, y nos dé la vida eterna teniendo unos con otros caridad, paz, y concordia, Dios nos la dé; y la vida eterna.

LAUS DEO.[105]

ruining our republic, and if I were to send you their followers, one hundred ships would not suffice."[103] The monarchs would do as well to clean their courts of these immoral people and be watchful of how they live.

David fell in love with Bathsheba upon seeing her in the bath and committed the great cruelty of killing her husband, Captain Urias. He later repented, wept for his sin (all people are familiar with David's tears, and he was a very holy man as we all know), and wrote all the psalms sung by the church.[104] God forgave him his sin, so merciful is He, as He will do with all of us who weepingly repent our sins; and we shall flee opportunities to offend Him, believing He watches everything we do. And so, Christians, I recommend this, so that God may forgive us and grant us eternal life, so long as we live in charity, peace, and harmony with one another. May God grant us that, and eternal life.

LAUS DEO.[105] *praise be to God*

# APPENDIX A

MEMORIAL DE LA CASA DE ESCALANTE Y SERVICIOS DE ELLA
AL REY NUESTRO SEÑOR POR DOÑA MARÍA DE GUEVARA
MANRIQUE, CONDESA DE ESCALANTE, Y DE TAHALÚ,
VISCONDESA DE TRECEÑO, SEÑORA DEL VALLE DE VALDALIAGA,
Y DEL MARQUESADO DE RUSCANDIO, Y DE LA VILLA DE VILLA
REAL DE ÁLAVA, Y DE LAS CASA DE ZEBALLOS Y CAVIEDES Y
AVENDAÑO, OLASO Y ORQUIZO, ARAZURI Y MONTALBÁN,
Y GAMBOA, ESPARZA Y ACOTAYN.

En Valladolid Año De 1654
Sumario De Mi Descendencia (19v–20v)

Diego Gutiérrez de Zeballos, Almirante de Castilla, casó con D. Juana Carrillo, tuvieron por hija a doña Elvira de Zeballos.

Doña Elvira de Zeballos casó con Hernán Pérez de Ayala el Fraile, tuvieron por hija a D. Mencía de Ayala.

Doña Mencía de Ayala, casó con don Beltrán de Guevara, tuvieron por hijo a don Beltrán de Guevara Conde de Tahalú.

Don Beltrán de Guevara casó con doña Juana de Quesada, hija del señor de Garcías, tuvieron por hijo a don Ladrón de Guevara.

Don Ladrón de Guevara casó con doña Sancha de Rojas, hija del Marqués de Poza, tuvieron por hijo a don Juan de Guevara.

Don Juan de Guevara casó con doña María de Ulloa, hija del señor de la Mota, tuvieron por hijo a don Juan de Guevara.

Don Juan de Guevara casó con doña Ana de Tobar, hija del señor de la casa de Tobar, y Villamizar, tuvieron por hijo a don José de Guevara.

Don José de Guevara casó con doña María Manrique, hija del Marqués de Aguilar, tuvieron por hijo a don Antonio de Guevara.

Don Antonio de Guevara casó con doña María de Avendaño y Belmonte, hija del señor de la casa de Avendaño, tuvieron por hijo a don Pedro de Guevara.

# APPENDIX A

MEMORIAL OF THE HOUSE OF ESCALANTE AND OF SERVICES RENDERED TO THE KING, OUR LORD, BY DOÑA MARÍA DE GUEVARA MANRIQUE, COUNTESS OF ESCALANTE AND OF TAHALÚ, VISCOUNTESS OF TRECEÑO, LADY OF THE VALLEY OF VALDALIGA AND THE MARQUISATE OF RUCANDIO AND OF THE VILLAGE OF VILLAREAL AT ALAVA, AND LADY OF THE HOUSES OF CEBALLOS AND CAVIEDES AND AVENDAÑO, OLASO, AND ORQUIZO, ARAZURI AND MONTALBÁN, AND GAMBOA, ESPARZA, AND ACOTAYN.

In Valladolid 1654
Summary Of My Lineage (19v–20v)

Diego Gutiérrez de Zevallos, Admiral of Castile, wed Doña Juana Carrillo, and they had a daughter, Doña Elvira de Zevallos.

Doña Elvira de Zevallos wed Hernán Pérez de Ayala the Friar, and they had a daughter, Doña Mencía de Ayala.

Doña Mencía de Ayala wed Don Beltrán de Guevara, and they had a son, Don Beltrán de Guevara, count of Tahalú.

Don Beltrán de Guevara wed Doña Juana de Quesada, daughter of the lord of Garcías, and they had a son, Don Ladrón de Guevara.

Don Ladrón de Guevara wed Doña Sancha de Rojas, daughter of the marquis of Poza, and they had a son, Don Juan de Guevara.

Don Juan de Guevara wed Doña María de Ulloa, daughter of the lord of Mota, and they had a son, Don Juan de Guevara.

Don Juan de Guevara wed Doña Ana Tobar, daughter of the lord of the house of Tobar and Villamizar, and they had a son, Don Joseph de Guevara.

Don Joseph de Guevara wed Doña María Manrique, daughter of the marquis of Aguilar, and they had a son, Don Antonio de Guevara.

Don Antonio de Guevara wed Doña María de Avendaño and Beamonte, daughter of the lord of the house of Avendaño, and they had a son, Don Pedro de Guevara.

Don Pedro de Guevara casó con doña Francisca de Mendoza, tuvieron por hija a doña María de Guevara Condesa de Escalante y Tahalú, Viscondesa de Treceño, señora del valle de Valdaliga, del Marquesado de Rucandio, y de la villa de Villareal de Álava, y de las casas de Zeballos y Avendaño, Olaso y Urquezo y Arazuri y Montalbán y Acotayn y Esparza, y de la casa de Caviedes, que casó con don Andrés Velázquez Velasco, que como está dicho está sirviendo a Vuestra Majestad.

A estas casas tan ilustres como antiguas, dieron los señores Reyes, por los grandes servicios de ellas a la de Guevara, como tengo dicho, el privilegio para hacer cincuenta hijosdalgo,[1] y no se le deja usar de él ni se le ha dado recompensa.

Y a las casas de Navarra, que es la de don Francés de Belmonte dio el lugar de Catarroso, año de 1479 por don Gastón y doña Leonor Príncipes de Navarra, y después se lo quitaron, sin haberle dado otra recompensa.[2] Y las casas de Avendaño y Gamboa, y Urquizo, dieron los señores Reyes muchas Merindades y Prebostrías y Patronazgos, y entre ellos el de Olaso, con todos los agregados a él, y habiéndolo perpetuado en la casa por tres Reyes. Con siniestra relación nos lo quitó Vuestra Majestad y nos quitó Vuestra Majestad la Prebostría de *Valbao* [sic] que era de cien mil ducados. Y el oficio de Ballestero mayor que estuvo más de 200 años en la casa de Avendaño, fue servido Vuestra Majestad de sacarlo de ella y dárselo al Duque de Ciudad Real, siendo estas casas más dignas de que vuestra Majestad las honre y haga merced, que de quitarles las que sus abuelos le dieron.

También el mayorazgo[3] de mi madre, que es 5 mil ducados de renta, está perdido por estar a la raya de Portugal, y consistir en dehesas y juros, la cual pasa necesidad, que me es preciso el alimentarla. Por todo lo cual me pongo a los Reales pies de Vuestra Majestad como humilde vasalla suya, suplico a Vuestra Sacra Real Majestad se sirva de honrarme, haciéndome la merced, que merecen los servicios de tan honradas casas, y pues el oficio de Ballestero mayor está hoy vaco, por muerte del Duque de Ciudad Real, se sirva de hacerme merced de volvérsele a mi casa, juntamente con los patronazgos, que el Duque tenía, pues eran de ella, que son los de Plasencia, e Ybar.

También suplico a Vuestra Majestad se sirva de darme licencia, para que use del privilegio que tiene la casa de Escalante, para hacer cincuenta hijosdalgo, o de darme otra cosa equivalente en recompensa.

En la villa de Osornillo, que antiguamente fue de mi casa como está dicho, tengo la casa más antigua del mayorazgo de Escalante, con todas las preeminencias de señor, como son pastar por dos veces, darme la paz diferente que al pueblo, poner Escribano: tengo un juro sobre las alcabalas, y la Olmeda y todas las tierras y viñas de aquel lugar.

Y el año de 53 entre otras jurisdicciones, que Vuestra Majestad vendió al Duque de Pastrana, fue servido de venderle ésta, que es el mayor agravio, que mi casa puede recibir, pues siendo de las más antiguas de España, no es razón sea vasalla de nadie. Y pues el Duque de Pastrana no ha acabado de pagar a Vuestra Majestad le suplico se sirva de dármele por el tanto que yo lo pagaré luego en la misma especie que el Duque, y será la mayor merced de cuantas Vuestra Majestad me hiciese.

Don Pedro de Guevara wed Doña Francisca de Mendoza, and they had a daughter, Doña María de Guevara, countess of Escalante and Tahalú, viscountess of Treceño, lady of the valley of Valdaliga and the marquisate of Rucandio and the village of Villareal at Álava, and lady of the houses of Zeballos and Avendaño, Olaso and Urquizo and Arazuri and Montalbán and Acotayn and Esparza, and of the house of Caviedes, who wed Don Andrés Velázquez de Velasco, who, as stated, is today serving your Majesty.

To these houses, which are as illustrious as they are old, the kings gave rewards befitting their great services. To the Guevara house, as I have stated, they gave the privilege of naming fifty *hijosdalgo*,[1] but the house is not allowed to name them nor has it received any compensation for them.

And in the year 1479, the prince and princess of Navarre, Don Gaston and Doña Leonor, gave the estate of Caparroso to the houses of Navarre, which belong to Don Francés de Beamonte, and later they took it away from him, without giving him any other compensation.[2] And to the houses of Avendaño and Gamboa, and Urquizo, the kings gave many rewards and provosts and patronages—among them that of Olaso with all its attachés, and all were maintained as such by three kings. Following an evil report, your Majesty took it from us, as well as the provostship of Valbao [*sic*], a position which is worth one hundred thousand ducats. And as for the post of crossbowman major, which for more than two hundred years belonged to the house of Avendaño, your Majesty decided to take it from us and give it to the duke of Ciudad Real, even though this house better merits your Majesty's honor and rewards than it does being deprived of what it inherited from its grandparents.

Also, my mother's *mayorazgo*,[3] which provides an income of five thousand ducats, is lost for being on the border with Portugal, and for consisting of pastureland and royal bonds. She therefore is in such dire need that I have to feed her. For all of this, I throw myself at the royal feet of your Majesty as your humble servant; I beg your Sacred Royal Majesty to be so kind as to honor me, rewarding me as befits the services of such honorable houses. And since the post of crossbowman major is vacant owing to the death of the duke of Ciudad Real, please be so kind as to reward me by returning it to my house, along with the patronages of Plasencia and Ybar, now held by the duke, but which once belonged to my house.

I also beg your Majesty to be so kind as to grant me license to use the privilege held by the house of Escalante to create fifty *hijosdalgo*, or to grant me the equivalent compensation.

In the town of Osornillo, which once belonged to my house as has been stated previously, I have the oldest house of the *mayorazgo* of Escalante, including all the privileges of a lord, such as having pastureland for two inhabitants, being greeted differently than the common people, having a notary, having the perpetual right to sales taxes and to the elm groves, and to all of the house's lands and vineyards.

And in the year 53, among other jurisdictions that your Majesty sold to the duke of Pastrana, it pleased you to sell this one—which is the greatest affront my house could ever receive. As it is among the oldest of Spain, it is not right that it should stand as vassal to anyone. And since the duke of Pastrana has not finished paying your Majesty, I beg you to see fit to return it to me, provided that I pay in the same manner as the duke. And that will be the highest honor your Majesty could bestow upon me.

También suplico a Vuestra Majestad, mande pagar a D. Francisca de Mendoza mi madre más de 20 mil ducados que se le están debiendo de quiebras de juros, pues no tiene otra cosa al presente de qué valerse. En todo espero recibir merced de la poderosa mano de Vuestra Sacra Real Majestad, cuya vida guarde Dios los muchos años, que estos Reinos han menester. Fecha en Valladolid a 16 de Marzo de 1654.

*La Condesa de Escalante y Tahalú*

I also beg your Majesty to order that Doña Francisca de Mendoza, my mother, be paid the more than twenty thousand ducats that she is owed for her failed royal bonds, as she has nothing else of which to avail herself right now. In all this I hope to be rewarded by the powerful hand of your Sacred Royal Majesty; may God grant you life for as many years as are needed by these kingdoms. In Valladolid, March 16, 1654.

*The Countess of Escalante and Tabalú*

# APPENDIX B

### RELACIÓN DE LA JORNADA QUE
### LA CONDESA DE ESCALANTE HIZO A LA CIUDAD
### DE VITORIA A BESAR LA MANO A SU MAJESTAD

Primero día de Mayo tuvo aviso que Su Majestad entraba en la ciudad de Vitoria a tres de Mayo y que venían muchos ladrones a so color de criados; proveyó un mandamiento por todos sus lugares que viniesen a cada lugar cuatro hombres con arcabuces a velar la fortaleza, porque quedasen guardadas sus criadas y hacienda, y el tamborín para que hiciese más ruido; vinieron y aguardaron mientras las Condesa estuvo en Vitoria, adonde estuvo tres días. Fue a palacio en silla; besó la mano a la Reina e hízole mil honras; hizo asentar y preguntole cómo se llamaba el lugar adonde estaba y en qué se entretenía en él y adónde estaba su marido; a todo le respondió la dicha Condesa, haciéndola reír un rato, aunque la Reina había menester poco, que va contenta; no lo va tanto el Rey con las cartas que cada día recibe de Francia, y aquella noche dicen que recibió una que le puso muy melancólico aunque disimuló.

Y estando entretenida la Reina haciendo estas preguntas a la Condesa vino la provincia de Álava a besarle la mano, habiéndosela besado antes al Rey, dándole una fuente de plata con dos mil doblones. La Reina sintió el que viniesen en aquella ocasión a estorbarle su conversación y dio una palmada y lo dijo, que en el camino no ha topado otra persona conocida; se holgó, según las apariencias de topar a la Condesa, la cual estuvo entre las damas a la puerta de la sala viendo el besamanos de la provincia y el de la ciudad y el del Cabildo,[4] que todos fueron uno tras otro; con que llegó la hora de comer y la Condesa se volvió a despedir de la Reina, y le dijo que en París le volvería a besar la mano; riéronse todas, pareciéndoles chanza, a que respondió que no lo era porque pensaba ir a pleitear la casa de Ortubia, que es suya y la posee un sobrino del de Agramonte que estuvo en Madrid. La camarera y las damas la agasajaron mucho, y la de Santa Marta la llevó a su posada y la dio chocolate y muy lindos dulces y medallas del Santo Cristo de Burgos; y al salir de la antecámara

# APPENDIX B

## REPORT ON THE DAY'S JOURNEY THAT THE COUNTESS OF ESCALANTE MADE TO THE CITY OF VITORIA TO KISS HER MAJESTY'S HAND

On the first day of May she received word that her Majesty was entering the city of Vitoria on May 3 and that many thieves were coming under the guise of servants; she issued a decree throughout her estates, ordering that four men with blunderbusses be sent from each town to keep watch over the fortress, so as to keep her female servants and wealth well protected, and also ordering that the drum sound more loudly. They came and kept watch while the countess was in Vitoria, where she spent three days. She went to the palace in a chair; she kissed the queen's hand and honored her profusely. The queen had her take a seat and asked her the name of the place she lived and how she entertained herself there and where her husband was. The aforementioned countess responded to every question, making the queen laugh for a while—even though the queen had little need, as she was already happy. But the king was not so, because of the letters he received from France every day, and it is said that that night he received a letter which made him quite sad, though he acted otherwise.

And while the queen was finding entertainment in asking the countess these questions, the province of Álava came to kiss the queen's hand, having kissed the king's hand previously, and gave her a silver platter with two thousand five hundred doubloons. The queen was sorry that their arrival had disturbed her conversation; she then clapped her hands and said so, adding that during her trip she had not come across any other well-known person. Apparently the queen enjoyed having encountered the countess, who remained among the ladies at the entrance to the hall, watching the royal audience with the province and with the city and with the chapter[1] one after another. And so then it was time to eat and the countess went to bid the queen farewell and told her that in Paris she would kiss her hand again; all the ladies laughed, believing it to be a joke, to which she responded that it was not, as she was planning to litigate the house of Ortubia, which is hers and is in the possession of a nephew of the lord of Agramonte, who was in Madrid. The queen's

llegaron a hablarla el Conde de el Real y el de *Pliego* [sic] y otros caballeros y hasta el Doctor Chabarra, y hasta los lacayos y cocheros y pajes de la de Osorno, haciéndole mil fiestas por las calles; y al salir de Santo Domingo llegó el Patriarca a hablarle, adonde estuvo un rato y llevaba un mozo de silla de la aldea; y el patriarca le compuso la valona[5] y correón y la dijo que llevaba muy aliñado mozo; y aquella noche fue el Duque de Medina a visitarla, haciéndole la merced que acostumbra, y la dijo que a la vuelta había de venir por Villarreal y llevarla por fuerza a Madrid.

Don Antonio de Benavides la visitó y envió la cena; y antes de entrar en Vitoria, en un campo topó a Don Luis de Haro con sus hijos, y le dijo: "Buen viaje, señor Don Luis;" y él respondió e hizo muchas cortesías; no la conoció porque llevaba mascarilla; quedó confuso, queriendo conocer la voz. Paseó la Condesa toda Vitoria en su silla con catorce gentiles hombres delante, los cinco clérigos, y todos vasallos suyos que fueron acompañándola desde su aldea; y como en Vitoria no andan sillas ni se han visto, decían las mujeres: "con todo cuanto el Rey ha traído, no hemos visto más linda litera."

Desde una ventana vio la entrada, que fue grande cosa; disparó la ciudad las piezas de artillería, y de ahí a media hora entró el Duque de Medina con tanta autoridad como el Rey, que se holgó de verle por ser Conde de Oñate.

Miércoles a las once salió el Rey de Vitoria y la Condesa una hora antes se fue a su jurisdicción que divide la provincia de Guipúzcoa, adonde de rebozo y con mascarilla, con todos sus vasallos y vasallas vio el recibimiento que la provincia hizo, que fue poner en un cuerpo en dos escuadrones seiscientos hombres con arcabuces y picas, de infantería todos, y dos capitanes a caballo; y en oyendo las chirimías de que venía el Rey, empezaron a disparar de una parte y de otra, que parecía darse la batalla, y las acémilas y el primer coche dispararon, que fue mucho poderle quitar las mulas; aprisa envió el Rey a Gavilla a mandar que no disparasen; y así le obedecieron hasta que pasó su Majestad; y después se hundía el campo a mosquetazos, batieron las diez banderas y las demás ceremonias acostumbradas.

Partió la Condesa hacia su casa con su escuadrón de aldeanos; topó al Duque de Medina con todo su acompañamiento, y aunque ella iba disfrazada y con mascarilla, la conoció y la dijo: "Servidor, señora, la de la mascarilla;" y ella besó la mano y no le respondió por no ser conocida de los que le acompañaban.

Llegó a su fortaleza, adonde halló las guardas que la aguardaban, y fiada en esta seguridad durmió muy bien toda la noche, aunque sus criadas le contaron que habían venido unos soldados, y que ellas estaban asomadas al castillo y que les dijeron desde abajo: "Madama queda en Vitoria, que vale por dos hombres;" y ellas tuvieron tanto

chamberlain and the other ladies regaled her greatly and that noblewoman of Santa Marta took her to her lodging and gave her chocolate and lovely sweets and medals of the Holy Christ of Burgos. When she left the antechamber, the count of El Real and the count of Pliego [sic] arrived to speak with her along with other gentlemen, and even Doctor Chabarra, along with the footmen and coachmen and pages from the house of Osorno, all of them praising her in the streets with thousands of flattering words. And when she left Santo Domingo, the Patriarch came out to talk to her, and she spent a while there. She had with her a chair servant from her village, and the Patriarch straightened the boy's *valona*[2] and his belt and told her that she had a very smart-looking boy. And that night the duke of Medina came to visit her, honoring her as was his custom, and told her that on her way home she was to come through Villarreal and he would oblige her to go with him to Madrid.

Don Antonio de Benavides visited her and sent her dinner. And before entering Vitoria, she came across Don Luis de Haro with his sons in a field and told him: "Have a pleasant trip, Don Luis." He nodded and responded with many courtesies, though he did not recognize her for the mask she was wearing; this confounded him, and he attempted to recognize the voice. The countess went about the entire city of Vitoria in her chair with fourteen elegant men in front, five clergymen, and all the vassals who had escorted her from her village. And since in Vitoria chairs are not used nor have they ever been seen, the women would say to her: "With all that the king has brought, we have never seen such a lovely litter."

From a window she saw the royal entrance, which was a marvelous sight. The city fired its artillery, and within half an hour the duke of Medina made his entrance with as much authority as the king; she was pleased to see him since he was also the count of Oñate.

Wednesday at eleven o'clock the king left Vitoria, and the countess, one hour before, went to her jurisdiction (which divides the province of Guipúzcoa) where— shawled and wearing a mask, and with all her male and female vassals—she witnessed the welcome the province gave the king. This was done by a body of six hundred men with blunderbusses and pikes, divided into two squadrons, all of them from the infantry, and two captains on horseback. Once they heard the flageolets announcing the king's arrival, they began to fire first from one place and then from another, as if a battle were under way. The mules and the first coach took off like a shot, and it was difficult to control the mules. Immediately the king sent Gavilla to order that they not fire, and so they obeyed until his Majesty had passed by, and then the place was overwhelmed with gunfire; and they flew their ten flags and the rest of the usual ceremonies took place.

The countess set off for home with her troop of villagers; she came across the duke of Medina with all his retinue, and though she was disguised and wearing a mask, he recognized her and said to her: "At your service, my lady, she of the mask"; and she kissed his hand but did not respond so as not to be recognized by those accompanying him.

She arrived at her fortress, where she found the female guards awaiting her, and trusting such safety she slept very well the whole night through. This, despite being told by the female servants that some soldiers had come while they were gazing out of the castle windows and that the soldiers had told them from below: "Your lady is in Vitoria, and she is worth two men." They were so frightened that they thought

miedo, que ya pensaron les faltaba la fortaleza y no se acostaron, haciendo que las guardas disparasen toda la noche y el tamborilero tocase la caja.

Esta es la relación verdadera; quiera Dios sea tan buena la de la vuelta de su Majestad. (Dios le guarde).

Y lo que la Condesa ha sentido de pesadumbre en esta ocasión es no tener un marido con la condición que requería tal caso, para que saliese a recibir a su Majestad, como cabeza del bando Gamboyno que es de todas tres provincias, Álava, Vizcaya y Guipúzcoa.

they had already lost the fortress and did not go to bed, insisting that the guards fire all night long and that the drummer continue to play.

This is the true account of what occurred; God willing, the account of your Majesty's return trip will be just as good (may God be with you).

And what grieved the countess most on this occasion was not having a husband as required by the situation, one who could come out to greet your Majesty as he should in his position, the head of the Ganboyno house, which is made up of three provinces, Álava, Vizcaya, and Guipúzcoa.

# NOTES

## CHAPTER ONE

1. *Corrida* has the double sense of "affronted" and also "embarrassed" (*Aut.*).

2. The addressee is Philip IV, Spanish monarch from 1621 to 1665.

3. The siege of Yelbes (also known as Yelves and Elvas) occurred at the end of October 1658, after the siege of Badajoz that same year. See Carlos Sánchez Rubio, *Coreographia y descripción del territorio de la plaza de Badaxoz y fronteras del Reyno de Portugal confinantes a ella* (Mérida: Junta de Extremadura, 2003), 11.

4. The year of the military campaign of Entremoz, in the province of Alentejo (Portugal), in which the battles of Évora and Ameixial took place. After these two battles, the army of Don Juan José of Austria was defeated and had to retreat definitively. See the account of this campaign by the Portuguese Antonio Alvares da Cunha, *Campanha de Portugal: Pella provincia do Alentejo. Ne primavera do Anno de 1663* (Lisbon: Henrique Valente de Oliveira, 1663), as well as the news as it appeared in the *Mercurio* (1663), included in the same volume along with Alvares's account.

5. As explained in the introduction, one of the characteristics of the crisis of seventeenth-century Spain is the refusal of noblemen to go to war. Here Guevara explains the unfortunate situation that results from such a refusal. See Antonio Maravall, *Poder, honor y élites en el siglo XVII* (Madrid: Siglo XXI, 1980), 201–14.

6. Is she referring to her own situation? The reader must be aware that her third and last husband, Luis Andrés de Velázquez, was imprisoned in Portugal after the Spanish defeat in the campaigns of Entremoz and Évora (1663); this is the topic that opens this treatise.

7. *Puestos en la paz*, in the sense of posts related to the *Consejo de la Paz*, also known as the *Consejo de Estado*, the Council of State.

8. The moment Guevara introduces the topic of Portugal specifically, the *we* of her statements becomes an *I*, and the general complaint about the Spanish army is transformed into a personal battle against the king on the one hand and the Portuguese on the other.

9. Portugal was one of the destinations for Jews and Christian converts expelled from Castile after 1492. During the sixteenth century, when the crowns of Portugal

and Spain came together under the rule of Philip II, the Inquisition acted strongly against the converted Jews in Portugal. Indeed, as Rafael Valladares explains, the intervention of the Inquisition in Portugal was harsher than in Spain, for which reason many of the "New Christians" from Portugal ran away to Holland and, after 1627, to Madrid. For instance, while in 1630 Spain was trying to carry out a policy of assimilation through marriages and royal post offerings for these "New Christians," Portugal was considering their expulsion. *Portugal y la Monarquía hispánica, 1580–1668* (Madrid: Arco Libros, 2000), 19–20.

10.    This woman is probably Luisa de Gusmão, queen regent of Portugal, 1652–62.

11.    As she has demonstrated with her own *Memorial* (1654).

12.    Probably Guevara is referring to the kings of England, France, Portugal, and Spain.

13.    Don Juan José of Austria complained of not having the right soldiers with him to fight. In a letter to King Philip IV in 1661, he requested, along with money, expert ministers from the Council of War who could help him in planning the war directly from the battlefield. *Carta de Don Juan de Austria desde Arroches, 11 de Julio de 1661,* [MSS 2.388, National Library, Madrid, 6. In a biography of Don Juan José of Austria, José Calvo Poyato refers to the army of Don Juan José as a group of soldiers with no experience, most of them coming from prison. *Juan José de Austria* (Barcelona: Mondadori, 2003), 87.

14.    *Cava* is an Arab word that means "prostituted." This name was given to Count Don Julian's daughter, Florinda. Legend says that the last Visigoth king of the Peninsula, Don Rodrigo, raped her, and for this reason her father allowed the Arab troops to enter Spain through the city of Tarifa in 711. Alfonso X, "Estoria de Espanna," in *Prosa Histórica*, ed. Benito Brancaforte (Madrid: Cátedra, 1999), 89–90. Guevara updates this legend and draws a parallel between the Arabs and the Portuguese.

15.    During the Thirty Years War (1618–48), French troops attacked the town of Fuenterrabia (Hondarrabia), 1638–39. Women took the image of the Virgin of Guadalupe and placed her at the entrance of the city to protect them. Then, under her protection, men and women of all ages formed an army that defeated the French. In the National Library in Madrid, there is a volume entitled *Papeles varios* (R/12212) that contains different accounts of this event along with *loas* (praising poems) and *romances* (ballads). See, for example, *Relación en que se declara lo que la ciudad de Fuenterrabia avisa a su Magestad del prodigio y milagro que ha sucedido con la imagen de Nuestra Señora de Guadalupe, 1638–1639* (Barcelona: Jaume Romeu, 1639).

16.    Women of Ávila in 1109, with Ximena Blásquez as their leader, disguised themselves as male warriors and defended the city against the Arabs. Fray Luis Ariz, *Historia de las grandezas de la ciudad de Ávila* (Alcalá de Henares: Luis Martínez Grande, 1607), 43–45. In this local history, Ximena, the leader, is compared to Ulysses, Hector, Cornelia, and Lucretia for her bravery.

17.    I have not been able to locate this character beyond Guevara's own account of her. She is probably the same Blanca de Guevara as appears in Guevara's *Disenchantments* (1664), that is, the daughter of the count of Oñate and widow of Ortuño de Lara. This Blanca participated in an event that freed the kingdom of Navarre from the Moors in 716. From Guevara's own *Memorial* (1654), we know that this event gave rise to the house of Guevara.

18.   As she establishes a difference between the valor of Castilian women and the cowardice of Castilian men.

19.   Prince Don Carlos of Austria (1607–32), brother of Philip III. According to Adolfo de Castro, there was a time during which it was thought he would be sent to govern Portugal. "Apuntes biográficos de algunos autores contenidos en este tomo," in *Poetas Líricos de los siglos XVI y XVII*, Biblioteca de Autores Españoles, vol. 42 (Madrid: Rivadeneyra, 1957), li.

20.   Francisco de Mora or Moura, third marquis of Castelo-Rodrigo (d. 1675), a Portuguese nobleman faithful to the Spanish crown. The historian Fernando Bouza explains that by 1640 the economic situation of this nobleman was very difficult, since he was loyal to a king to whom his kingdom of birth was denying obedience. However, he was always on the Spanish side, and for that reason he was well rewarded by being assigned important posts as ambassador in Vienna (1652), as viceroy of the Low Countries (1656) and Catalonia (1663), as governor of the Low Countries (1664), and until the end of his life in 1675, as Master of the King's Horse. *Portugal no tempo dos Felipes. Política, cultura e representações (1580–1668)*, trans. Ângela Barreto Xavier and Pedro Cardim (Lisbon: Cosmos, 2000), 275–95.

21.   *Morisco:* Christianized Moor *(EC)*.

22.   Évora was taken during the battle of 1663, mentioned at the beginning of this treatise.

23.   Regarding the defeat of Spanish troops in 1663.

24.   *Juros:* bonds issued by the crown *(EC)*.

25.   *Real:* a standard silver coin of the time *(EC)*.

26.   Probably Count Miranda and not Mirandel. Both the count of Miranda and Francisco d'Azevedo are among the Portuguese noblemen who left Madrid to return to Portugal right before the rebellion in 1640 (Bouza, *Portugal*).

27.   Francisco d'Azevedo and the brothers of Peñalba appear to be fundamental to the Portuguese army in Alvares's account of the battle of Alentejo (*Campanha de Portugal*, 33 and 39, respectively).

28.   As James Boyajian explains, "The prevailing anti-semitic and anti-Portuguese mood of the court in the post-Olivarean period and the heightened Inquisitorial activity contributed to an atmosphere in which the least credible rumors and claims about the Portuguese gained rapid acceptance. A populace that suspected the Portuguese New Christians of *Judaizing* was easily convinced that the Portuguese committed other crimes, ranging from earning usurious profits from the interest charges in the *asientos* and extracting wealth from the peninsula to enrich Spain's enemies, to sabotaging Spain's foreign policy and military offensives in Flanders." *Portuguese Bankers at the Court of Spain, 1626–50* (New Brunswick, NJ: Rutgers University Press, 1983), 164.

29.   With the accession of Emperor Charles I (V in Germany), many Burgundian and Flemish people were assigned to important official posts. Among them was the prime minister, or favorite, Monsieur Xevres, whose power became so great that, as the chronicler Father Prudencio de Sandoval says, "it seemed that Xevres was the king and the king his son." *Historia de la vida y hechos del emperador Carlos V* (1604–6), ed. Carlos Seco Serrano, Biblioteca de Autores Españoles, vol. 80 (Madrid: Atlas,

1955), 192. This situation, along with the excessive taxation and the absence of the king from Spain, provoked the people into revolting all over the country from 1517 to 1522; popularly, this was known as the revolt of the *Comunidades* (Communities). Henry Kamen, *Spain 1469–1714: A Society of Conflict* (London: Longman, 1983), 73–81. In his history, Father Prudencio de Sandoval explains the reasons for these revolts and presents a contemporary account of them (192–451).

30.    For a summary of the popular revolts that took place during the reign of Philip IV, see R. A. Stradling, *Philip IV and the Government of Spain, 1621–1665* (Cambridge: Cambridge University Press, 1988), 189–206.

31.    Although the members of the Council of Finance changed often during these years, by 1660 Juan de Góngora was the president and his councilors were Manuel Pantoja, Gerónimo Sanvítores, Don Juan Otáñez, Don Diego de Argote, the marquis of Monasterio, Don Sebastián Cortizos, Andrea Piquenotti, and the count of la Roca. Antonio Domínguez Ortiz, *Política y hacienda de Felipe IV* (Madrid: Ed. de Derecho Financiero, 1960), 176.

32.    Probably Queen Catalina of Lancaster (1373–1418), wife of Henry III and mother of John II.

33.    *Hacanea:* a type of horse, larger than a mare but smaller than a male horse *(EC).*

34.    *Caballero:* member of the middle nobility, usually propertied *(Aut.).*

## CHAPTER TWO

1.    According to Covarrubias, a "modern author" refers to an author who "has been writing for only a few years and who therefore does not have as much authority as those from antiquity" *(Cov.).* Guevara is making use of the rhetoric of false humility from the beginning of her text, by indicating that she does not possess sufficient authority. Despite the anonymity sought by the author, one can read "This book was made by the countess of Escalante. Year 1664" handwritten at the bottom of the text.

2.    Franciscan monk (1395–1463). He was the guardian at the Franciscan convent in the Canary Islands. After being in Rome in charge of the infirmary in the convent of Ara Coeli, Saint Diego retired to Alcalá de Henares where he died. Before his death, his reputation was already widespread. He was known to have miraculously cured both King Henry IV of Castile and, even more famously, in 1562, Prince Carlos, the unfortunate son of Philip II (although he later died). For these miracles, he was canonized. In 1661, Saint Diego of Alcalá's body was moved to Madrid in order to cure Prince Baltasar Carlos, son of Philip IV. Under the saint's protection this prince died, but Charles Joseph was born, the future king Charles II, to whom this work is dedicated. For more information about this famous saint, see his life in Father Antonio Fiol Borrás, *Vida de San Diego de Alcalá* (Madrid: n.p., 1958). Lope de Vega immortalized his life with a play entitled *San Diego de Alcalá*, probably written around 1613 and published in *Parte tercera de los mejores ingenios de España* in 1653. There is a modern edition of the play by Thomas Case (Kassel: Reichenberger, 1988).

3.    "Small but giant in intentions" is a common topos in the rhetoric of the time. Specifically see the prologue to the reader by Baltasar Gracián in his *El Héroe* (1639):

"I undertake with a small book to educate a giant man." Facsimile edition (Zaragoza: Institución "Fernando El Católico," Diputación de Zaragoza, 2001).

4.  The author refers to Prince Baltasar Carlos, the only male offspring of the marriage of Philip IV and his first wife, Elizabeth of Bourbon. The prince died in 1646 before he turned seventeen.

5.  Spanish warrior (1357–1428). As constable of Castile, he served King John I, King Henry III, and King John II. Dávalos fought in every military campaign of his time as a valorous captain. He participated in different political events but fell into disgrace, lost his posts and honors, saw his wealth confiscated, and had to flee as an exile to Valencia, where he died (*EC*).

6.  Father Antonio de Guevara was María de Guevara's great-great-uncle. See the volume editor's introduction for more details on influences and relationships.

7.  It is important to notice that Guevara has not chosen the Virgin's immaculate conception as the characteristic to highlight. Along with being a model of humility (for giving birth in a manger), the Virgin Mary is a model of valor (she was not afraid of making a long trip while pregnant). Indeed, from this point forward, valor is the feature Guevara intends to emphasize, a valor related to physical and moral aspects as well as to intelligence and wit.

8.  Guevara is self-conscious about being an author, mainly with respect to theological subjects such as the Virgin. However, she makes those declarations and, in a way, becomes another Saint Augustine.

9.  1 Samuel 19: 11–17. Queen Michal is also included in the catalogue of women by Álvaro de Luna, well known at the end of the fifteenth century, entitled *Libro de las virtuosas y claras mujeres* (Madrid: Sociedad de Bibliófilos Españoles, 1891), 1.25.

10.  Zenobia, queen of Palmyra (third century BCE). Always attracted to masculine pastimes, as an adult she reconquered part of the Roman Empire fighting alongside her husband as a brave captain. Guevara might have used as a source Antonio de Guevara's *Epístolas familiares*, ed. José María de Cossío (Madrid: Real Academia Española, 1950–52), 2: 26, although Queen Zenobia was very famous during her time owing, in part, to Calderón de la Barca's play *La gran Cenobia*, performed in 1625. Zenobia's life and valorous deeds were already an official entry in books of illustrious women such as Giovanni Boccaccio's *De mulieribus claris*, ed. and trans. Virginia Brown (Cambridge: Harvard University Press, 2001), 100; Christine de Pizan's *The Book of the City of Ladies*, trans. Earl Jeffrey Richards (New York: Persea Books, 1982), 1.20.1; and Álvaro de Luna's *Libro de las virtuosas y claras mujeres*, 3.74.

11.  María de Guevara may be referring to one of the two very famous French regents of the time: Catherine de Medici, married to Henry II (1547–59), who gave birth to Isabel of Valois, spouse of Philip II of Spain; and Marie de Medici, married to Henry IV (1589–1610), who gave birth to the Louis XIII, spouse of Anne of Austria, a daughter of Philip III.

12.  As noted in the *Treatise,* Spanish queen Catalina of Lancaster (1373–1418) was married to Spanish king Henry III. After his death, she was the regent queen until their son John II came of age.

13.  María de Guevara is basing her account of Count Fernán González on a legendary thirteenth-century epic in which the real events have been altered (e.g.,

historically, Fernán González was first imprisoned in León and then in Navarre). The king of Navarre who was killed by the count is Sancho de Abarca, and his son was García Sanchez II, brother of Sancha, Fernán González's wife. The other sister of García Sanchez II is Teresa, married to the king of León, Sancho Ordóñez (Sancho I, the Fat King). For a complete account of this epic, see *Poema de Fernán González,* ed. Emilio Alarcos Llorach (Madrid: Gredos, 1982).

14. For the legend of this historical character, Queen Giovanna I of Anjou, known as Queen Giovanna of Naples, I refer to Benedetto Croce's *Storia del Regno di Napoli* (Bari: Laterza, 1925), 43–56, and his "I ricordi della Regina Giovanna a Napoli," in *Leggende Napoletane* (Napoli: Morano, 1905). The legend was popularized in Spain by Lope de Vega's *comedia, La reina Juana de Nápoles* (written between 1597 and 1602 and published in 1615).

15. From Antonio de Guevara's *Relox de Príncipes* (n.p.: ABL/Conferencia de Ministros Provinciales Franciscanos de España, 1994), 2.27–28.

16. In the *Comedia Primera* of the *Mocedades del Cid* (1621), by Gillén de Castro, ed. Víctor Said Armesto (Madrid: La Lectura, 1913), there is an episode similar to this: Before Ximena and the Cid were married, he visited her house, handed his knife to her, and told her to use it, but first she was to listen to the explanation he had to offer in regard to her father's death. At the end of his explanation, and with tears in her eyes, Ximena returned the knife to the Cid and asked him to leave. In the scene, it is said that the Cid fell in love with Ximena and admired her valor and courage (vv. 1105–1208).

17. 1 Samuel 25:2–25. Also in Álvaro de Luna's *Libro,* 1.14.

18. I have not been able to locate this episode. However, it could be that we are dealing with a misspelling (there is no Moorish king Marfidio in the history of Al-Andalus that I have been able to find) or with a historical anachronism (the lordship of Oñate was not converted into an earldom until 1469, and by that time the kingdom of Navarre was in its last years of existence as such; also during this time the presence of Moors in the Peninsula was limited to the kingdom of Granada). The participation of Blanca de Guevara in the liberation of Navarre from the Moors means that there is a connection between the house of Guevara and the kingdom of Navarre, and that Navarre owes much to the Guevara family.

19. This episode is repeated in her two writings. The event took place in 1109, when women of Ávila, with Ximena Blasquez as their leader, disguised themselves as male warriors and defended their city (see *Treatise,* note 16).

20. Unless María de Guevara is talking about another Antona García, we are faced with another possible anachronism. The only Antona that I have located is a famous *toresana* (from Toro) who died after giving entrance to the Castilians into a fortified town that was occupied by the Portuguese during the fifteenth century. The Catholic Queen, Isabella of Castile, exalted her memory (*EC*). This story was popularized in Tirso de Molina's *Antona García* (ca. 1623), first published in the *Cuarta Parte* of Tirso's collected works in 1635 (ed. Margaret Wilson [Manchester: Manchester University Press, 1957]).

21.  Possibly King Alfonso VI. However, there is no recorded information related to this episode.

22.  Saint Anthony's fire is a deadly skin disease (erysipelas).

23.  The Catholic King and Queen, Ferdinand of Aragon and Isabella of Castile, subdued the last Muslim redoubt in the Peninsula in 1492 and were able to unify Spain. The personal participation of the queen in battle is well known. See Barbara Weissberger's analysis of Isabella in her *Isabel Rules: Constructing Queenship, Wielding Power* (Minneapolis: University of Minnesota Press, 2004).

24.  Simancas is a town in the province of Valladolid. It is said that once, when the town had to offer a hundred Christian women to the Moors as taxes, seven of the hundred maidens cut off a hand in order to be less desirable to the supposed Muslim lust. On display in one of the castles of the town is the coat of arms with seven hands; thus the origin of the name "Simancas" (seven [*seti*] one-armed [*manca*] maidens) (*EC*). This story first appeared in the thirteenth century in the *Vida de San Millán*, by Gonzalo de Berceo, (*Obra Completa*, ed. C. García Turza et al. [Madrid: Espasa-Calpe, 1992], vv. 369–74), and became the theme of Lope de Vega's *Las doncellas de Simancas* (Madrid: Biblioteca Nacional, 1992).

25.  Legend says that during the time of the Moors' domination, when Christians were confined in the mountains of Asturias and Galicia, a young Galician man of the Figueroa lineage was in love with Rosarda. When Rosarda was chosen by the Moors as one of the hundred maidens, the young man, helped by four friends, decided to fight the Moors. Since they did not have any arms, they attacked the Moors with the branches of a fig tree and defeated them. This legend is included in the eleventh book of the epic poem by Cristóbal Suárez de Figueroa, *La España defendida* (Madrid: Juan de la Cuesta, 1612).

26.  In Greek mythology, Queen Penelope, King Ulysses' wife, represents a symbol of conjugal fidelity. In Homer's *Odyssey*, she is one of the main characters in book 19, where she tells Odysseus about her weaving and the suitors. She is also included among the virtuous women of Boccaccio (40), Christine de Pizan (2.41.1), and Álvaro de Luna (2.66).

27.  Also quoted in Guevara's treatise: in 1638–39, these women defended Fuenterrabia (Hondarrabia) from the French troops (See *Treatise*, note 15.)

28.  Antonio de Guevara, *Relox*, 2.17.

29.  Dido, queen of Carthage (end of the eleventh century BCE). According to Virgil's *Aeneid* (books 1 and 4), she killed herself after being abandoned by Aeneas, prince of Troy, with whom she was in love. In Boccaccio, 42; Pizan, 2.55.1; Álvaro de Luna, 2.35.

30.  The Roman Lucretia (d. ca. 509 BCE) killed herself after being raped by Tarquin the Proud, son of King Tarquin. See Boccaccio's account (48); Pizan's version, 2.44.1. Also in Antonio de Guevara's *Epístolas familiares*, ed. Augusto Cortina (Buenos Aires: Espasa-Calpe, 1942), 2.8, and Álvaro de Luna, 2.1.

31.  In contrast to other accounts of these stories (Boccaccio, Pizan, Álvaro de Luna, and Father Antonio de Guevara, for example), the characteristics of loving constancy, in the case of Dido, and virtuous chastity, in the case of Lucretia, are not

* the ones praised. For María de Guevara, their suicides were in vain because they were not guilty and therefore had nothing to prove to anybody.

32.    According to the legend, the *Cava*, or Florinda, daughter of Count Don Julian, was raped by Rodrigo, the last Visigoth king, and this event provoked the invasion of Arabs in Spain. See note 14 of the *Treatise* for more information on the *Cava*. Unlike the classic assaulted woman, she did not kill herself after being raped.

33.    Judith 10–13.

34.    It corresponds to the parable of the ten virgins, not fourteen as Guevara says. See Matthew 25: 1–13.

35.    Aristotle talks about the divine substance in his *Metaphysics*, trans. A.D. Melville (Oxford: Oxford University Press, 1986), 2.12.

36.    Not clear in the original. It may say *faula* but the word does not exist in Spanish. Judging by the context in which it appears, I think this may be a misspelling of "*fabla = habla*," meaning that all men are the same.

37.    In Greek mythology, Orpheus, a Thracian prince, was married to Eurydice and traveled to the underworld to rescue her. His story has been told by many writers; among others, the Latin Ovid in his *Metamorphoses*, book 10.

38.    Antón Martín, disciple of Saint John of God, founded the Hospital of Our Lady of the Love of God, also known as the Hospital of Antón Martín, in Madrid during the sixteenth century. The hospital was dedicated to the treatment of venereal and contagious diseases (*EC*).

39.    From Guevara's *Relox*, 2.15.

40.    Ibid., 3.12–16 and 27.

41.    Ibid., 2.15.

42.    King Fernando I divided his kingdom among his sons and daughter: Castile went to Sancho, León to Alfonso, Galicia to García, Zamora to Urraca, and Toro to Elvira. Unhappy with the division, Sancho began to reconquer all the kingdoms from his brothers and sisters. In the siege of Zamora, which he was going to take from his sister Urraca, he was betrayed by his brother Alfonso and killed by Bellido de Orfos (or Dolfos), on October 7, 1072. Urraca kept her kingdom and Alfonso kept the rest; he became Alfonso IV of Castile and León (with Galicia and Toro included) (*EC*). There are many *romances* (ballads) about this historical event, like "A pesar del aviso que Arias Gonzalo da al rey, éste se fía de Bellido y muere alevosamente a sus manos," in Agustín Durán's compilation of ballads, *Romancero general o Colección de romances castellanos* Biblioteca de Autores Españoles, vol. 10 (Madrid: Atlas, 1945), 504–5. See the historical account by King Alfonso X, the Wise, in his *Primera Crónica General de España*, ed. Ramón Menéndez Pidal (Madrid: Gredos, 1977), 2: 509 ff.

43.    Guevara refers to the biblical episode of the destruction of Sodom and Gomorrah, in which Abraham and his family were saved. Genesis 18–19.

44.    The *Magnificat* in Luke 1: 52 says exactly: "He has deposed the mighty from their thrones / and raised the lowly to high places."

45.    "Cause of causes, take pity on me." Not by Aristotle, this aphorism is attributed to Cicero, who pronounced it when he was attacked in December of 43 BCE by assassins hired by Mark Antony.

46.   Genesis 41.

47.   Probably Prince Pedro of Aragon (1406–38), son of King Ferdinand I and Leonor of Alburquerque. However, the expression attributed to him by the trickster seems to be a popular one, and it appears in a variety of documents of the time, such as *El viage de Hierusalem que hizo Francisco Guerrero, Racionero, y Maestro de capilla de la Santa Iglesia de Sevilla* (Valencia: Joan Navarro, 1593), 13v.

48.   Virgil blames Helen for the destruction of Troy, since she left her husband voluntarily to run away with Paris (*Aeneid*, books 1 and 7). Also Homer's *Odyssey*, book 23. See also Boccaccio, *De mulieribus*, 36, and, particularly, Pizan (2.61.6), who, instead of using the description to blame her, praises her beauty.

49.   While trying to escape from a burning Troy, Creusa, Aeneas's wife, died in the confusion (*Aeneid*, book 2).

50.   Genesis 22.

51.   2 Samuel 11.

52.   King Henry VIII's first marriage was to the princess of Castile, Catherine of Aragon, daughter of the king and queen of Spain. Anne Boleyn (1507–36) was one of her ladies-in-waiting. This marriage between Henry VIII and Anne Boleyn provoked the schism of the English church.

53.   Boabdil, last king of the Moorish kingdom of Granada, was known as King Chico.

54.   The plot of the well-known first part of *Guerras civiles de Granada*, by Ginés Pérez de Hita, ed. Shasta Bryant (Newark: Juan de la Cuesta, 1982), deals mainly with the civil war between Abencerrajes and Zegríes. This work was published at least seventy-two times before 1700, which demonstrates the popularity of the story. The confrontation is also known because of a story, also very popular in the seventeenth century, called *El Abencerraje*, ed. Francisco López Estrada (Madrid: Cátedra, 1992), popularized through ballads and a short novel of the same title.

55.   Daniel 6: 1–18.

56.   According to both the Guevaras (Antonio and María), the fall of Rome resulted from not giving the right posts to the right people. See Guevara, *Relox*, 1.13–15.

57.   Guevara, *Relox*, 1.13–15. María mistakenly writes "Aurelius" where she should have said "Tiberius."

58.   In the chronicles, we find the Cid, Ruy Díaz de Vivar, fighting the Moors after his death. See, for example, *Crónica del famoso caballero Cid Ruy Diez campeador* (Burgos: Fadrique Alemán de Basilea, 1512), chaps. 281 ff.

59.   There is no gender mark, but she is probably referring to herself as the head of her estates. She may be using the structure "I know a person" in order to make the threat to the king less strong.

60.   Saint Julian, bishop of Cuenca, was very popular in the seventeenth century. Father Bartolomé Alcázar wrote his life, *Vida, virtudes y milagros de San Julián, Obispo segundo de Cuenca* (Madrid: Juan García Infanzón, 1692). In this account of the saint's life, it is noted that Philip II had faith in him (438–39).

61.   This happened in 1580 when the Cortes were held in Tomar and Philip II was named king of Spain and Portugal.

62.   Owing to a probable misspelling, "Seminides" could refer to either of two Greek poets: Semonides, originally from Samos (seventh century BCE) or Simonides, from Ceos (sixth century BCE). Both, very famous during their times, wrote many elegies and epigrams. I am inclined to think that the one in this case is Semonides from Samos because some of his fragments that have survived contain ideas that distinguish different types of women, and others refer to pessimistic moralizing (OCD).

63.   Gorgias of Leontini (ca. 485–ca. 380 BCE), one of the most influential sophists, also an important thinker and stylist. Founder of the art of Greek prose, he was concerned with the language and communication of being (OCD).

64.   Archytas of Tarentum (fourth century BCE), Pythagorean philosopher and mathematician. He invented the pulley and was the first to apply geometry to mechanics. Of his writings we have only some fragments of mathematics and physics; those on philosophical themes seem to be apocryphal (OCD).

65.   Battle of Yelves (Elvas), in 1658–59. See volume editor's introduction.

66.   In the *Comedia Primera* of the *Mocedades del Cid* (1621), Guillén de Castro dramatizes this episode of the Cid with his father and brothers (vv. 333–585). Guevara might have been familiar with this episode from de Castro's version or from the *romances* (ballads) popular at the time. One example is entitled "Diego Laines prueba a sus hijos para saber a cual puede fiar la venganza de la afrenta que le hizo el Conde Lozano" [Diego Laines tests his sons to find out to whom he will entrust the affront against him by Count Lozano]. This ballad is included in the "Romances relativos a la historia de España," compiled by Agustín Durán in *Romancero general* (Madrid: Rivadeneyra, 1851), 478–79.

67.   Semimythical figure of the ninth century. According to the ballads of Roncesvalles and the heroic anonymous chronicle *Bernardo del Carpio* (thirteenth century), Bernardo del Carpio, son of Alfonso II's sister, defeated Charlemagne and his knight Roland in the battle of Roncesvalles. Bernardo freed Spain from the danger of being taken by France, since King Alfonso did not have a successor. In 1624 Bernardo de Balbuena published an epic poem on this hero, entitled *El Bernardo o victoria de Roncesvalles*, ed. Cayetano Rosell, Biblioteca de Autores Españoles, vol. 17 (Madrid: Atlas, 1945), 139–399.

68.   Juan de Labrit (or Albrit) married Queen Catalina of Navarre (1483–1515). This marriage revived the confrontation between "Agramonteses" and "Beamonteses," two Navarre factions that were formed at the beginning of the century, during the reign of Charles, prince of Viana, who was supported by the "Beamonteses" against his father, John I of Aragon, and the "Agramonteses." The confrontation originated when the king of Aragon tried to impose his power over the kingdom of Navarre.

69.   The *escudo* became a new gold coin after 1537. The value changed depending on the economy.

70.   I have not been able to locate these archives in the town of Salvatierra.

71.   *Crónica de Pedro* (1353), by Pero López de Ayala (1332–1407), ed. Constance Wilkins and Heanon Wilkins (Madison: Medieval Studies Seminar, 1985). This episode is included in chapter 9 on the second year of his reign. It corresponds to the fight against Pedro I and Don Nuño (and not Don Uño), last lord of Vizcaya. Don

Nuño, son of Don Juan Núñez de Lara (d. 1350) and María López de Haro (d. 1348), was born in 1348 and inherited the lordship of Vizcaya in 1350 against the opposition of Pedro I. Chapter 7 of the chronicle speaks of a "lady who raised Don Nuño de Lara, who was called Doña Mencía." Her son, Don Juan de Avendaño, defended Don Nuño from Pedro I (chap. 8). Both Juan de Avendaño and his mother, Doña Mencía, are ancestors of Guevara, belonging to the house of Gamboa. Luis de Salazar y Castro, *Historia Genealógica de la Casa de Lara*, (Madrid: Imprenta Real, for Mateo de Llanos y Guzmán, 1797), 3: 219.

72.    I have been unable to locate this episode.

73.    Don Juan, prince of Spain, son of Ferdinand and Isabella, died in 1497.

74.    "[L]e trespas du prince de Castille . . . . Et, à la verité, je n'oys jamais parler de plus grand dueil qu'il en a esté faict par tous leurs royaulmes, car toutes gens de mestier ont cessé par quarante jours (comme leurs ambaxadeours me disrent despuys), tout homme vestu de noir, de ces gros bureaulx; et les nobles et gens de bien chevauchrient les mulles couvertz jusques aux genoulx dudit trap; et ne leur paressoit que les yeulx; et banières noyres partout sur les portes des villes." Philippe de Commynes, *Mémoires*, ed. Joseph Calmette (Paris: Librairie Ancienne Honoré Champion, 1924), 294–95.

75.    Ferdinand, son of Juana I (also known as Juana the Mad Queen, daughter of Ferdinand and Isabella) and Philip the Beautiful, became emperor of Germany. His baptism was in Alcalá de Henares in 1503.

76.    Father Prudencio de Sandoval's *Historia de la vida y hechos del emperador Carlos V* (1604–6), ed. Carlos Seco Serrano, Biblioteca de Autores Españoles, vol. 80 (Madrid: Atlas, 1955), 22.

77.    *Maravedí* is not a coin but a sum composed by smaller coins (*Cov.*). By the end of the fifteenth century, accounting in Castile was done in *maravedíes*.

78.    Antisthenes of Athens, founder of the Cynic school, pupil of Gorgias the rhetorician (ca. 446–366 BCE). As an associate of Socrates, he continued the sophistic tradition. He elaborated on the need of virtue to ensure happiness (*OCD*).

79.    Probably Polemon of Athens (314–270 BCE), head of the Academy. A moralist who stated that the ideal life is that according to nature, he was mainly concerned with Platonic ethics (*OCD*).

80.    Heraclitus of Ephesus (ca. 504–ca. 478 BCE). His central concept is that of the *logos*. His philosophy deals with the movements that result from the contradiction between two different states of matter. In politics, he is inclined to aristocratic ideas but insists on the importance of public law (*OCD*).

81.    The episode of the villager became very famous through Antonio de Guevara's account. This episode appears, in fact, in book 3 of his *Relox*, chaps. 3–6.

82.    *Vasallages*: A type of tax or tribute that the vassal must pay his lord (*Aut.*).

83.    Genesis 6–8.

84.    From this point on, María de Guevara refers to Christian values (charity, humility, and penance) and highlights the lives of different saints. Most of the saints she includes were well known during her time, thanks to a popular genre, "the lives of saints," particularly Alonso de Villegas's *Flos sanctorum*, which—after its publica-

tion in 1580—saw many reprints. All the saints Guevara chooses to illustrate those Christian values are found in the *Flos* by Villegas. *Flos sanctorum. Historia general de la vida y hechos de Jesucristo y de todos los sanctos* (Toledo: widow of Juan Rodriguez, 1591). It is very likely that she owned one or more volumes on the lives of saints by Villegas, Martín de Lilio, or Father Ribadeneyra. since these were some of the most commonly found texts discovered in private libraries in Spain during the sixteenth and seventeenth centuries.

85.   Saint Isabel, princess of Hungary (1207–1231), married Louis IV, landgrave of Thuringia. After her husband's death, she gave all her possessions to the poor and retired to a monastery (Villegas, *Flos*, 133–34).

86.   Order founded in 1209 by Saint Francis of Assisi (*EC*).

87.   Book of Job in the Old Testament. Despite all the bad things that happened to his estates, his family, and himself, he still believed in God and trusted in his compassion.

88.   Saint Francis of Assisi (1182–1226), founded the Franciscan order (or the "friars minor"). Touched by divine grace, he divided up his goods among the needy, wore rough woolen cloth, and became the apostle of the poor (Villegas, *Flos*, 339–343v).

89.   This event is included in Villegas's account of Saint Francis's life.

90.   Saint Clare of Assisi (1193–1253), Italian nun, founded the order of Saint Clare. She was canonized by Pope Alexander IV (Villegas, *Flos*, 279v–282). When speaking of her, Villegas refers to this false testimony.

91.   Genesis 24. Pizan includes Rebecca in her city of ladies and also praises her chastity and humility (2.39.1).

92.   Egyptian monk of the fourth century who did penance in the desert (Villegas, *Flos*, 85–86).

93.   Saint Jerome, father of the Latin church (ca. 345–420), spent most of his life in the Middle East as a penitent in the desert. He worked on biblical studies (e.g., translated the Bible into Latin) (Villegas, *Flos*, 332–336v). In Villegas's *Flos*, the possible false testimony against him and Saint Paula is noted. Making Saint Jerome a cardinal is a medieval anachronism not contained in Villegas's account of his life. For a historical and legendary account of Saint Jerome's life and his cult in the Renaissance, see Eugene F. Rice Jr., *Saint Jerome in the Renaissance* (Baltimore: Johns Hopkins University Press, 1985).

94.   Saint Paula (347–404), patroness of widows. Saint Paula was a very wealthy Roman noble who decided to join the circle of followers of Saint Jerome (Villegas, *Flos*, 72–74). She accompanied him to the Holy Land and founded monastic communities for men and for women (Rice, *Saint Jerome*, 12–20). During their time, there was a rumor of a possible scandalous relationship between her and Saint Jerome. See John Delaney, *Dictionary of Saints* (Garden City, NY: Doubleday, 1980), 312. Álvaro de Luna includes her in his catalogue of virtuous women (3.4).

95.   *Roquete:* article of clothing that is worn by people of the church over the cassock (*Cov.*).

96.   Louis IX or Saint Louis (1215–1270), king of France, was crowned when he was eleven. His mother as regent prepared the kingdom for her son by eliminating

the feudal coalitions. He signed a peace treaty with England, was the mediator between the pope and the Holy Roman Emperor Frederick II, and supported Robert Sorbonne in the foundation of the University of Paris (Villegas, *Flos*, 295–98).

97.   Saint Anthony of Padua (1195–1231), Franciscan friar, great orator, diligent nurse, and eminent theologian. He connected the Augustinian tradition with the new Franciscan school (Villegas, *Flos*, 191–193v).

98.   Mary Magdalene accompanied Jesus through his life and was the first to see him after he was resurrected (John 20: 11–18). She is also identified with the sinner who washed Jesus' feet and perfumed them (Luke 7: 36–50). See also Álvaro de Luna (3.14). Included in Villegas, *Flos*, 231–234v.

99.   Fifth-century penitent Saint Mary of Egypt became very popular with the *jongleurs* in Europe; her life was written during the thirteenth and fourteenth centuries. See, for example, the first manuscript ever written in Spanish, the early thirteenth-century MSS Escorial III-K-4. Also in Álvaro de Luna's catalogue (3.8) and in Villegas's *Flos* (62v–66).

100.   Luke 22: 54–62.

101.   Matthew 27: 3–10.

102.   Bias of Priene (fifth century BCE), head of the seven sages of Greece. Some of his maxims have survived (*EC*). One of his recommendations is to measure life as if we had both a short time and a long time to live.

103.   In Guevara's *Relox*, 3.43–47.

104.   2 Samuel 11.

105.   Praise be to God.


### APPENDIX A

1.   *Hijosdalgo:* title of nobility (*Cov.*)

2.   Doña Leonor de Foix, daughter of John and Blanca of Navarre, was queen after the death of her sister Blanca, poisoned by orders of Doña Leonor herself in 1479.

3.   *Mayorazgo:* entailed estate (*Aut.*)


### APPENDIX B

1.   *Chapter* in the sense of the members of the Alavan church and orders.

2.   *Valona:* boy's shirt collar (*EC*).

# SERIES EDITORS'
# BIBLIOGRAPHY

## PRIMARY SOURCES

Alberti, Leon Battista (1404–72). *The Family in Renaissance Florence*. Trans. Renée Neu Watkins. Columbia, SC: University of South Carolina Press, 1969.

Arenal, Electa, and Stacey Schlau, eds. *Untold Sisters: Hispanic Nuns in Their Own Works*. Trans. Amanda Powell. Albuquerque, NM: University of New Mexico Press, 1989.

Astell, Mary (1666–1731). *The First English Feminist: Reflections on Marriage and Other Writings*. Ed. and Introd. Bridget Hill. New York: St. Martin's Press, 1986.

Atherton, Margaret, ed. *Women Philosophers of the Early Modern Period*. Indianapolis, IN: Hackett Publishing Co., 1994.

Aughterson, Kate, ed. *Renaissance Woman: Constructions of Femininity in England: A Source Book*. London and New York: Routledge, 1995.

Barbaro, Francesco (1390–1454). *On Wifely Duties*. Trans. Benjamin Kohl in Kohl and R. G. Witt, eds., *The Earthly Republic*. Philadelphia: University of Pennsylvania Press, 1978, 179–228. Translation of the preface and book 2.

Behn, Aphra. *The Works of Aphra Behn*. 7 vols. Ed. Janet Todd. Columbus, OH: Ohio State University Press, 1992–96.

Blamires, Alcuin, ed. *Woman Defamed and Woman Defended: An Anthology of Medieval Texts*. Oxford: Clarendon Press, 1992.

Boccaccio, Giovanni (1313–75). *Famous Women*. Ed. and trans. Virginia Brown. The I Tatti Renaissance Library. Cambridge, MA: Harvard University Press, 2001.

———. *Corbaccio or the Labyrinth of Love*. Trans. Anthony K. Cassell. Second revised edition. Binghamton, NY: Medieval and Renaissance Texts and Studies, 1993.

Booy, David, ed. *Autobiographical Writings by Early Quaker Women*. Aldershot and Brookfield: Ashgate Publishing Co., 2004.

Brown, Sylvia. *Women's Writing in Stuart England: The Mother's Legacies of Dorothy Leigh, Elizabeth Joscelin and Elizabeth Richardson*. Thrupp, Stroud, Gloceter: Sutton, 1999.

Bruni, Leonardo (1370–1444). "On the Study of Literature (1405) to Lady Battista Malatesta of Moltefeltro." In *The Humanism of Leonardo Bruni: Selected Texts*. Trans. and Introd. Gordon Griffiths, James Hankins, and David Thompson. Binghamton, NY: Medieval and Renaissance Studies and Texts, 1987, 240–51.

Castiglione, Baldassare (1478–1529). *The Book of the Courtier.* Trans. George Bull. New York: Penguin, 1967; *The Book of the Courtier.* Ed. Daniel Javitch. New York: W. W. Norton & Co., 2002.

Christine de Pizan (1365–1431). *The Book of the City of Ladies.* Trans. Earl Jeffrey Richards. Foreward Marina Warner. New York: Persea Books, 1982.

———. *The Treasure of the City of Ladies.* Trans. Sarah Lawson. New York: Viking Penguin, 1985. Also trans. and introd. Charity Cannon Willard. Ed. and introd. Madeleine P. Cosman. New York: Persea Books, 1989.

Clarke, Danielle, ed. *Isabella Whitney, Mary Sidney and Aemilia Lanyer: Renaissance Women Poets.* New York: Penguin Books, 2000.

Couchman, Jane, and Ann Crabb, eds. *Women's Letters Across Europe, 1400–1700.* Aldershot and Brookfield: Ashgate Publishing Co., 2005.

Crawford, Patricia and Laura Gowing, eds. *Women's Worlds in Seventeenth-Century England: A Source Book.* London and New York: Routledge, 2000.

*"Custome Is an Idiot": Jacobean Pamphlet Literature on Women.* Ed. Susan Gushee O'Malley. Afterword Ann Rosalind Jones. Chicago and Urbana: University of Illinois Press, 2004.

Daybell, James, ed. *Early Modern Women's Letter Writing, 1450–1700.* Houndmills, England and New York: Palgrave, 2001.

De Erauso, Catalina. *Lieutenant Nun: Memoir of a Basque Transvestite in the New World.* Trans. Michele Ttepto and Gabriel Stepto; foreword by Marjorie Garber. Boston: Beacon Press, 1995.

*Elizabeth I: Collected Works.* Ed. Leah S. Marcus, Janel Mueller, and Mary Beth Rose. Chicago: University of Chicago Press, 2000.

Elyot, Thomas (1490–1546). *Defence of Good Women: The Feminist Controversy of the Renaissance.* Facsimile Reproductions. Ed. Diane Bornstein. New York: Delmar, 1980.

Erasmus, Desiderius (1467–1536). *Erasmus on Women.* Ed. Erika Rummel. Toronto: University of Toronto Press, 1996.

*Female and Male Voices in Early Modern England: An Anthology of Renaissance Writing.* Ed. Betty S. Travitsky and Anne Lake Prescott. New York: Columbia University Press, 2000.

Ferguson, Moira, ed. *First Feminists: British Women Writers 1578–1799.* Bloomington, IN: Indiana University Press, 1985.

Galilei, Maria Celeste. *Sister Maria Celeste's Letters to her father, Galileo.* Ed. and trans. Rinaldina Russell. Lincoln, NE, and New York: Writers Club Press of Universe.com, 2000; *To Father: The Letters of Sister Maria Celeste to Galileo, 1623–1633.* Trans. Dava Sobel. London: Fourth Estate, 2001.

Gethner, Perry, ed. *The Lunatic Lover and Other Plays by French Women of the 17th and 18th Centuries.* Portsmouth, NH: Heinemann, 1994.

Glückel of Hameln (1646–1724). *The Memoirs of Glückel of Hameln.* Trans. Marvin Lowenthal. New Introd. Robert Rosen. New York: Schocken Books, 1977.

Harline, Craig, ed. *The Burdens of Sister Margaret: Inside a Seventeenth-Century Convent.* Abridged ed. New Haven: Yale University Press, 2000.

Henderson, Katherine Usher, and Barbara F. McManus, eds. *Half Humankind: Contexts and Texts of the Controversy about Women in England, 1540–1640.* Urbana: University of Illinois Press, 1985.

Hoby, Margaret. *The Private Life of an Elizabethan Lady: The Diary of Lady Margaret Hoby 1599–1605.* Phoenix Mill: Sutton Publishing, 1998.

*Humanist Educational Treatises.* Ed. and trans. Craig W. Kallendorf. The I Tatti Renaissance Library. Cambridge, MA: Harvard University Press, 2002.

Hunter, Lynette, ed. *The Letters of Dorothy Moore, 1612–64.* Aldershot and Brookfield: Ashgate Publishing Co., 2004.

Joscelin, Elizabeth. *The Mothers Legacy to her Unborn Childe.* Ed. Jean leDrew Metcalfe. Toronto: University of Toronto Press, 2000.

Kaminsky, Amy Katz, ed. *Water Lilies, Flores del agua: An Anthology of Spanish Women Writers from the Fifteenth Through the Nineteenth Century.* Minneapolis: University of Minnesota Press, 1996.

Kempe, Margery (1373–1439). *The Book of Margery Kempe.* Trans. and ed. Lynn Staley. A Norton Critical Edition. New York: W. W. Norton, 2001.

King, Margaret L., and Albert Rabil, Jr., eds. *Her Immaculate Hand: Selected Works by and about the Women Humanists of Quattrocento Italy.* Binghamton, NY: Medieval and Renaissance Texts and Studies, 1983; second revised paperback edition, 1991.

Klein, Joan Larsen, ed. *Daughters, Wives, and Widows: Writings by Men about Women and Marriage in England, 1500–1640.* Urbana, IL: University of Illinois Press, 1992.

Knox, John (1505–72). *The Political Writings of John Knox: The First Blast of the Trumpet against the Monstrous Regiment of Women and Other Selected Works.* Ed. Marvin A. Breslow. Washington: Folger Shakespeare Library, 1985.

Kors, Alan C., and Edward Peters, eds. *Witchcraft in Europe, 400–1700: A Documentary History.* Philadelphia: University of Pennsylvania Press, 2000.

Krämer, Heinrich, and Jacob Sprenger. *Malleus Maleficarum* (ca. 1487). Trans. Montague Summers. London: Pushkin Press, 1928; reprinted New York: Dover, 1971.

Larsen, Anne R., and Colette H. Winn, eds. *Writings by Pre-Revolutionary French Women: From Marie de France to Elizabeth Vigée-Le Brun.* New York and London: Garland Publishing Co., 2000.

de Lorris, William, and Jean de Meun. *The Romance of the Rose.* Trans. Charles Dahlbert. Princeton: Princeton University Press, 1971; reprinted University Press of New England, 1983.

Marcus, Leah S., Janel Mueller, and Mary Beth Rose, eds. *Elizabeth I: Collected Works.* Chicago: University of Chicago Press, 2000.

Marguerite d'Angoulême, Queen of Navarre (1492–1549). *The Heptameron.* Trans. P. A. Chilton. New York: Viking Penguin, 1984.

Mary of Agreda. *The Divine Life of the Most Holy Virgin.* Abridgment of *The Mystical City of God.* Abr. by Fr. Bonaventure Amedeo de Caesarea, M.C. Trans. from French by Abbé Joseph A. Boullan. Rockford, IL: Tan Books, 1997.

Mullan, David George. *Women's Life Writing in Early Modern Scotland: Writing the Evangelical Self, c. 1670–c. 1730.* Aldershot and Brookfield: Ashgate Publishing Co., 2003.

Myers, Kathleen A., and Amanda Powell, eds. *A Wild Country Out in the Garden: The Spiritual Journals of a Colonial Mexican Nun.* Bloomington: Indiana University Press, 1999.

Russell, Rinaldina, ed. *Sister Maria Celeste's Letters to Her Father, Galileo.* San Jose and New York: Writers Club Press, 2000.

Teresa of Avila, Saint (1515–82). *The Life of Saint Teresa of Avila by Herself.* Trans. J. M. Cohen. New York: Viking Penguin, 1957.

————. *The Collected Letters of St. Teresa of Avila. Volume One: 1546–1577*, trans. Kieran Kavanaugh. Washington, DC: Institute of Carmelite Studies, 2001.

Travitsky, Betty, ed. *The Paradise of Women: Writings by Entlishwomen of the Renaissance.* Westport, CT: Greenwood Press, 1981.

Weyer, Johann (1515–88). *Witches, Devils, and Doctors in the Renaissance: Johann Weyer, De praestigiis daemonum.* Ed. George Mora with Benjamin G. Kohl, Erik Midelfort, and Helen Bacon. Trans. John Shea. Binghamton, NY: Medieval and Renaissance Texts and Studies, 1991.

Wilson, Katharina M., ed. *Medieval Women Writers.* Athens: University of Georgia Press, 1984.

————, ed. *Women Writers of the Renaissance and Reformation.* Athens: University of Georgia Press, 1987.

————, and Frank J. Warnke, eds. *Women Writers of the Seventeenth Century.* Athens: University of Georgia Press, 1989.

Wollstonecraft, Mary. *A Vindication of the Rights of Men and a Vindication of the Rights of Women.* Ed. Sylvana Tomaselli. Cambridge: Cambridge University Press, 1995. Also *The Vindications of the Rights of Men, The Rights of Women.* Ed. D. L. Macdonald and Kathleen Scherf. Peterborough, Ontario, Canada: Broadview Press, 1997.

*Woman Defamed and Woman Defended: An Anthology of Medieval Texts.* Ed. Alcuin Blamires. Oxford: Clarendon Press, 1992.

*Women Critics 1660–1820: An Anthology.* Edited by the Folger Collective on Early Women Critics. Bloomington, IN: Indiana University Press, 1995.

*Women Writers in English 1350–1850:* 15 published through 1999 (projected 30-volume series suspended). Oxford University Press.

*Women's Letters Across Europe, 1400–1700.* Ed. Jane Couchman and Ann Crabb. Aldershot and Brookfield: Ashgate Publishing Co., 2005.

Wroth, Lady Mary. *The Countess of Montgomery's Urania.* 2 parts. Ed. Josephine A. Roberts. Tempe, AZ: MRTS, 1995, 1999.

————. *Lady Mary Wroth's "Love's Victory": The Penshurst Manuscript.* Ed. Michael G. Brennan. London: The Roxburghe Club, 1988.

————. *The Poems of Lady Mary Wroth.* Ed. Josephine A. Roberts. Baton Rouge: Louisiana State University Press, 1983.

de Zayas Maria. *The Disenchantments of Love.* Trans. H. Patsy Boyer. Albany: State University of New York Press, 1997.

————. *The Enchantments of Love: Amorous and Exemplary Novels.* Trans. H. Patsy Boyer. Berkeley: University of California Press, 1990.

## SECONDARY SOURCES

Abate, Corinne S., ed. *Privacy, Domesticity, and Women in Early Modern England.* Aldershot and Brookfield: Ashgate Publishing Co., 2003.

Ahlgren, Gillian. *Teresa of Avila and the Politics of Sanctity.* Ithaca: Cornell University Press, 1996.

Akkerman, Tjitske, and Siep Sturman, eds. *Feminist Thought in European History, 1400–2000.* London and New York: Routledge, 1997.

Allen, Sister Prudence, R.S.M. *The Concept of Woman: The Aristotelian Revolution, 750 B.C.–A.D. 1250.* Grand Rapids, MI: William B. Eerdmans Publishing Company, 1997.

————. *The Concept of Woman: Volume II: The Early Humanist Reformation, 1250–1500.* Grand Rapids, MI: William B. Eerdmans Publishing Company, 2002.

Altmann, Barbara K., and Deborah L. McGrady, eds. *Christine de Pizan: A Casebook.* New York: Routledge, 2003.

*Ambiguous Realities: Women in the Middle Ages and Renaissance.* Ed. Carole Levin and Jeanie Watson. Detroit: Wayne State University Press, 1987.

Amussen, Susan D, and Adele Seeff, eds. *Attending to Early Modern Women.* Newark: University of Delaware Press, 1998.

Andreadis, Harriette. *Sappho in Early Modern England: Female Same-Sex Literary Erotics 1550–1714.* Chicago: University of Chicago Press, 2001.

*Architecture and the Politics of Gender in Early Modern Europe.* Ed. Helen Hills. Aldershot and Brookfield: Ashgate Publishing Co., 2003.

Armon, Shifra. *Picking Wedlock: Women and the Courtship Novel in Spain.* New York: Rowman and Littlefield Publishers, Inc., 2002.

*Attending to Early Modern Women.* Ed. Susan D. Amussen and Adele Seeff. Newark: University of Delaware Press, 1998.

Backer, Anne Liot. *Precious Women.* New York: Basic Books, 1974.

Ballaster, Ros. *Seductive Forms.* New York: Oxford University Press, 1992.

Barash, Carol. *English Women's Poetry, 1649–1714: Politics, Community, and Linguistic Authority.* New York and Oxford: Oxford University Press, 1996.

Barker, Alele Marie, and Jehanne M. Gheith, eds. *A History of Women's Writing in Russia.* Cambridge: Cambridge University Press, 2002.

Battigelli, Anna. *Margaret Cavendish and the Exiles of the Mind.* Lexington: University of Kentucky Press, 1998.

Beasley, Faith. *Revising Memory: Women's Fiction and Memoirs in Seventeenth-Century France.* New Brunswick: Rutgers University Press, 1990.

————. *Salons, History, and the Creation of Seventeenth-Century France.* Aldershot and Brookfield: Ashgate Publishing Co., 2006.

Becker, Lucinda M. *Death and the Early Modern Englishwoman.* Aldershot and Brookfield: Ashgate Publishing Co., 2003.

Beilin, Elaine V. *Redeeming Eve: Women Writers of the English Renaissance.* Princeton: Princeton University Press, 1987.

Bennett, Lyn. *Women Writing of Divinest Things: Rhetoric and the Poetry of Pembroke, Wroth, and Lanyer.* Pittsburgh: Duquesne University Press, 2004.

Benson, Pamela Joseph. *The Invention of Renaissance Woman: The Challenge of Female Independence in the Literature and Thought of Italy and England.* University Park: Pennsylvania State University Press, 1992.

———— and Victoria Kirkham, eds. *Strong Voices, Weak History? Medieval and Renaissance Women in their Literary Canons: England, France, Italy.* Ann Arbor: University of Michigan Press, 2003.

Berry, Helen. *Gender, Society and Print Culture in Late-Stuart England.* Aldershot and Brookfield: Ashgate Publishing Co., 2003.

*Beyond Isabella: Secular Women Patrons of Art in Renaissance Italy.* Ed. Sheryl E. Reiss and David G. Wilkins. Kirksville, MO: Turman State University Press, 2001.

*Beyond Their Sex: Learned Women of the European Past.* Ed. Patricia A. Labalme. New York: New York University Press, 1980.

Bicks, Caroline. *Midwiving Subjects in Shakespeare's England.* Aldershot and Brookfield: Ashgate Publishing Co., 2003.

Bilinkoff, Jodi. *The Avila of Saint Teresa: Religious Reform in a Sixteenth-Century City.* Ithaca: Cornell University Press, 1989.

———. *Related Lives: Confessors and Their Female Penitents, 1450–1750.* Ithaca, NY: Cornell University Press, 2005.

Bissell, R. Ward. *Artemisia Gentileschi and the Authority of Art.* University Park: Pennsylvania State University Press, 2000.

Blain, Virginia, Isobel Grundy, and Patricia Clements, eds. *The Feminist Companion to Literature in English: Women Writers from the Middle Ages to the Present.* New Haven: Yale University Press, 1990.

Blamires, Alcuin. *The Case for Women in Medieval Culture.* Oxford: Clarendon Press, 1997.

Bloch, R. Howard. *Medieval Misogyny and the Invention of Western Romantic Love.* Chicago: University of Chicago Press, 1991.

Bogucka, Maria. *Women in Early Modern Polish Society, Against the European Background.* Aldershot and Brookfield: Ashgate Publishing Co., 2004.

Bornstein, Daniel, and Roberto Rusconi, eds. *Women and Religion in Medieval and Renaissance Italy.* Trans. Margery J. Schneider. Chicago: University of Chicago Press, 1996.

Brant, Clare, and Diane Purkiss, eds. *Women, Texts and Histories, 1575–1760.* London and New York: Routledge, 1992.

Briggs, Robin. *Witches and Neighbours: The Social and Cultural Context of European Witchcraft.* New York: HarperCollins, 1995; Viking Penguin, 1996.

Brink, Jean R., ed. *Female Scholars: A Traditioin of Learned Women before 1800.* Montréal: Eden Press Women's Publications, 1980.

———, Allison Coudert, and Maryanne Cline Horowitz. *The Politics of Gender in Early Modern Europe.* Sixteenth Century Essays and Studies, 12. Kirksville, MO: Sixteenth Century Journal Publishers, 1989.

Broude, Norma, and Mary D. Garrard, eds. *The Expanding Discourse: Feminism and Art History.* New York: HarperCollins, 1992.

Brown, Judith C. *Immodest Acts: The Life of a Lesbian Nun in Renaissance Italy.* New York: Oxford University Press, 1986.

——— and Robert C. Davis, eds. *Gender and Society in Renaisance Italy.* London: Addison Wesley Longman, 1998.

Burke, Victoria E. Burke, ed. *Early Modern Women's Manuscript Writing.* Aldershot and Brookfield: Ashgate Publishing Co., 2004.

Burns, Jane E., ed. *Medieval Fabrications: Dress, Textiles, Cloth Work, and Other Cultural Imaginings.* New York: Palgrave Macmillan, 2004.

Bynum, Carolyn Walker. *Fragmentation and Redemption: Essays on Gender and the Human Body in Medieval Religion.* New York: Zone Books, 1992.

———. *Holy Feast and Holy Fast: The Religious Significance of Food to Medieval Women.* Berkeley: University of California Press, 1987.

Campbell, Julie DeLynn. "Renaissance Women Writers: The Beloved Speaks her Part." Ph.D diss., Texas A&M University, 1997.

Catling, Jo, ed. *A History of Women's Writing in Germany, Austria and Switzerland.* Cambridge: Cambridge University Press, 2000.

Cavallo, Sandra, and Lyndan Warner. *Widowhood in Medieval and Early Modern Europe.* New York: Longman, 1999.

Cavanagh, Sheila T. *Cherished Torment: The Emotional Geography of Lady Mary Wroth's Urania.* Pittsburgh: Duquesne University Press, 2001.

Cerasano, S. P., and Marion Wynne-Davies, eds. *Readings in Renaissance Women's Drama: Criticism, History, and Performance 1594–1998.* London and New York: Routledge, 1998.

Cervigni, Dino S., ed. *Women Mystic Writers. Annali d'Italianistica* 13 (1995) (entire issue).

——— and Rebecca West, eds. *Women's Voices in Italian Literature.* Special issue. *Annali d'Italianistica* 7 (1989).

Charlton, Kenneth. *Women, Religion and Education in Early Modern England.* London and New York: Routledge, 1999.

Chojnacka, Monica. *Working Women in Early Modern Venice.* Baltimore: Johns Hopkins University Press, 2001.

Chojnacki, Stanley. *Women and Men in Renaissance Venice: Twelve Essays on Patrician Society.* Baltimore: Johns Hopkins University Press, 2000.

Cholakian, Patricia Francis. *Rape and Writing in the* Heptameron *of Marguerite de Navarre.* Carbondale and Edwardsville: Southern Illinois University Press, 1991.

———. *Women and the Politics of Self-Representation in Seventeenth-Century France.* Newark: University of Delaware Press, 2000.

*Christine de Pizan: A Casebook.* Ed. Barbara K. Altmann and Deborah L. McGrady. New York: Routledge, 2003.

Clogan, Paul Maruice, ed. *Medievali et Humanistica: Literacy and the Lay Reader.* Lanham, MD: Rowman & Littlefield, 2000.

Clubb, Louise George (1989). *Italian Drama in Shakespeare's Time.* New Haven: Yale University Press

Clucas, Stephen, ed. *A Princely Brave Woman: Essays on Margaret Cavendish, Duchess of Newcastle.* Aldershot and Brookfield: Ashgate Publishing Co., 2003.

Conley, John J., S.J. *The Suspicion of Virtue: Women Philosophers in Neoclassical France.* Ithaca, NY: Cornell University Press, 2002.

Crabb, Ann. *The Strozzi of Florence: Widowhood and Family Solidarity in the Renaissance.* Ann Arbor: University of Michigan Press, 2000.

*The Crannied Wall: Women, Religion, and the Arts in Early Modern Europe.* Ed. Craig A. Monson. Ann Arbor: University of Michigan Press, 1992.

*Creative Women in Medieval and Early Modern Italy.* Ed. E. Ann Matter and John Coakley. Philadelphia: University of Pennsylvania Press, 1994.

Crowston, Clare Haru. *Fabricating Women: The Seamstresses of Old Regime France, 1675–1791.* Durham, NC: Duke University Press, 2001.

Cruz, Anne J. and Mary Elizabeth Perry, eds. *Culture and Control in Counter-Reformation Spain.* Minneapolis: University of Minnesota Press, 1992.

Datta, Satya. *Women and Men in Early Modern Venice.* Aldershot and Brookfield: Ashgate Publishing Co., 2003.

Davis, Natalie Zemon. *Society and Culture in Early Modern France.* Stanford: Stanford University Press, 1975.

————. *Women on the Margins: Three Seventeenth-Century Lives.* Cambridge, MA: Harvard University Press, 1995.

DeJean, Joan. *Ancients against Moderns: Culture Wars and the Making of a Fin de Siècle.* Chicago: University of Chicago Press, 1997.

————. *Fictions of Sappho, 1546–1937.* Chicago: University of Chicago Press, 1989.

————. *The Reinvention of Obscenity: Sex, Lies, and Tabloids in Early Modern France.* Chicago: University of Chicago Press, 2002.

————. *Tender Geographies: Women and the Origins of the Novel in France.* New York: Columbia University Press, 1991.

D'Elia, Anthony F. *The Renaissance of Marriage in Fifteenth-Century Italy.* Cambridge, MA: Harvard University Press, 2004.

*Dictionary of Russian Women Writers.* Ed. Marina Ledkovsky, Charlotte Rosenthal, and Mary Zirin. Westport, CT: Greenwood Press, 1994.

Dixon, Laurinda S. *Perilous Chastity: Women and Illness in Pre-Enlightenment Art and Medicine.* Ithaca: Cornell University Press, 1995.

Dolan, Frances, E. *Whores of Babylon: Catholicism, Gender and Seventeenth-Century Print Culture.* Ithaca: Cornell University Press, 1999.

Donovan, Josephine. *Women and the Rise of the Novel, 1405–1726.* New York: St. Martin's Press, 1999.

*Early [English] Women Writers: 1600–1720.* Ed. Anita Pacheco. New York and London: Longman, 1998.

Eigler, Friederike and Susanne Kord, eds. *The Feminist Encyclopedia of German Literature.* Westport, CT: Greenwood Press, 1997.

*Engendering the Early Modern Stage: Women Playwrights in the Spanish Empire.* Ed. Valeria (Oakey) Hegstrom and Amy R. Williamsen. New Orleans: University Press of the South, 1999.

Erdmann, Axel. *My Gracious Silence: Women in the Mirror of Sixteenth-Century Printing in Western Europe.* Luzern: Gilhofer and Rauschberg, 1999.

Erickson, Amy Louise. *Women and Property in Early Modern England.* London and New York: Routledge, 1993.

*Extraordinary Women of the Medieval and Renaissance World: A Biographical Dictionary.* Ed. Carole Levin, et al. Westport, CT: Greenwood Press, 2000.

Ezell, Margaret J. M. *The Patriarch's Wife: Literary Evidence and the History of the Family.* Chapel Hill: University of North Carolina Press, 1987.

————. *Social Authorship and the Advent of Print.* Baltimore: Johns Hopkins University Press, 1999.

————. *Writing Women's Literary History.* Baltimore: Johns Hopkins University Press, 1993.

Farrell, Michèle Longino. *Performing Motherhood: The Sévigné Correspondence.* Hanover, NH and London: University Press of New England, 1991.

*Feminism and Renaissance Studies.* Ed. Lorna Hutson. New York: Oxford University Press, 1999.

*The Feminist Companion to Literature in English: Women Writers from the Middle Ages to the Present.* Ed. Virginia Blain, Isobel Grundy, and Patricia Clements. New Haven: Yale University Press, 1990.

*Feminist Encyclopedia of Italian Literature.* Edited by Rinaldina Russell. Westport, CT: Greenwood Press, 1997.

*Feminist Thought in European History, 1400–2000.* Ed. Tjitske Akkerman and Siep Sturman. London and New York: Routledge, 1997.

Ferguson, Margaret W. *Dido's Daughters: Literacy, Gender, and Empire in Early Modern England and France.* Chicago: University of Chicago Press, 2003.

———, Maureen Quilligan, and Nancy J. Vickers, eds. *Rewriting the Renaissance: The Discourses of Sexual Difference in Early Modern Europe.* Chicago: University of Chicago Press, 1987.

Ferraro, Joanne M. *Marriage Wars in Late Renaissance Venice.* Oxford: Oxford University Press, 2001.

Fletcher, Anthony. *Gender, Sex and Subordination in England 1500–1800.* New Haven: Yale University Press, 1995.

Franklin, Margaret. *Boccaccio's Heroines.* Aldershot and Brookfield: Ashgate Publishing Co., 2006.

*French Women Writers: A Bio-Bibliographical Source Book.* Ed. Eva Martin Sartori and Dorothy Wynne Zimmerman. Westport, CT: Greenwood Press, 1991.

Frye, Susan and Karen Robertson, eds. *Maids and Mistresses, Cousins and Queens: Women's Alliances in Early Modern England.* Oxford: Oxford University Press, 1999.

Gallagher, Catherine. *Nobody's Story: The Vanishing Acts of Women Writers in the Marketplace, 1670–1820.* Berkeley: University of California Press, 1994.

Garrard, Mary D. *Artemisia Gentileschi: The Image of the Female Hero in Italian Baroque Art.* Princeton: Princeton University Press, 1989.

Gelbart, Nina Rattner. *The King's Midwife: A History and Mystery of Madame du Coudray.* Berkeley: University of California Press, 1998.

Giles, Mary E., ed. *Women in the Inquisition: Spain and the New World.* Baltimore: Johns Hopkins University Press, 1999.

Gill, Catie. *Somen in the Seventeenth-Century Quaker Community.* Aldershot and Brookfield: Ashgate Publishing Co., 2005.

Glenn, Cheryl. *Rhetoric Retold: Regendering the Tradition from Antiquity Through the Renaissance.* Carbondale and Edwardsville, IL: Southern Illinois University Press, 1997.

Goffen, Rona. *Titian's Women.* New Haven: Yale University Press, 1997.

*Going Public: Women and Publishing in Early Modern France.* Ed. Elizabeth C. Goldsmith and Dena Goodman. Ithaca: Cornell University Press, 1995.

Goldberg, Jonathan. *Desiring Women Writing: English Renaissance Examples.* Stanford: Stanford University Press, 1997.

Goldsmith, Elizabeth C. *Exclusive Conversations: The Art of Interaction in Seventeenth-Century France.* Philadelphia: University of Pennsylvania Press, 1988.

———, ed. *Writing the Female Voice.* Boston: Northeastern University Press, 1989.

——— and Dena Goodman, eds. *Going Public: Women and Publishing in Early Modern France.* Ithaca: Cornell University Press, 1995.

Grafton, Anthony, and Lisa Jardine. *From Humanism to the Humanities: Education and the Liberal Arts in Fifteenth- and Sixteenth-Century Europe.* London: Duckworth, 1986.

*The Graph of Sex and the German Text: Gendered Culture in Early Modern Germany 1500–1700.* Ed. Lynne Tatlock and Christiane Bohnert. Amsterdam and Atlanta: Rodolphi, 1994.

Grassby, Richard. *Kinship and Capitalism: Marriage, Family, and Business in the English-Speaking World, 1580–1740.* Cambridge: Cambridge University Press, 2001.

Greer, Margaret Rich. *Maria de Zayas Tells Baroque Tales of Love and the Cruelty of Men.* University Park: Pennsylvania State University Press, 2000.

Grossman, Avraham. *Pious and Rebellious: Jewish Women in Medieval Europe.* Trans. Jonathan Chipman. Brandeis/University Press of New England, 2004.

Gutierrez, Nancy A. *"Shall She Famish Then?" Female Food Refusal in Early Modern England.* Aldershot and Brookfield: Ashgate Publishing Co., 2003.

Habermann, Ina. *Staging Slander and Gender in Early Modern England.* Aldershot and Brookfield: Ashgate Publishing Co., 2003.

Hacke, Daniela. *Women Sex and Marriage in Early Modern Venice.* Aldershot and Brookfield: Ashgate Publishing Co., 2004.

Hackel, Heidi Brayman. *Reading Material in Early Modern England: Print, Gender, Literacy.* Cambridge: Cambridge University Press, 2005.

Hackett, Helen. *Women and Romance Fiction in the English Renaissance.* Cambridge: Cambridge University Press, 2000.

Hall, Kim F. *Things of Darkness: Economies of Race and Gender in Early Modern England.* Ithaca, NY: Cornell University Press, 1995.

Hamburger, Jeffrey. *The Visual and the Visionary: Art and Female Spirituality in Late Medieval Germany.* New York: Zone Books, 1998.

Hampton, Timothy. *Literature and the Nation in the Sixteenth Century: Inventing Renaissance France.* Ithaca, NY: Cornell University Press, 2001.

Hannay, Margaret, ed. *Silent But for the Word.* Kent, OH: Kent State University Press, 1985.

Hardwick, Julie. *The Practice of Patriarchy: Gender and the Politics of Household Authority in Early Modern France.* University Park: Pennsylvania State University Press, 1998.

Harris, Barbara J. *English Aristocratic Women, 1450–1550: Marriage and Family, Property and Careers.* New York: Oxford University Press, 2002.

Harth, Erica. *Ideology and Culture in Seventeenth-Century France.* Ithaca: Cornell University Press, 1983.

———. *Cartesian Women. Versions and Subversions of Rational Discourse in the Old Regime.* Ithaca: Cornell University Press, 1992.

Harvey, Elizabeth D. *Ventriloquized Voices: Feminist Theory and English Renaissance Texts.* London and New York: Routledge, 1992.

Haselkorn, Anne M., and Betty Travitsky, eds. *The Renaissance Englishwoman in Print: Counterbalancing the Canon.* Amherst: University of Massachusetts Press, 1990.

Hawkesworth, Celia, ed. *A History of Central European Women's Writing.* New York: Palgrave Press, 2001.

Hegstrom (Oakey), Valerie, and Amy R. Williamsen, eds. *Engendering the Early Modern Stage: Women Playwrights in the Spanish Empire.* New Orleans: University Press of the South, 1999.

Hendricks, Margo, and Patricia Parker, eds. *Women, "Race," and Writing in the Early Modern Period.* London and New York: Routledge, 1994.

Herlihy, David. *"Did Women Have a Renaissance? A Reconsideration." Medievalia et Humanistica* 13 n.s. (1985): 1–22.

Hill, Bridget. *The Republican Virago: The Life and Times of Catharine Macaulay, Historian.* New York: Oxford University Press, 1992.

Hills, Helen, ed. *Architecture and the Politics of Gender in Early Modern Europe.* Aldershot and Brookfield: Ashgate Publishing Co., 2003.

*A History of Central European Women's Writing.* Ed. Celia Hawkesworth. New York: Palgrave Press, 2001.

*A History of Women in the West.*
Volume 1: *From Ancient Goddesses to Christian Saints.* Ed. Pauline Schmitt Pantel. Cambridge, MA: Harvard University Press, 1992.
Volume 2: *Silences of the Middle Ages.* Ed. Christiane Klapisch-Zuber. Cambridge, MA: Harvard University Press, 1992.
Volume 3: *Renaissance and Enlightenment Paradoxes.* Ed. Natalie Zemon Davis and Arlette Farge. Cambridge, MA: Harvard University Press, 1993.

*A History of Women Philosophers.* Ed. Mary Ellen Waithe. 3 vols. Dordrecht: Martinus Nijhoff, 1987.

*A History of Women's Writing in France.* Ed. Sonya Stephens. Cambridge: Cambridge University Press, 2000.

*A History of Women's Writing in Germany, Austria and Switzerland.* Ed. Jo Catling. Cambridge: Cambridge University Press, 2000.

*A History of Women's Writing in Italy.* Ed. Letizia Panizza and Sharon Wood. Cambridge: University Press, 2000.

*A History of Women's Writing in Russia.* Edited by Alele Marie Barker and Jehanne M. Gheith. Cambridge: Cambridge University Press, 2002.

Hobby, Elaine. *Virtue of Necessity: English Women's Writing, 1646–1688.* London: Virago Press, 1988.

Horowitz, Maryanne Cline. "Aristotle and Women." *Journal of the History of Biology* 9 (1976): 183–213.

Howell, Martha. *The Marriage Exchange: Property, Social Place, and Gender in Cities of the Low Countries, 1300–1550.* Chicago: University of Chicago Press, 1998.

Hufton, Olwen H. *The Prospect before Her: A History of Women in Western Europe, 1: 1500–1800.* New York: HarperCollins, 1996.

Hull, Suzanne W. *Chaste, Silent, and Obedient: English Books for Women, 1475–1640.* San Marino, CA: Huntington Library, 1982.

Hunt, Lynn, ed. *The Invention of Pornography: Obscenity and the Origins of Modernity, 1500–1800.* New York: Zone Books, 1996.

Hutner, Heidi, ed. *Rereading Aphra Behn: History, Theory, and Criticism.* Charlottesville: University Press of Virginia, 1993.

Hutson, Lorna, ed. *Feminism and Renaissance Studies.* New York: Oxford University Press, 1999.

*The Invention of Pornography: Obscenity and the Origins of Modernity, 1500–1800.* Ed. Lynn Hunt. New York: Zone Books, 1996.

*Italian Women Writers: A Bio-Bibliographical Sourcebook.* Edited by Rinaldina Russell. Westport, CT: Greenwood Press, 1994.

Jaffe, Irma B., with Gernando Colombardo. *Shining Eyes, Cruel Fortune: The Lives and Loves of Italian Renaissance Women Poets.* New York: Fordham University Press, 2002.

James, Susan E. *Kateryn Parr: The Making of a Queen.* Aldershot and Brookfield: Ashgate Publishing Co., 1999.

Jankowski, Theodora A. *Women in Power in the Early Modern Drama.* Urbana, IL: University of Illinois Press, 1992.

Jansen, Katherine Ludwig. *The Making of the Magdalen: Preaching and Popular Devotion in the Later Middle Ages.* Princeton: Princeton University Press, 2000.

Jed, Stephanie H. *Chaste Thinking: The Rape of Lucretia and the Birth of Humanism.* Bloomington: Indiana University Press, 1989.

Jones, Ann Rosalind and Peter Stallybrass. *Renaissance Clothing and the Materials of Memory.* Cambridge: Cambridge University Press, 2000.

Jordan, Constance. *Renaissance Feminism: Literary Texts and Political Models.* Ithaca: Cornell University Press, 1990.

Kagan, Richard L. *Lucrecia's Dreams: Politics and Prophecy in Sixteenth-Century Spain.* Berkeley: University of California Press, 1990.

Kehler, Dorothea and Laurel Amtower, eds. *The Single Woman in Medieval and Early Modern England: Her Life and Representation.* Tempe, AZ: MRTS, 2002.

Kelly, Joan. "Did Women Have a Renaissance?" In her *Women, History, and Theory.* Chicago: University of Chicago Press, 1984. Also in Renate Bridenthal, Claudia Koonz, and Susan M. Stuard, eds., *Becoming Visible: Women in European History.* Third edition. Boston: Houghton Mifflin, 1998.

———. "Early Feminist Theory and the *Querelle des Femmes.*" In *Women, History, and Theory.*

Kelso, Ruth. *Doctrine for the Lady of the Renaissance.* Foreword by Katharine M. Rogers. Urbana: University of Illinois Press, 1956, 1978.

Kendrick, Robert L. *Celestical Sirens: Nuns and their Music in Early Modern Milan.* New York: Oxford University Press, 1996.

Kermode, Jenny, and Garthine Walker, eds. *Women, Crime and the Courts in Early Modern England.* Chapel Hill: University of North Carolina Press, 1994.

King, Catherine E. *Renaissance Women Patrons: Wives and Widows in Italy, c. 1300–1550.* New York and Manchester: Manchester University Press (distributed in the U.S. by St. Martin's Press), 1998.

King, Margaret L. *Women of the Renaissance.* Foreword by Catharine R. Stimpson. Chicago: University of Chicago Press, 1991.

Krontiris, Tina. *Oppositional Voices: Women as Writers and Translators of Literature in the English Renaissance.* London and New York: Routledge, 1992.

Kuehn, Thomas. *Law, Family, and Women: Toward a Legal Anthropology of Renaissance Italy.* Chicago: University of Chicago Press, 1991.

Kunze, Bonnelyn Young. *Margaret Fell and the Rise of Quakerism.* Stanford: Stanford University Press, 1994.

Labalme, Patricia A., ed. *Beyond Their Sex: Learned Women of the European Past.* New York: New York University Press, 1980.

Lalande, Roxanne Decker, ed. *A Labor of Love: Critical Reflections on the Writings of Marie-Catherine Desjardina (Mme de Villedieu).* Madison, NJ: Fairleigh Dickinson University Press, 2000.

Lamb, Mary Ellen. *Gender and Authorship in the Sidney Circle.* Madison: University of Wisconsin Press, 1990.

Laqueur, Thomas. *Making Sex: Body and Gender from the Greeks to Freud.* Cambridge, MA: Harvard University Press, 1990.

Larsen, Anne R., and Colette H. Winn, eds. *Renaissance Women Writers: French Texts/American Contexts.* Detroit, MI: Wayne State University Press, 1994.

Laven, Mary. *Virgins of Venice: Enclosed Lives and Broken Vows in the Renaissance Convent.* London: Viking, 2002.

Ledkovsky, Marina, Charlotte Rosenthal, and Mary Zirin, eds. *Dictionary of Russian Women Writers.* Westport, CT: Greenwood Press, 1994.

Lehfeldt, Elizabeth A. *Religious Women in Golden Age Spain: The Permeable Cloister.* Aldershot and Brookfield: Ashgate Publishing Co., 2005.

Lerner, Gerda. *The Creation of Patriarchy and Creation of Feminist Consciousness, 1000–1870.* Two vols. New York: Oxford University Press, 1986, 1994.

Levack. Brian P. *The Witch Hunt in Early Modern Europe.* London: Longman, 1987.

Levin, Carole, and Jeanie Watson, eds. *Ambiguous Realities: Women in the Middle Ages and Renaissance.* Detroit: Wayne State University Press, 1987.

Levin, Carole, Jo Eldridge Carney, and Debra Barrett-Graves. *Elizabeth I: Always Her Own Free Woman.* Aldershot and Brookfield: Ashgate Publishing Co., 2003.

Levin, Carole, et al. *Extraordinary Women of the Medieval and Renaissance World: A Biographical Dictionary.* Westport, CT: Greenwood Press, 2000.

Levy, Allison, ed. *Widowhood and Visual Culture in Early Modern Europe.* Aldershot and Brookfield: Ashgate Publishing Co., 2003.

Lewalsky, Barbara Kiefer. *Writing Women in Jacobean England.* Cambridge, MA: Harvard University Press, 1993.

Lewis, Gertrud Jaron. *By Women for Women about Women: The Sister-Books of Fourteenth-Century Germany.* Toronto: University of Toronto Press, 1996.

Lewis, Jayne Elizabeth. *Mary Queen of Scots: Romance and Nation.* London: Routledge, 1998.

Lindenauer, Leslie J. *Piety and Power: Gender and Religious Culture in the American Colonies, 1630–1700.* London and New York: Routledge, 2002.

Lindsey, Karen. *Divorced Beheaded Survived: A Feminist Reinterpretation of the Wives of Henry VIII.* Reading, MA: Addison-Wesley Publishing Co., 1995.

Lochrie, Karma. *Margery Kempe and Translations of the Flesh.* Philadelphia: University of Pennsylvania Press, 1992.

Longino Farrell, Michèle. *Performing Motherhood: The Sévigné Correspondence.* Hanover, NH: University Press of New England, 1991.

Lougee, Carolyn C. *Le Paradis des Femmes: Women, Salons, and Social Stratification in Seventeenth-Century France.* Princeton: Princeton University Press, 1976.

Love, Harold. *The Culture and Commerce of Texts: Scribal Publication in Seventeenth-Century England.* Amherst: University of Massachusetts Press, 1993.

Lowe, K. J. P. *Nuns' Chronicles and Convent Culture in Renaissance and Counter-Reformation Italy.* Cambridge: Cambridge University Press, 2003.

Lux-Sterritt, Laurence. *Redefining Female Religious Life: French Ursulines and English Ladies in Seventeenth-Century Catholicism.* Aldershot and Brookfield: Ashgate Publishing Co., 2005.

MacCarthy, Bridget G. *The Female Pen: Women Writers and Novelists 1621–1818.* Preface by Janet Todd. New York: New York University Press, 1994. (Originally published by Cork University Press, 1946–47).

Mack, Phyllis. *Visionary Women: Ecstatic Prophecy in Seventeenth-Century England.* Berkeley: University of California Pres, 1992.

Maclean, Ian. *Woman Triumphant: Feminism in French Literature, 1610–1652.* Oxford: Clarendon Press, 1977.

———. *The Renaissance Notion of Woman: A Study of the Fortunes of Scholasticism and Medical Science in European Intellectual Life.* Cambridge: Cambridge University Press, 1980.

MacNeil, Anne. *Music and Women of the Commedia dell'Arte in the Late Sixteenth Century.* New York: Oxford University Press, 2003.

Maggi, Armando. *Uttering the Word: The Mystical Performances of Maria Maddalena de' Pazzi, a Renaissance Visionary.* Albany: State University of New York Press, 1998.

*Maids and Mistresses, Cousins and Queens: Women's Alliances in Early Modern England.* Ed. Susan Frye and Karen Robertson. Oxford: Oxford University Press, 1999.

Marshall, Sherrin, ed. *Women in Reformation and Counter-Reformation Europe: Public and Private Worlds.* Bloomington: Indiana University Press, 1989.

Masten, Jeffrey. *Textual Intercourse: Collaboration, Authorship, and Sexualities in Renaissance Drama.* Cambridge: Cambridge University Press, 1997.

Matter, E. Ann, and John Coakley, eds. *Creative Women in Medieval and Early Modern Italy.* Philadelphia: University of Pennsylvania Press, 1994.

McGrath, Lynette. *Subjectivity and Women's Poetry in Early Modern England.* Aldershot and Brookfield: Ashgate Publishing Co., 2002.

McIver, Katherine A. *Women, Art, and Architecture in Northern Italy, 1520–1580.* Aldershot and Brookfield: Ashgate Publishing Co., 2006.

McLeod, Glenda. *Virtue and Venom: Catalogs of Women from Antiquity to the Renaissance.* Ann Arbor: University of Michigan Press, 1991.

McTavish, Lianne. *Childbirth and the Display of Authority in Early Modern France.* Aldershot and Brookfield: Ashgate Publishing Co., 2005.

*Medieval Women's Visionary Literature.* Ed. Elizabeth A. Petroff. New York: Oxford University Press, 1986.

Medwick, Cathleen. *Teresa of Avila: The Progress of a Soul.* New York: Doubleday, 1999.

Meek, Christine, ed. *Women in Renaissance and Early Modern Europe.* Dublin and Portland: Four Courts Press, 2000.

Mendelson, Sara, and Patricia Crawford. *Women in Early Modern England, 1550–1720.* Oxford: Clarendon Press, 1998.

Merchant, Carolyn. *The Death of Nature: Women, Ecology and the Scientific Revolution.* New York: HarperCollins, 1980.

Merrim, Stephanie. *Early Modern Women's Writing and Sor Juana Inés de la Cruz.* Nashville, TN: Vanderbilt University Press, 1999.

Messbarger, Rebecca. *The Century of Women: The Representations of Women in Eighteenth-Century Italian Public Discourse.* Toronto: University of Toronto Press, 2002.

Miller, Nancy K. *The Heroine's Text: Readings in the French and English Novel, 1722–1782.* New York: Columbia University Press, 1980.

Miller, Naomi J. *Changing the Subject: Mary Wroth and Figurations of Gender in Early Modern England.* Lexington: University Press of Kentucky, 1996.

——— and Gary Waller, eds. *Reading Mary Wroth: Representing Alternatives in Early Modern England.* Knoxville: University of Tennessee Press, 1991.

Monson, Craig A. *Disembodied Voices: Music and Culture in an Early Modern Italian Convent.* Berkeley: University of California Press, 1995.

———., ed. *The Crannied Wall: Women, Religion, and the Arts in Early Modern Europe.* Ann Arbor: University of Michigan Press, 1992.

Moore, Cornelia Niekus. *The Maiden's Mirror: Reading Material for German Girls in the Sixteenth and Seventeenth Centuries.* Wiesbaden: Otto Harrassowitz, 1987.

Moore, Mary B. *Desiring Voices: Women Sonneteers and Petrarchism.* Carbondale: Southern Illinois University Press, 2000.

Mujica, Bárbara. *Women Writers of Early Modern Spain.* New Haven: Yale University Press, 2004.

Musacchio, Jacqueline Marie. *The Art and Ritual of Childbirth in Renaissance Italy.* New Haven: Yale University Press, 1999.

Newman, Barbara. *God and the Goddesses: Vision, Poetry, and Belief in the Middle Ages.* Philadelphia: University of Pennsylvania Press, 2003.

Newman, Karen. *Fashioning Femininity and English Renaissance Drama.* Chicago: University of Chicago Press, 1991.

O'Donnell, Mary Ann. *Aphra Behn: An Annotated Bibliography of Primary and Secondary Sources.* Aldershot and Brookfield: Ashgate Publishing Co., 2nd ed., 2004.

Okin, Susan Moller. *Women in Western Political Thought.* Princeton: Princeton University Press, 1979.

Ozment, Steven. *The Bürgermeister's Daughter: Scandal in a Sixteenth-Century German Town.* New York: St. Martin's Press, 1995.

———. *Flesh and Spirit: Private Life in Early Modern Germany.* New York: Penguin Putnam, 1999.

———. *When Fathers Ruled: Family Life in Reformation Europe.* Cambridge, MA: Harvard University Press, 1983.

Pacheco, Anita, ed. *Early [English] Women Writers: 1600–1720.* New York and London: Longman, 1998.

Pagels, Elaine. *Adam, Eve, and the Serpent.* New York: Harper Collins, 1988.

Panizza, Letizia, and Sharon Wood, eds. *A History of Women's Writing in Italy.* Cambridge: University Press, 2000.

Panizza, Letizia, ed. *Women in Italian Renaissance Culture and Society.* Oxford: European Humanities Research Centre, 2000.

Parker, Patricia. *Literary Fat Ladies: Rhetoric, Gender and Property.* London and New York: Methuen, 1987.

Pernoud, Regine, and Marie-Veronique Clin. *Joan of Arc: Her Story.* Rev. and trans. Jeremy DuQuesnay Adams. New York: St. Martin's Press, 1998.

Perry, Mary Elizabeth. *Crime and Society in Early Modern Seville.* Hanover, NH: University Press of New England, 1980.

———. *Gender and Disorder in Early Modern Seville.* Princeton: Princeton University Press, 1990.

———. *The Handless Maiden: Moriscos and the Politics of Religion in Early Modern Spain.* Princeton: Princeton University Press, 2005.

Petroff, Elizabeth A., ed. *Medieval Women's Visionary Literature.* New York: Oxford University Press, 1986.

Perry, Ruth. *The Celebrated Mary Astell: An Early English Feminist.* Chicago: University of Chicago Press, 1986.

*The Practice and Representation of Reading in England.* Ed. James Raven, Helen Small, and Naomi Tadmor. Cambridge: University Press, 1996.

Quilligan, Maureen. *Incest and Agency in Elizabeth's England.* Philadelphia: University of Pennsylvania Press, 2005.

Rabil, Albert. *Laura Cereta: Quattrocento Humanist.* Binghamton, NY: MRTS, 1981.

Ranft, Patricia. *Women in Western Intellectual Culture, 600–1500.* New York: Palgrave, 2002.

Rapley, Elizabeth. *A Social History of the Cloister: Daily Life in the Teaching Monasteries of the Old Regime.* Montreal: McGill-Queen's University Press, 2001.

———. *The Devotés: Women and Church in Seventeenth-Century France.* Kingston, Ontario: McGill-Queen's University Press, 1989.

Raven, James, Helen Small, and Naomi Tadmor, eds. *The Practice and Representation of Reading in England.* Cambridge: University Press, 1996.

*Reading Mary Wroth: Representing Alternatives in Early Modern England.* Ed. Naomi Miller and Gary Waller. Knoxville: University of Tennessee Press, 1991.

Reardon, Colleen. *Holy Concord within Sacred Walls: Nuns and Music in Siena, 1575–1700.* Oxford: Oxford University Press, 2001.

*Recovering Spain's Feminist Tradition.* Ed. Lisa Vollendorf. New York: MLA, 2001.

Reid, Jonathan Andrew. "King's Sister—Queen of Dissent: Marguerite of Navarre (1492–1549) and Her Evangelical Network." Ph.D diss., University of Arizona, 2001.

Reiss, Sheryl E,. and David G. Wilkins, ed. *Beyond Isabella: Secular Women Patrons of Art in Renaissance Italy.* Kirksville, MO: Turman State University Press, 2001.

*The Renaissance Englishwoman in Print: Counterbalancing the Canon.* Ed. Anne M. Haselkorn and Betty Travitsky. Amherst: University of Massachusetts Press, 1990.

*Renaissance Women Writers: French Texts/American Contexts.* Ed. Anne R. Larsen and Colette H. Winn. Detroit, MI: Wayne State University Press, 1994.

*Rereading Aphra Behn: History, Theory, and Criticism.* Ed. Heidi Hutner. Charlottesville: University Press of Virginia, 1993.

Rheubottom, David. *Age, Marriage, and Politics in Fifteenth-Century Ragusa.* Oxford: Oxford University Press, 2000.

Richardson, Brian. *Printing, Writers and Readers in Renaissance Italy.* Cambridge: University Press, 1999.

Riddle, John M. *Contraception and Abortion from the Ancient World to the Renaissance.* Cambridge, MA: Harvard University Press, 1992.

———. *Eve's Herbs: A History of Contraception and Abortion in the West.* Cambridge, MA: Harvard University Press, 1997.

Roper, Lyndal. *The Holy Household: Women and Morals in Reformation Augsburg.* New York: Oxford University Press, 1989.

Rose, Mary Beth. *The Expense of Spirit: Love and Sexuality in English Renaissance Drama.* Ithaca, NY: Cornell University Press, 1988.

———. *Gender and Heroism in Early Modern English Literature.* Chicago: University of Chicago Press, 2002.

———, ed. *Women in the Middle Ages and the Renaissance: Literary and Historical Perspectives.* Syracuse: Syracuse University Press, 1986.

Rosenthal, Margaret F. *The Honest Courtesan: Veronica Franco, Citizen and Writer in Sixteenth-Century Venice.* Foreword by Catharine R. Stimpson. Chicago: University of Chicago Press, 1992.

Rublack, Ulinka, ed. *Gender in Early Modern German History.* Cambridge: Cambridge University Press, 2002.

Russell, Rinaldina, ed. *Feminist Encyclopedia of Italian Literature.* Westport, CT: Greenwood Press, 1997.

———. *Italian Women Writers: A Bio-Bibliographical Sourcebook.* Westport, CT: Greenwood Press, 1994.

Sackville-West, Vita. *Daughter of France: The Life of La Grande Mademoiselle.* Garden City, NY: Doubleday, 1959.

Sage, Lorna, ed. *Cambridge Guide to Women's Writing in English.* Cambridge: University Press, 1999.

Sánchez, Magdalena S. *The Empress, the Queen, and the Nun: Women and Power at the Court of Philip III of Spain*. Baltimore: Johns Hopkins University Press, 1998.

Sartori, Eva Martin, and Dorothy Wynne Zimmerman, eds. *French Women Writers: A Bio-Bibliographical Source Book*. Westport, CT: Greenwood Press, 1991.

Scaraffia, Lucetta, and Gabriella Zarri. *Women and Faith: Catholic Religious Life in Italy from Late Antiquity to the Present*. Cambridge, MA: Harvard University Press, 1999.

Scheepsma, Wybren. *Medieval Religious Women in the Low Countries: The 'Modern Devotion', the Canonesses of Windesheim, and Their Writings*. Rochester, NY: Boydell Press, 2004.

Schiebinger, Londa. *The Mind has no sex?: Women in the Origins of Modern Science*. Cambridge, MA: Harvard University Press, 1991.

———. *Nature's Body: Gender in the Making of Modern Science*. Boston: Beacon Press, 1993.

Schutte, Anne Jacobson, Thomas Kuehn, and Silvana Seidel Menchi, eds. *Time, Space, and Women's Lives in Early Modern Europe*. Kirksville, MO: Truman State University Press, 2001.

Schofield, Mary Anne, and Cecilia Macheski, eds. *Fetter'd or Free? British Women Novelists, 1670–1815*. Athens: Ohio University Press, 1986.

Schutte, Anne Jacobson. *Aspiring Saints: pretense of Holiness, Inquisition, and Gender in the Republic of Venice, 1618–1750*. Baltimore: Johns Hopkins University Press, 2001.

———, Thomas Kuehn, and Silvana Seidel Menchi, eds. *Time, Space, and Women's Lives in Early Modern Europe*. Kirksville, MO: Truman State University Press, 2001.

Seifert, Lewis C. *Fairy Tales, Sexuality and Gender in France 1690–1715: Nostalgic Utopias*. Cambridge, UK: Cambridge University Press, 1996.

Shannon, Laurie. *Sovereign Amity: Figures of Friendship in Shakespearean Contexts*. Chicago: University of Chicago Press, 2002.

Shemek, Deanna. *Ladies Errant: Wayward Women and Social Order in Early Modern Italy*. Durham, NC: Duke University Press, 1998.

*Silent But for the Word*. Ed. Margaret Hannay. Kent, OH: Kent State University Press, 1985.

*The Single Woman in Medieval and Early Modern England: Her Life and Representation*. Ed. Dorothea Kehler and Laurel Amtower. Tempe, AZ: MRTS, 2002.

Smarr, Janet L. *Joining the Conversation: Dialogues by Renaissance Women*. Ann Arbor: University of Michigan Press, 2005.

Smith, Hilda L. *Reason's Disciples: Seventeenth-Century English Feminists*. Urbana: University of Illinois Press, 1982.

———. *Women Writers and the Early Modern British Political Tradition*. Cambridge: Cambridge University Press, 1998.

Snook, Edith. *Women, Reading, and the Cultural Politics of Early Modern England*. Aldershot and Brookfield: Ashgate Publishing Co., 2005.

Sobel, Dava. *Galileo's Daughter: A Historical Memoir of Science, Faith, and Love*. New York: Penguin Books, 2000.

Sommerville, Margaret R. *Sex and Subjection: Attitudes to Women in Early-Modern Society*. London: Arnold, 1995.

Soufas, Teresa Scott. *Dramas of Distinction: A Study of Plays by Golden Age Women*. Lexington: The University Press of Kentucky, 1997.

Spencer, Jane. *The Rise of the Woman Novelist: From Aphra Behn to Jane Austen*. Oxford: Basil Blackwell, 1986.

Spender, Dale. *Mothers of the Novel: 100 Good Women Writers Before Jane Austen.* London and New York: Routledge, 1986.

Sperling, Jutta Gisela. *Convents and the Body Politic in Late Renaissance Venice.* Foreword by Catharine R. Stimpson. Chicago: University of Chicago Press, 1999.

Steinbrügge, Lieselotte. *The Moral Sex: Woman's Nature in the French Enlightenment.* Trans. Pamela E. Selwyn. New York: Oxford University Press, 1995.

Stephens, Sonya, ed. *A History of Women's Writing in France.* Cambridge: Cambridge University Press, 2000.

Stephenson, Barbara. *The Power and Patronage of Marguerite de Navarre.* Aldershot and Brookfield: Ashgate Publishing Co., 2004.

Stocker, Margarita. *Judith, Sexual Warrior: Women and Power in Western Culture.* New Haven: Yale University Press, 1998.

Straznacky, Marta. *Privacy, Playreading, and Women's Closet Drama, 1550–1700.* Cambridge: Cambridge University Press, 2004.

Stretton, Timothy. *Women Waging Law in Elizabethan England.* Cambridge: Cambridge University Press, 1998.

*Strong Voices, Weak History: Early Women Writers and Canons in England, France, and Italy.* Ed. Pamela J. Benson and Victoria Kirkham. Ann Arbor: University of Michigan Press, 2005.

Stuard, Susan M. "The Dominion of Gender: Women's Fortunes in the High Middle Ages." In Renate Bridenthal, Claudia Koonz, and Susan M. Stuard, eds. *Becoming Visible: Women in European History.* Third edition. Boston: Houghton Mifflin, 1998.

Summit, Jennifer. *Lost Property: The Woman Writer and English Literary History, 1380–1589.* Chicago: University of Chicago Press, 2000.

Surtz, Ronald E. *The Guitar of God: Gender, Power, and Authority in the Visionary World of Mother Juana de la Cruz (1481–1534).* Philadelphia: University of Pennsylvania Press, 1991.

———. *Writing Women in Late Medieval and Early Modern Spain: The Mothers of Saint Teresa of Avila.* Philadelphia: University of Pennsylvania Press, 1995.

Suzuki, Mihoko. *Subordinate Subjects: Gender, the Political Nation, and Literary Form in England, 1588–1688.* Aldershot and Brookfield: Ashgate Publishing Co., 2003.

Tatlock, Lynne, and Christiane Bohnert, eds. *The Graph of Sex* (q.v.).

*Teaching Tudor and Stuart Women Writers.* Ed. Susanne Woods and Margaret P. Hannay. New York: MLA, 2000.

Teague, Frances. *Bathsua Makin, Woman of Learning.* Lewisburg, PA: Bucknell University Press, 1999.

Thomas, Anabel. *Art and Piety in the Female Religious Communities of Renaissance Italy: Iconography, Space, and the Religious Woman's Perspective.* New York: Cambridge University Press, 2003.

Tinagli, Paola. *Women in Italian Renaissance Art: Gender, Representation, Identity.* Manchester: Manchester University Press, 1997.

Todd, Janet. *The Secret Life of Aphra Behn.* London, New York, and Sydney: Pandora, 2000.

———. *The Sign of Angelica: Women, Writing and Fiction, 1660–1800.* New York: Columbia University Press, 1989.

Tomas, Natalie R. *The Medici Women: Gender and Power in Renaissance Florence.* Aldershot and Brookfield: Ashgate Publishing Co., 2004.

Traub, Valerie. *The Renaissance of Lesbianism in Early Modern England*. Cambridge: Cambridge University Press, 2002.

Valenze, Deborah. *The First Industrial Woman*. New York: Oxford University Press, 1995.

Van Dijk, Susan, Lia van Gemert, and Sheila Ottway, eds. *Writing the History of Women's Writing: Toward an International Approach*. Proceedings of the Colloquium, Amsterdam, 9–11 September. Amsterdam: Royal Netherlands Academy of Arts and Sciences, 2001.

Vickery, Amanda. *The Gentleman's Daughter: Women's Lives in Georgian England*. New Haven: Yale University Press, 1998.

Vollendorf, Lisa. *The Lives of Women: A New History of Inquisitional Spain*. Nashville, TN: Vanderbilt University Press, 2005.

Walker, Claire. *Gender and Politics in Early Modern Europe: English Convents in France and the Low Countries*. New York: Palgrave, 2003.

Wall, Wendy. *The Imprint of Gender: Authorship and Publication in the English Renaissance*. Ithaca, NY: Cornell University Press, 1993.

Walsh, William T. *St. Teresa of Avila: A Biography*. Rockford, IL: TAN Books & Publications, 1987.

Warner, Marina. *Alone of All Her Sex: The Myth and Cult of the Virgin Mary*. New York: Knopf, 1976.

Warnicke, Retha M. *The Marrying of Anne of Cleves: Royal Protocol in Tudor England*. Cambridge: Cambridge University Press, 2000.

Watt, Diane. *Secretaries of God: Women Prophets in Late Medieval and Early Modern England*. Cambridge, England: D. S. Brewer, 1997.

Weaver, Elissa. *Convent Theatre in Early Modern Italy: Spiritual Fun and Learning for Women*. New York: Cambridge University Press, 2002.

Weber, Alison. *Teresa of Avila and the Rhetoric of Femininity*. Princeton: Princeton University Press, 1990.

Welles, Marcia L. *Persephone's Girdle: Narratives of Rape in Seventeenth-Century Spanish Literature*. Nashville: Vanderbilt University Press, 2000.

Whitehead, Barbara J., ed. *Women's Education in Early Modern Europe: A History, 1500–1800*. New York and London: Garland Publishing Co., 1999.

*Widowhood and Visual Culture in Early Modern Europe*. Ed. Allison Levy. Aldershot and Brookfield: Ashgate Publishing Co., 2003.

*Widowhood in Medieval and Early Modern Europe*. Ed. Sandra Cavallo and Lydan Warner. New York: Longman, 1999.

Wiesner, Merry E. *Working Women in Renaissance Germany*. New Brunswick, NJ: Rutgers University Press, 1986.

Wiesner-Hanks, Merry E. *Christianity and Sexuality in the Early Modern World: Regulating Desire, Reforming Practice*. New York: Routledge, 2000.

———. *Gender, Church, and State in Early Modern Germany: Essays*. New York: Longman, 1998.

———. *Gender in History*. Malden, MA: Blackwell, 2001.

———. *Women and Gender in Early Modern Europe*. Cambridge: Cambridge University Press, 1993.

———. *Working Women in Renaissance Germany*. New Brunswick, NJ: Rutgers University Press, 1986.

Willard, Charity Cannon. *Christine de Pizan: Her Life and Works.* New York: Persea Books, 1984.

Wilson, Katharina, ed. *Encyclopedia of Continental Women Writers.* 2 vols. New York: Garland, 1991.

Winn, Colette, and Donna Kuizenga, eds. *Women Writers in Pre-Revolutionary France.* New York: Garland Publishing, 1997.

Winston-Allen, Anne. *Convent Chronicles: Women Writing about Women and Reform in the Late Middle Ages.* University Park: Pennsylvania State University Press, 2004.

*Women and Monasticism in Medieval Europe: Sisters and Patrons of the Cistercian Reform,* ed. Constance H. Berman. Kalamazoo: Western Michigan University Press, 2002.

*Women, Crime and the Courts in Early Modern England.* Ed. Jenny Kermode and Garthine Walker. Chapel Hill: University of North Carolina Press, 1994.

*Women in Italian Renaissance Culture and Society.* Ed. Letizia Panizza. Oxford: European Humanities Research Centre, 2000.

*Women in Reformation and Counter-Reformation Europe: Public and Private Worlds.* Ed. Sherrin Marshall. Bloomington, IN: Indiana University Press, 1989.

*Women in Renaissance and Early Modern Europe.* Ed. Christine Meek. Dublin-Portland: Four Courts Press, 2000.

*Women in the Inquisition: Spain and the New World.* Ed. Mary E. Giles. Baltimore: Johns Hopkins University Press, 1999.

*Women in the Middle Ages and the Renaissance: Literary and Historical Perspectives.* Ed. Mary Beth Rose. Syracuse: Syracuse University Press, 1986.

*Women Players in England, 1500–1660: Beyond the All-Male Stage.* Ed. Pamela Allen Brown and Peter Parolin. Aldershot and Brookfield: Ashgate Publishing Co., 2005.

*Women, "Race," and Writing in the Early Modern Period.* Ed. Margo Hendricks and Patricia Parker. London and New York: Routledge, 1994.

Woodbridge, Linda. *Women and the English Renaissance: Literature and the Nature of Womankind, 1540–1620.* Urbana: University of Illinois Press, 1984.

Woodford, Charlotte. *Nuns as Historians in Early Modern Germany.* Oxford: Clarendon Press, 2002.

Woods, Susanne. *Lanyer: A Renaissance Woman Poet.* New York: Oxford University Press, 1999.

———— and Margaret P. Hannay, eds. *Teaching Tudor and Stuart Women Writers.* New York: MLA, 2000.

*Writing the Female Voice.* Ed. Elizabeth C. Goldsmith. Boston: Northeastern University Press, 1989.

*Writing the History of Women's Writing: Toward an International Approach.* Ed. Susan Van Dijk, Lia van Gemert and Sheila Ottway Proceedings of the Colloquium, Amsterdam, 9–11 September. Amsterdam: Royal Netherlands Academy of Arts and Sciences, 2001.

# INDEX